Julia Szota-Pachowicz

BPMN
Course

Learn and practice on examples

MODELING VIEW PRESS

www.modelingview.com

BPMN Course

Learn and practice on examples

Copyright @ 2019 by Julia Szota-Pachowicz

All rights reserved. No part of this book may be reproduced, stored in a retrieval system, or transmitted in any form or by any means without the prior written permission of the publisher, except in the case of brief quotations embedded in critical articles or reviews.

Every effort has been made in the preparation of this book to ensure the accuracy of the information presented. However, the information contained in this book is sold without warranty, either express or implied. The author and publisher will not be held liable for any damages caused or alleged to be caused directly or indirectly by this book.

Cover design by GroupMedia

First published: July 2019

ISBN 978-83-953432-0-9

Published by Modeling View Press

www.modelingview.com

Table of Contents

Introduction /7
OMG & BPMN /7
Scope and construction /8

Example 1: Chocolate cake /11

    Learning outcomes /11
1.1. Bake chocolate cake /12
    THEORY: Subprocess /14
    Using subprocesses /15
    AND-Split and AND-Join /16
    THEORY: Parallel gateway /17
    Using start and end events /18
    THEORY: Subprocesses, start and end events – modeling rules /19
1.2. Make cake process /20
    Irrelevant order of tasks /20
    THEORY: Ad-Hoc subprocess /22
    Ad-Hoc subprocess vs. AND-split / AND-join /24
    Parallel activities /24
    Activity with additional restrictions /25
    THEORY: Timer event /26
    Activity restrictions and process levels /30
    Use of text annotations to make the model unambiguous /31
    THEORY: Text annotations /32
1.3. Make cream process /33
    Identify tasks and subprocesses within the top-level process /33
    Activity interrupted by other activity /34
    THEORY: Conditional event /37
1.4. Data flow /39
    THEORY: Data flow elements /39
    Data object modeling rules /41

Example 2: Scrum /43

    Learning outcomes /43
2.1. Scrum process /44
    Multi-instance process /44
    THEORY: Loop subprocess characteristics /45

　　　　Subprocess called within execution of another activity /47
　　　　THEORY: Event subprocess /48
　　　　Introducing subprocesses and process levels /53
　　　　Boundary event /55
　　　　THEORY: Boundary event /55
　　　　Process participant /58
　　　　THEORY: Pool /58
2.2. Planning Meeting /59
　　　　Decision point /60
　　　　Number of end events in the process /60
　　　　THEORY: Exclusive gateway /61
　　　　Process organization /62
　　　　THEORY: Lanes /63
　　　　Collaborative activities /64
2.3. Daily Scrum /67
　　　　Activity deadline /67
　　　　Event subprocess deadline /68
　　　　Loop vs. multi-instance subprocess /70
　　　　Sequential tasks vs. multi-instance task /71
　　　　THEORY: Loop task characteristics /72
2.4. Review Meeting /73
　　　　Message event and process participants /75
　　　　THEORY: Message event /75
　　　　Catch events in the process /78
　　　　Event subprocess vs. boundary event /79
　　　　Explicit goals of activities /81
2.5. BPMN Collaboration /83
　　　　THEORY: Collaboration /83
　　　　THEORY: Message flow /84
　　　　Review meeting process – collaborative or not? /85
　　　　Identifying external process participants /88
　　　　Review meeting collaboration /89
　　　　Multiplicity of Participant /91
　　　　When and how use Message flows /91
　　　　Black box or white box? /93
2.6. Retrospective meeting /94
2.7. Process levels models /95

Example 3: Library /99

  Learning outcomes /99
3.1. Borrow book process /101
  Define top-level process elements /101
  Define transition conditions between top-level process elements /105
  Activity performance dependent on conditions /106
  Wrong usage of exclusive gateway /107
  Model alternative process flows using exclusive gateway /108
  Including all possible process ends /110
3.2. Reserve book process /113
  THEORY: Event-based gateways /115
  Undo changes /118
  THEORY: Compensation /120
  Ending the whole process from the child level /123
  Joining throw intermediate event and none end event /125
  THEORY: End events – their effect and usage within processes /126
3.3. Manage book order /135
  Use of event-based gateway – advanced /136
  Compensation of many tasks within the same process /138
3.4. Manage borrowed book /141
  Loop subprocess without end event /142
  Process designed as a loop vs. loop activity marker /143
  Breaking the loop process /144
  Conditions on exclusive gateway leading to the same results /146
  Consistency with parent process model /148
3.5. Return book /149
3.6. Collaboration – advanced /151
  Black box external process /151
  Different instances of external processes have influence on the internal process /152
  Subprocess within a pool – what to do with boundary events /155
  Message flow associated with collapsed subprocesses /158
  System-driven and human-driven processes /159

Would you like to learn more? /165
References /166

Introduction

The book teaches how to model processes using BPMN 2.0 based on design problems that arise during the modeling of a specific issue. The book is in the form of a course aimed at those who know the basics of BPMN. There are three fully explained examples. We first present the problem and then try to solve it with different modeling approaches so you can also learn how to approach the analysis of processes.

Every process can be modeled in number of ways, from model interpretation to the use and naming of different BPMN elements. This book shows the most common solutions. It also presents the most common mistakes and incorrect interpretation of BPMN modeling rules. Each solution is explained, supported by theory and compared with others. All the BPMN elements and approaches are described theoretically on the basis of the official BPMN specification. The reader will gain knowledge about what solutions to use in a specific case, which interpretational traps to avoid and how to skillfully read models.

This book doesn't teach BPMN from scratch so you should ideally have some basic knowledge of BPMN notation and its main concepts before beginning. The book also doesn't introduce all BPMN concepts – it explains the BPMN elements used and needed to resolve the modeling issues presented.

The book presents examples of non-executable processes, which are commonly used for documenting business processes within organizations. Within the examples, we will model both private and public processes and collaboration.

I'm confident that, through reading this book

… you will learn how to solve common issues related to process modeling using BPMN
… you will understood what aspects should you pay attention to when analyzing and modeling processes
… BPMN elements and modeling rules will become clearer to you
… you will start to create better models.

OMG & BPMN

The Business Process Model and Notation (BPMN) was developed by the Object Management Group (OMG) [1]. The OMG provides a free formal specification, guides and tutorials of BPMN. All information can be found at: http://www.bpmn.org/

Scope and construction

The book uses three fully explained business process examples:

- Baking a chocolate cake[1]
- The (software development) Scrum process[2]
- Library – borrowing a book process[1]

All three processes have been adjusted for the purpose of practicing BPMN rules and creating BPMN models.

The book is organized as follows

Every example starts with a process description. We start with high level analysis of the process description to model the top-level process. Next, we analyze more detailed elements and model child-level processes. Every child-level process may also contain subprocesses that are modeled as child-level process within a particular subsection. So the approach is as follows:

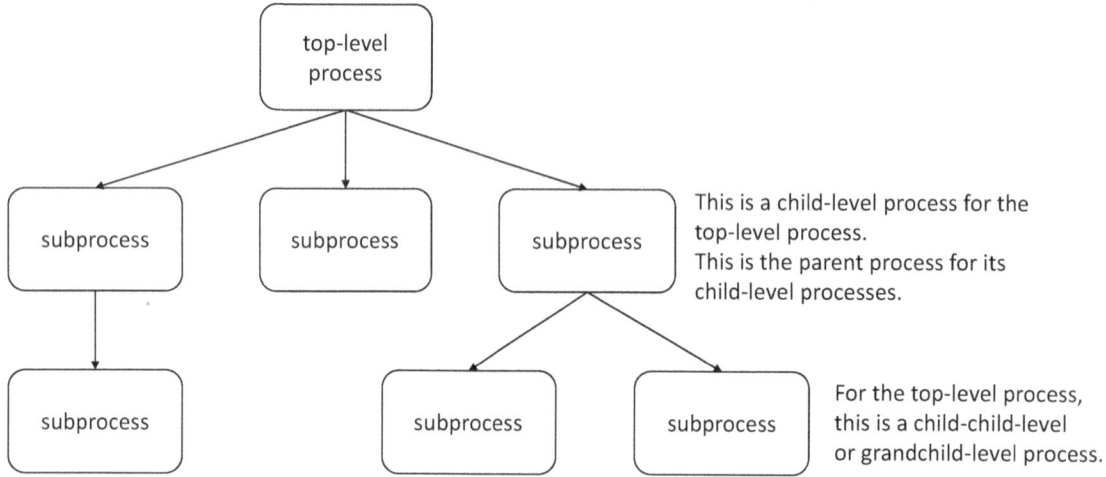

Figure 1: Process levels

---

[1] The Baking a chocolate cake and Library process descriptions have been prepared by the author.
[2] The Scrum process description has been prepared based on *The Scrum Guide* [2].

For every level of the process, you will find:

- Process analysis and a detailed explanation of why it is modeled in such a way;
- If applicable, different possible solutions as well as common modeling and interpretation mistakes.

In each example you will find:

- **TIP** – useful tips and information that is worth remembering. General TIPs are in the summary of the discussion and can be used in similar design problems.
- **THEORY** – subsections that present the full theory about a given BPMN element, design pattern or modeling approach. These are prepared based on the free official BPMN 2.0 specification [1].

Within the examples, we will model private and public processes and collaboration.

More examples and theory can be found at: **www.modelingview.com**

Example 1: Chocolate cake

Let's start with the process of baking a chocolate cake, which we model based on a recipe.

Learning outcomes

Based on this example we discuss and learn

- How to divide a process and organize a model within process levels
- When it's worth using subprocesses
- AND-join and AND-split modeling patterns
- AND gateway theory and modeling rules
- What is a parallel box and an Ad-Hoc subprocess, and when use them
- Activity naming conventions
- What are Text Annotations and when to use them
- How to use and interpret Timer events
- How to model additional restrictions related to tasks
- What are Conditional events
- What makes a model explicit and unambiguous
- Data flow modeling elements and rules

Process description

Chocolate cake recipe

Chocolate cake	Ingredients
Mix the margarine with the sugar; add the eggs, vanilla, cocoa powder and flour. Mix everything together adding the water. Bake for 1 hour at 180 degrees C. After cooling, decorate cake with egg white cream (see below).	250g margarine 2 cups sugar 2 eggs 3-4 teaspoons cocoa powder 2 ½ cups flour 1 cup water 1 ¼ teaspoons vanilla sugar
Egg white cream	**Ingredients**
Dissolve 2 teaspoons of gelatin in 3 tablespoons of water. Pour sugar into boiling water; boil to dissolve the sugar. Pour the hot syrup onto the egg whites while whipping. At the end, add the dissolved gelatin, a pinch of salt and the vanilla sugar.	250g margarine 2 cups powdered sugar 2 eggs (whites only) 3-4 teaspoons cocoa powder 2 ½ cups flour 1 cup water ½ teaspoons salt 1 ¼ teaspoons vanilla sugar

1.1. Bake chocolate cake

We start by creating a model of the top-level *Bake chocolate cake* process. In order to do this, we must extract the basic top-level elements of the process. For a baking example, it could simply be the preparation of the individual main dough ingredients.

> **TIP:** When modeling a top-level process, try to distinguish the main parts first, and next find dependences between them.

According to the recipe, we can distinguish two basic steps of chocolate cake preparation:
- Make cake
- Make cream

The next question is how these steps, *Make cake* and *Make cream*, are related to each other. In which order they should be performed? Going through the recipe once again, two solutions arise. We may model the process in the order that it's written in the recipe: first make the cake then make the cream. We can also interpret these steps as independent as there is no obstacle to these processes being carried out in any order.

The next question is, are there any other dependences and activities that may be classified as top-level process elements and influence the process flow? The common element that can be performed after cake and cream are ready is decoration of the cake with the cream. From the recipe: *"After cooling, decorate cake with the egg white cream."* We decide to model this activity within the top-level process as it's performed only after other top-level activities have been completed.

Look at the top-level process examples below. In the first case we don't enforce which activity should be done first – cake or cream – as these activities are completely independent (Figure 2A). If you want to model the process as it is written exactly in the recipe, use solution B (Figure 2B). The decision is up to you and what you want to achieve by the model: give the cake maker a free hand or suggest that he/she should start with cake preparation.

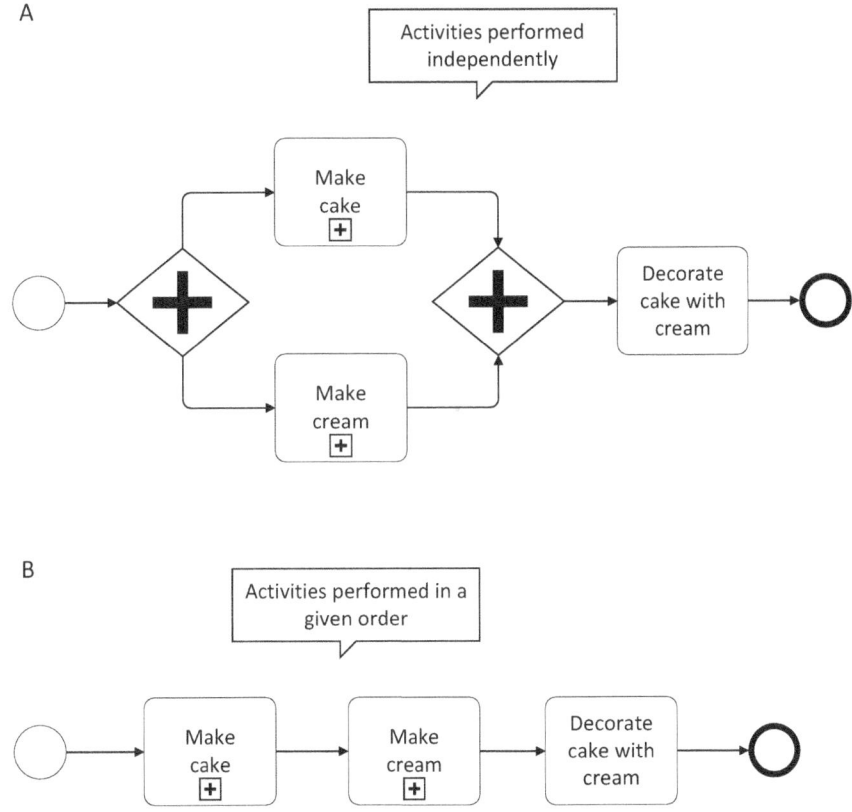

Figure 2: Bake chocolate cake top-level process examples

The *Make cake* and *Make cream* steps are modeled as **collapsed subprocesses** as we consider them as separate processes, each consisting of tasks.

THEORY: Subprocess

A subprocess is a lower-level process within a process called a child-level process and may include activities, gateways, events and sequence flows. A standard subprocess is part of a sequence flow. It has incoming and outgoing flows.

We can hide or show details of a subprocess by modeling it as collapsed or expanded.

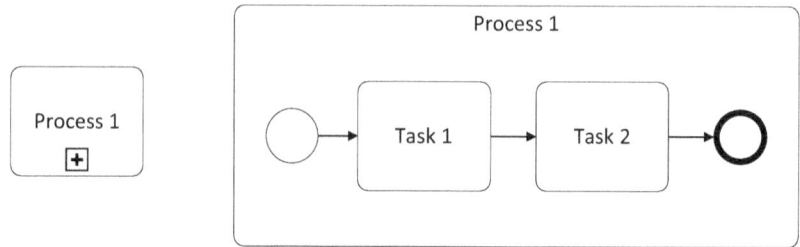

A standard subprocess that lacks more complex behavior such as boundary events or compensation mechanisms is just a container that groups activities needed to achieve some specific goal/behavior. This means that if we move the 'subprocess boundary' and put subprocess elements directly into the parent process, the flow of the parent process won't change.

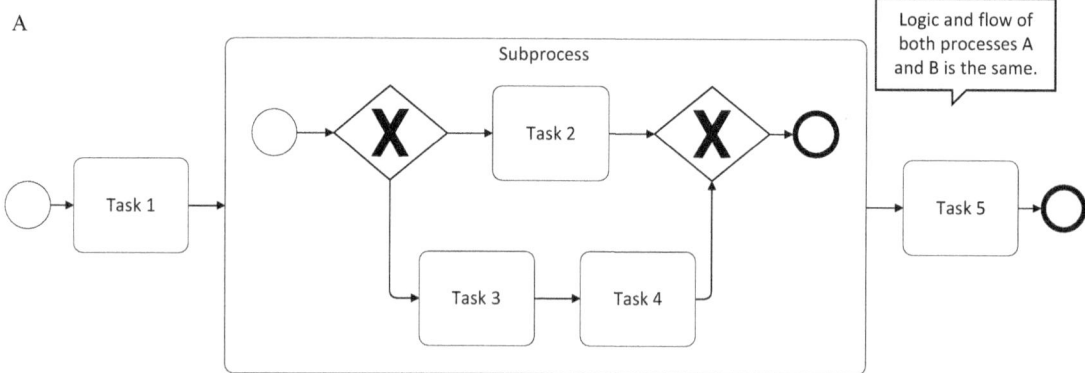

B

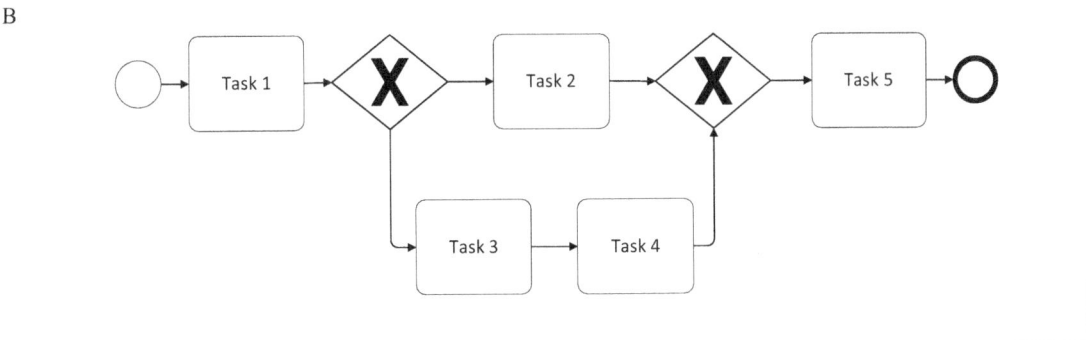

Using subprocesses

Using subprocesses makes the higher level process easier to read and understand. It makes the process easier to develop as you focus on and model smaller parts at a time.

> **TIP:** To show only high a level view of the process or hide some details, use collapsed sub-processes.

Do we always need to model a top-level process using subprocesses? Only if it consists of many activities. A good practice is to create process models that have no more than a few steps. This results in process simplicity.

Always try to look at the process as simply as possible. Creating a simple top-level process doesn't mean simplifying it. It's rather showing the process in a readable and easy to analyze way. This also gives you better understanding of the end-to-end process.

Deciding what steps are shown directly within a top-level process can be a really hard task that influences the child-level models. It's really worth thinking it over carefully. The are no strict rules on how to distinguish subprocesses from the parent process. However, these tips may help you:

- The distinguished part should not change the logic and sense of the process. In other words, if you remove the 'subprocess boundary,' the parent process shouldn't change.
- Think about the purpose of the subprocess. It should group activities that lead to some defined goal.
- Does the subprocess improve the readability of the parent process?

AND-Split and AND-Join

As a further example, we will model a solution saying that there are no dependences for what should be prepared first: cake or cream (Figure 3). Let's discuss this in more detail. To model activities that are performed independently we use the **AND-split** (also called **fork**), which is a **parallel gateway**. AND-split is very often misinterpreted as a place in the process that indicates activities performed in parallel. However, AND-split is used to model independent activities, rather than parallel activities.

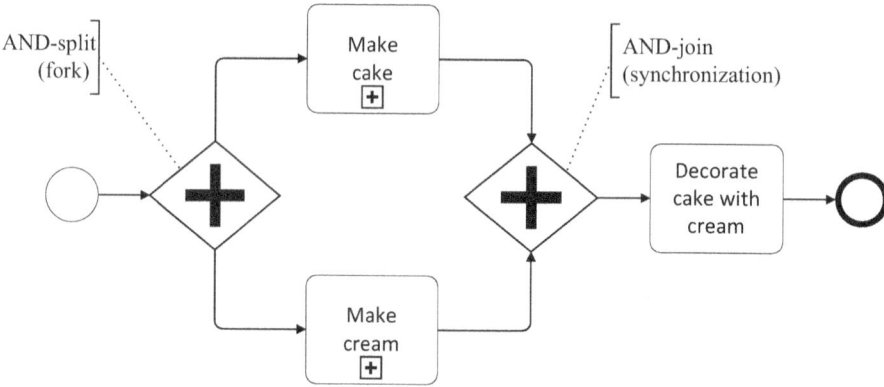

Figure 3: AND-Split and And-Join in Bake chocolate cake process

To decorate a cake with a cream we need to have both: cake and cream. When two or more flows need to reach some point in the process so the flow can go further, we can use a parallel gateway that joins independent paths into one. It's called **AND-join** or **synchronization**. AND-join is a place in a process that waits for all input paths.

THEORY: Parallel gateway

When we branch the flow using a parallel gateway (also called AND gateway), all outgoing paths are chosen – and that's all you need to know. There is no condition or rule for what happens later on each path, so we cannot use this gateway to force activities to be performed in parallel.

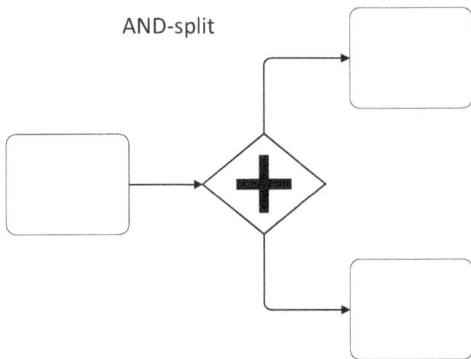

Because we don't declare any conditions for a parallel gateway, all outgoing and all incoming paths are in some sense equal. For this reason you cannot use default and conditional sequence flows as outgoing flows from an AND gateway.

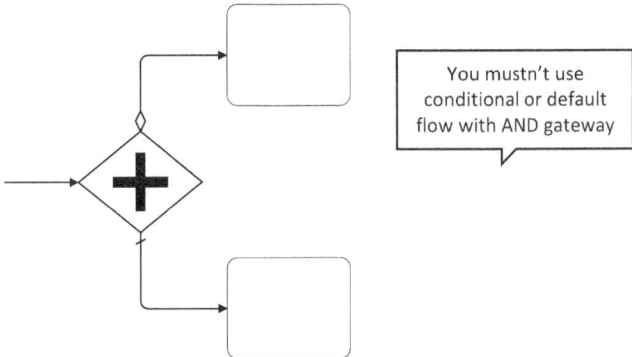

When we use a parallel gateway to join independent paths, this is then a synchronization point. The AND gateway waits for all incoming flows, which may come in at different times, before flow can go further through the gateway. Only once all the paths reach the gateway can the process go further. We can interpret this as a synchronization of flows, rather than an activity itself.

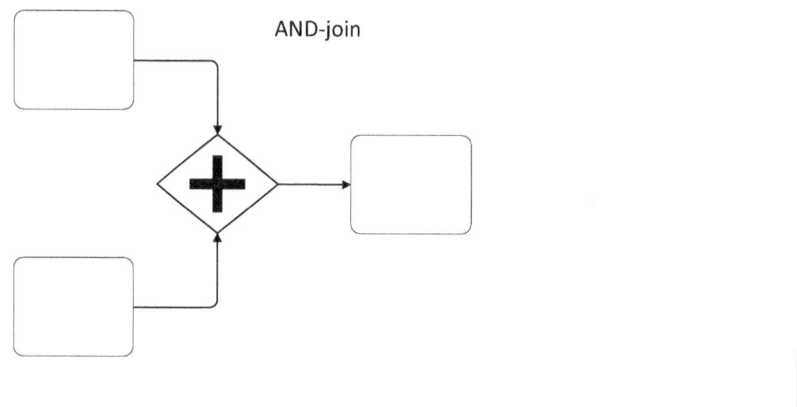

Using start and end events

In the *Bake chocolate cake* process we also use **start event** and **end event**. Use of a start event and end event are optional – you may choose not to include them on your diagram. However, it's recommended to use them because they make the process clearer.

> **TIP:** Clear beginning and end! Use start and end events to make the model unambiguous.

> **TIP:** Use the minimum number of start events. It makes the process easier to understand.

General rules relating to the use of start and end events within standard processes and subprocesses are as follows:
- You can use one or more start events and one or more end events in the process. Just remember that you must use both types of events or neither.
- It's not allowed to use a start event without ending the process with an end event.
- It's not allowed to end a process with an end event without starting it using at least one start event.

1.1. Bake chocolate cake

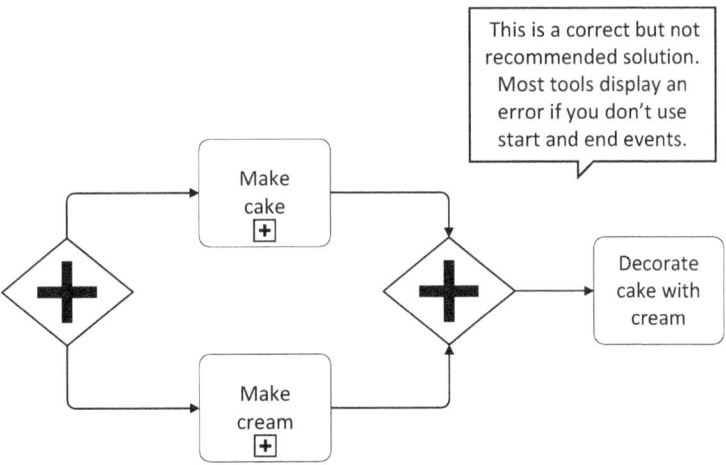

Figure 4: Bake chocolate cake process without start and end event

THEORY: Subprocesses, start and end events – modeling rules

We can use start and end events independently for each level of our model. By 'level of the model' we mean top-level process, subprocess or other process called by a call activity.

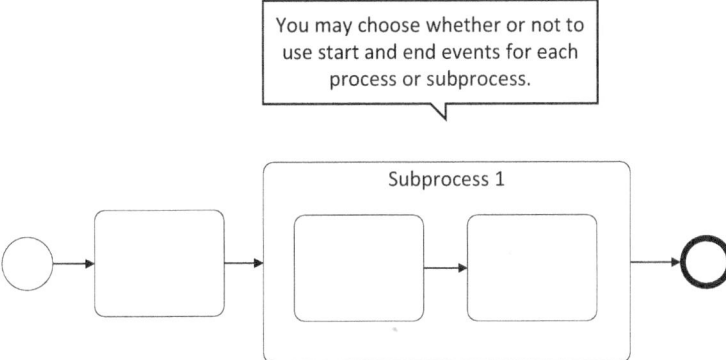

A subprocess is part of a standard flow within its parent process. That's why you can use only the **none start event** to trigger a subprocess. No other types are allowed!

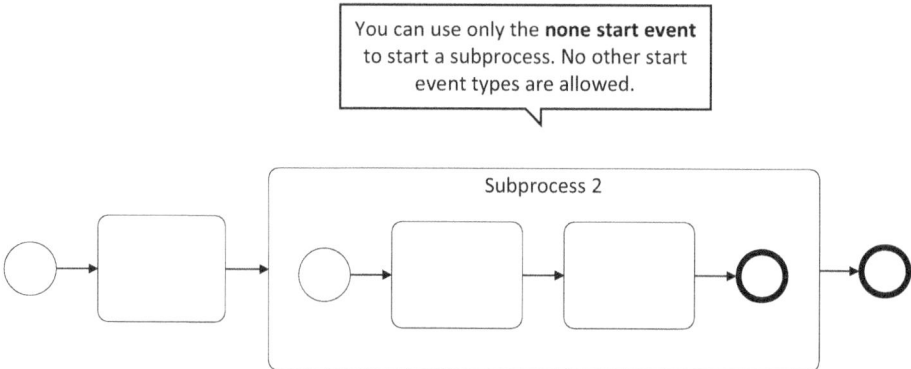

You can additionally use other types of start events within a subprocess, but if they are triggered, they would instantiate the top-level process so this is not recommended. It's simply unclear and can cause misunderstanding.

1.2. Make cake process

Irrelevant order of tasks

Let's now analyze the *Make cake* process in more detail.

Follow the recipe: "*Mix the margarine with the sugar; add the eggs, vanilla, cocoa powder and flour. Mix everything together adding water. Bake for 1 hour at 180 degrees C. After cooling, decorate the cake with the egg white cream.*"

The first question is: what are the steps of this process? According to the recipe, we may distinguish three main steps: add ingredients, mix ingredients and bake dough. The first thing we need to do is to mix the margarine with the sugar; next we add the other ingredients: eggs, vanilla cocoa powder and flour.

The next question is: what's the order (dependencies) between these activities? First we add ingredients, then we mix everything – so it seems that the order of adding ingredients doesn't matter. Again, we are faced with the decision of whether we model according to the way ingredients are listed in the recipe or whether we let the cook decide what should be added first. Look below at three sample solutions (Figure 5). Let's discuss them.

1.2. Make cake process

A

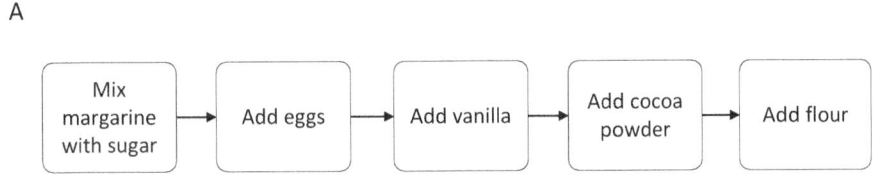

B

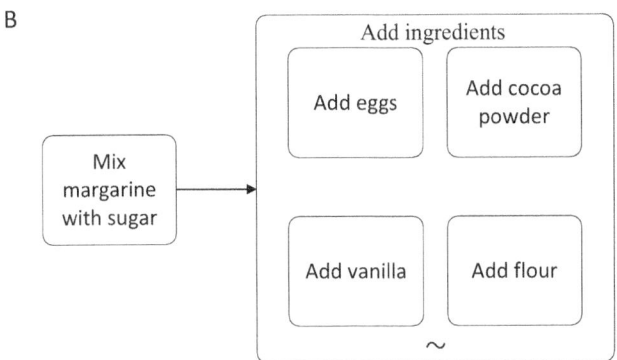

C

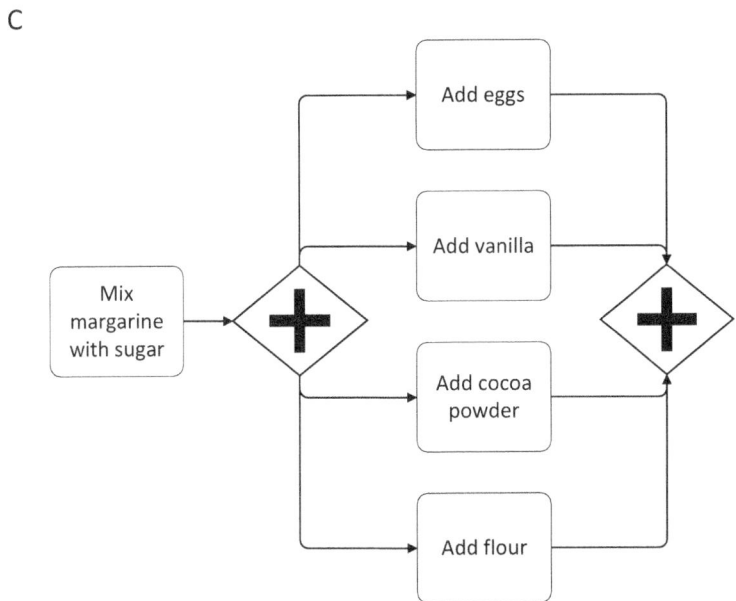

Figure 5: Model examples of tasks related to adding ingredients

1.2. Make cake process

All three models represent the same part of the flow and have the same tasks. All of them are correct and do not change the general flow of the process which follows from the recipe. So what are the differences between them? The first diagram (Figure 5A) enforces task order by using a sequence flow. If you want to say to the reader that some tasks have some defined order that can't be changed, use a simple sequence flow.

If the order of two or more activities doesn't matter, is unknown or unspecified, you can use the **Ad-Hoc subprocess** (Figure 5B). Note that the task *Mix margarine with sugar* could also be included within the Ad-Hoc subprocess; however, our intention is to explicitly show that this is the first thing you should do. The other ingredients can be added in any order the cook chooses.

> **TIP:** Use the Ad-Hoc subprocess when the order of tasks is irrelevant, unknown or when tasks are optional.

If activities are independent and all should be performed, we may use AND-split / AND-join (Figure 5C).

Don't use fewer tasks to avoid ordering (Figure 6). A common mistake is to present similar activities within one task. For such a simple process, it even makes the process clearer at first glance. However, this is not a recommended approach as we pack four activities into one task.

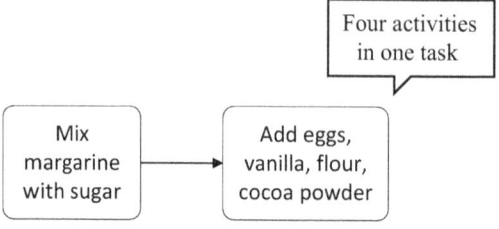

Figure 6: Example of packing many activities into one task

> **TIP:** One activity per BPMN task.

THEORY: Ad-Hoc subprocess

The Ad-Hoc subprocess gives the performer the ability to decide how and which activities are performed. It means that some activities may be performed sequentially, some in parallel, and some can be omitted and not executed.

For non-executable processes, the Ad-Hoc subprocess is used when the order of activities is irrelevant and there is no execution dependency between them. The decision of how to perform the activities is up to the performer.

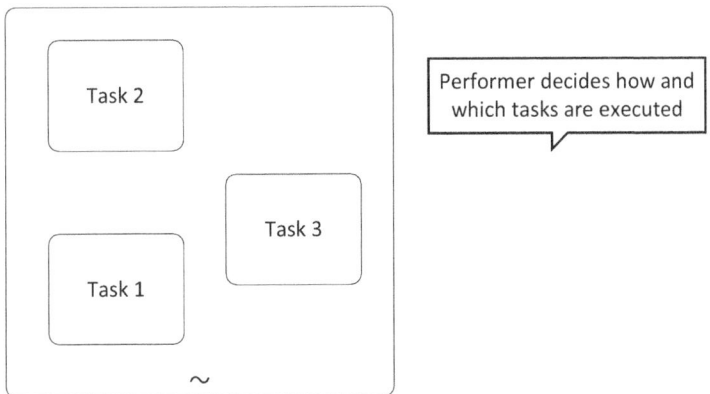

When we use a subprocess without the Ad-Hoc marker, all activities that don't have incoming flows are instantiated when the subprocess starts. For a subprocess with the Ad-Hoc marker, this rule doesn't apply.

You may use sequence flows between particular activities in an Ad-Hoc subprocess to enforce the order of execution for some selected activities.

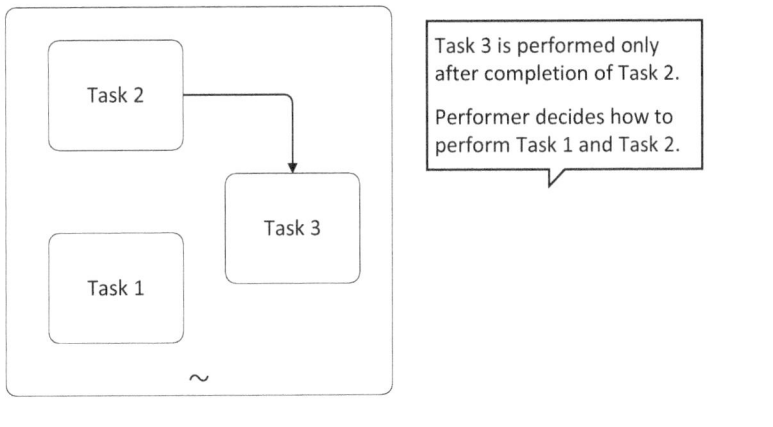

Ad-Hoc subprocess vs. AND-split / AND-join

Previously we used AND gateways to model independent steps, but now we additionally propose the Ad-Hoc subprocess. So what's the difference between the Ad-Hoc subprocess and the AND-split / AND-join pattern?

When using the AND-split / AND-join pattern, we provide information that all activities between the AND gateways must be performed and the order of performing them is unimportant. When we use the Ad-Hoc subprocess, we say to the reader that the performer decides how activities are performed. In this case, the performer may also not perform some of the activities. Usually the Ad-Hoc subprocess is used to say: it's up to you how to perform all these steps.

Remember that we want learn different BPMN modeling approaches. In real life processes, such modeling decisions make a difference so you need to be sure how exactly the process flow is interpreted.

In this example, to organize the adding ingredients tasks we will use solution B, with an Ad-Hoc subprocess.

Parallel activities

Let's go further. After the ingredients have been added, we mix all the ingredients together adding water at the same time. This is an example of tasks performed in parallel. To model this, we may use a subprocess without start and end events. It's called a **parallel box**.

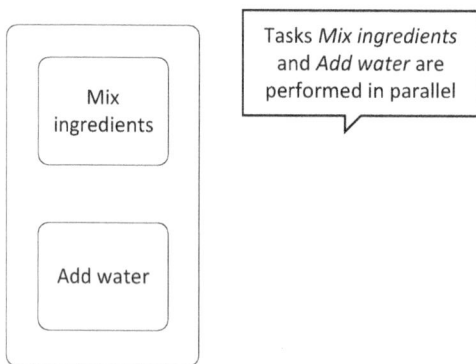

Figure 7: Activities performed in parallel

Why do we use a subprocess without start and end events to model parallel activities? According to the BPMN specification, all flow elements without incoming sequence flows are instantiated when the process is instantiated. So when our subprocess starts, all included tasks without an incoming flow also start. The process ends when all included tasks end; this is a synchronization mechanism. This solution is adopted in BPMN to model activities performed in parallel.

Activity with additional restrictions

The last task in the *Make cake* process is to bake the dough for 1 hour at 180 degrees C. This is an example of a task that can be performed if some requirement is met and is performed till another requirement is met. You can model such a task directly:

> Bake dough for 1 hour at 180 degrees

Figure 8: Task with restrictions introduced within task title

From a semantic point of view and also considering the process flow, this is an acceptable solution. However, good practice is to pull out and separately model restrictions related to an activity. Let's exercise such an approach.

The *Bake dough* activity has two additional requirements:
- Baking time – 1 hour
- Baking temperature – 180 degrees C.

We may interpret this as follows: we can start the baking once the oven is heated to 180 degrees, and we should bake the dough for 1 hour – so after one hour the activity should end. The first of these is an input requirement. The second restriction is an output requirement.

> **TIP:** If a task has additional restrictions, use additional BPMN elements like events or gateways to model them explicitly.

To explicitly model when we can start baking, we can use a conditional intermediate event. A conditional event is triggered when a condition becomes *true* – in our case when the oven temperature reaches 180 degrees. Then, the process proceeds and we can start to bake the dough.

We can generalize this example and say that if some activity has an external input requirement, then to check if it's met, you may first use a conditional intermediate event in the flow.

1.2. Make cake process

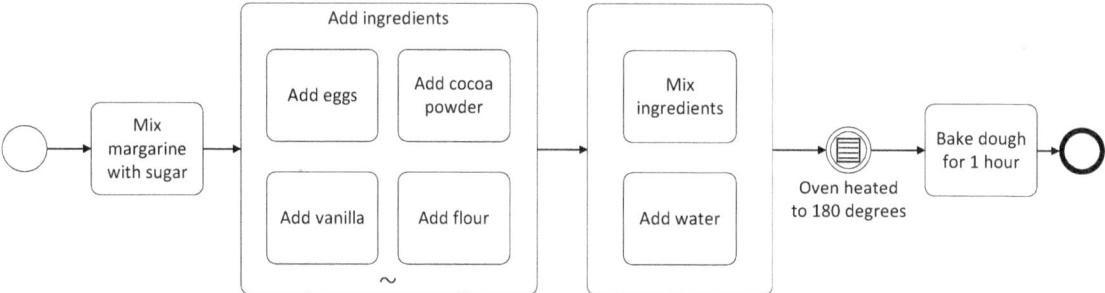

Figure 9: Make cake process with conditional intermediate event

And what about second requirement – bake for 1 hour? This is related to time, so the use of the timer event arises. Let's consider the behavior of the **timer event** first.

THEORY: Timer event

A timer intermediate event used in a sequence flow informs about a delay in a process, not about how long a specific activity lasts. For a timer event, we may define a specific date/time or a cycle. It's interpreted as follows:

Task 1 ends and the process waits for 4 days before continuing the flow and starting Task 2.

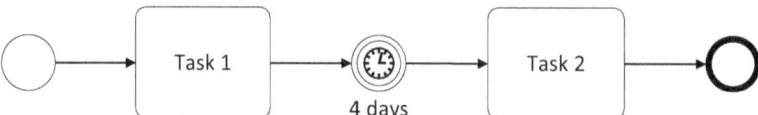

Task 3 ends and the process waits till 09:00 before continuing the flow and starting Task 4.

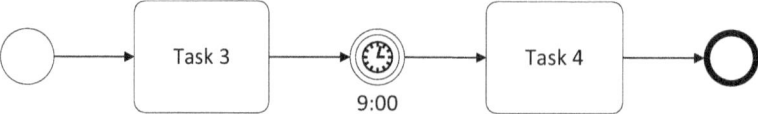

A timer intermediate event attached to the boundary of an activity is used to activate an exception flow. The event is triggered after a specified time or at specified time if the activity is still active. An activity itself can be interrupted or not. It's interpreted as follows:

Interrupted case: During execution of Task 1 and after 20 minutes from its start, the timer event fires. Task 1 is interrupted (cancelled) and the process is continues through an exception flow to Task 3.

1.2. Make cake process

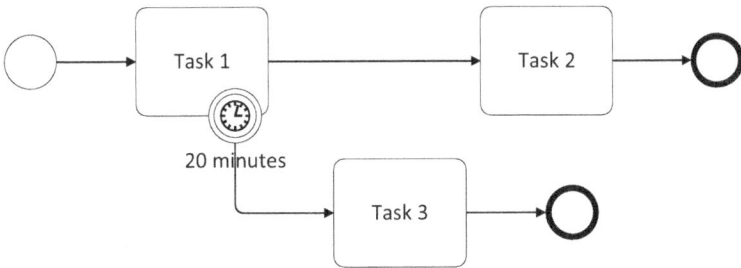

Non-interrupted case: During execution of Task 4, at 07:00 the timer event fires and the process goes through an exception flow to Task 6. In this case, Task 4 is still active, so after it ends the process goes to Task 5.

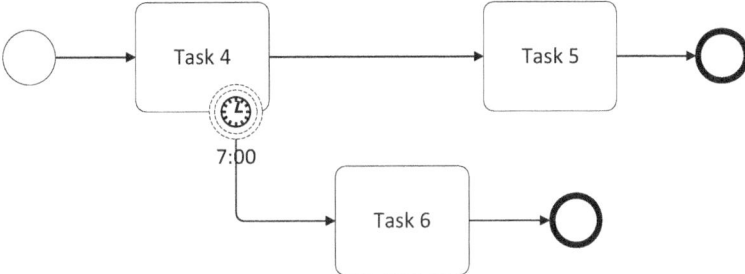

When using a timer event as a process trigger, the event behavior is the same. The timer event triggers a process for a specific date/time or on a specific cycle.

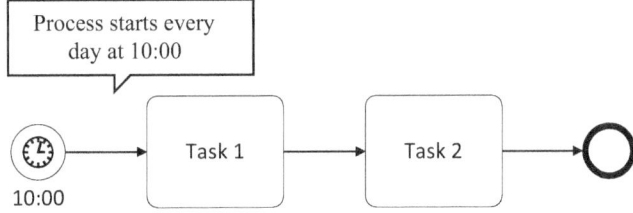

A timer start event may also be used as a trigger for an event subprocess. It may be defined as an interrupting or non-interrupting start event. Read more about event subprocesses in section **2.1. THEORY: Event subprocess.**

The timer event is trigger event – that's why you cannot use it to end a process. BPMN doesn't define a timer end event element.

Let's go back to our example. We cannot use a timer intermediate event directly in a flow to indicate that a cake should be baked for 1 hour. This would mean that before starting baking or after finishing baking, we need to wait for 1 hour (Figure 10).

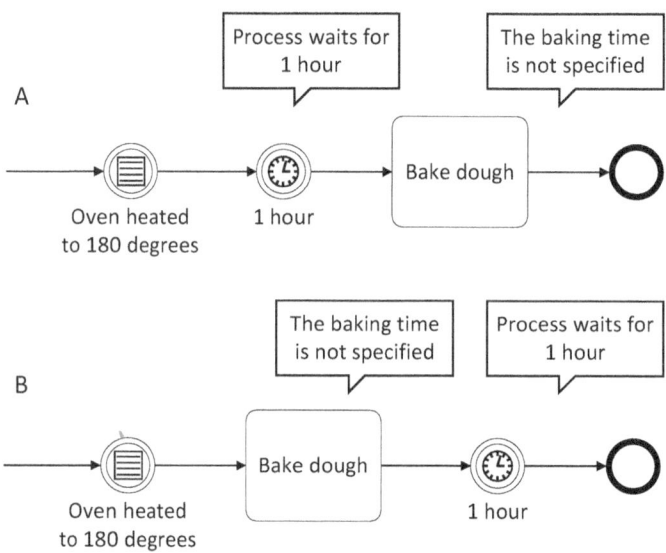

Figure 10: Timer event in a sequence flow

We may use an interrupting timer event attached to the boundary of the *Bake dough* task. This means that after 1 hour of baking, we terminate this task. If we want this task to have an enforced (automatic) deadline, it's a good solution.

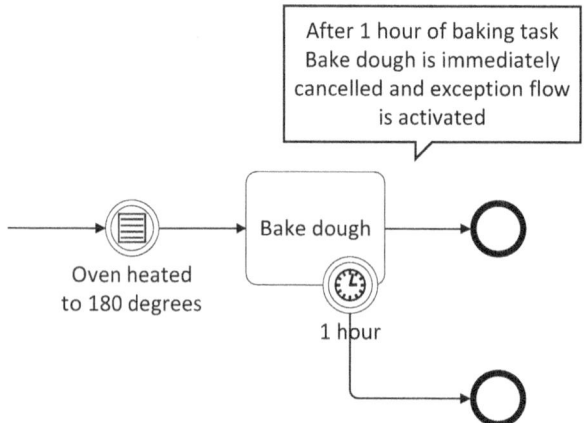

Figure 11: Interrupting timer event attached to activity boundary

If we used a non-interrupting timer event attached to the boundary of the *Bake dough* task, it would mean that after 1 hour we fire the additional flow. The question is what happens then? We are not able to answer this question looking at the recipe, so there is simply no point in firing an additional flow.

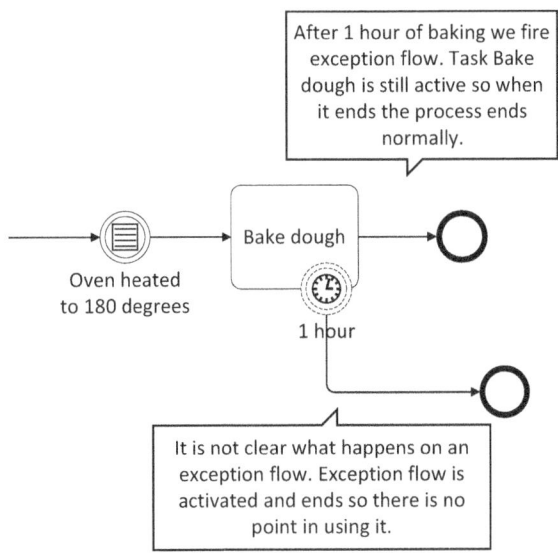

Figure 12: Non-interrupting timer event attached to activity boundary

So how should we model our 1 hour restriction? We may leave it as part of the task name, which is not recommended as the name should be simple – still, this is acceptable ('Bake for 1 hour'). We may use an interrupted timer event to show that after 1 hour, the task must end. Or we simply transfer additional information through **text annotation** (Figure 13).

Let's assume that we don't want to provide a deadline for the Bake dough task but only to inform the reader about the baking time. Using text annotation, we can achieve this: we inform that we should bake for one hour, but finishing the task is not enforced and depends on the performer.

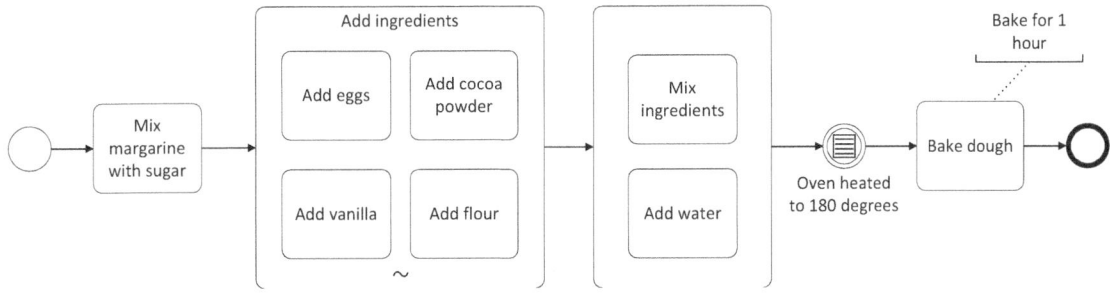

Figure 13: Bake cake process with information about baking temperature and time

Restrictions related to activities could be also modeled using other BPMN elements, not only events. A common way is to use an **exclusive gateway**. Read more about exclusive gateway in section **2.1. THEORY: Exclusive gateway.**

Activity restrictions and process levels

Let's discuss one more topic related to the 'right place in the process' for an activity input requirement. Going back to our top-level process, we haven't yet included the information that a cake needs to be cool before you can decorate it with cream. We may consider this fact as an input requirement: *cake is cool* for task *Decorate cake with cream*. In this case let's use a conditional event.

And what about the right place in the process for the conditional event: cake is cool? We can model it in three ways:
- within the *Make a cake* process (as the last element),
- just after the *Make a cake* process and before the AND-join, or
- after the AND-join.

In all three cases it won't change the cake recipe and the logic of the process. However, this is important for process readability. Putting the conditional event directly before the *Decorate cake with cream* task suggests to the reader that this rule should be met in order to start performing the task.

> **TIP:** An input requirement modeled using an event should be placed directly before the activity it's related to.

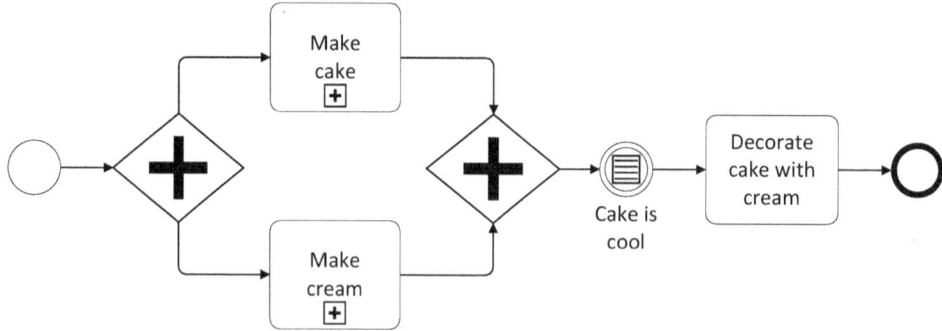

Figure 14: Bake chocolate cake top-level process with cake is cool condition

Why we don't use a task like *Cool cake*? There is no additional action needed to cool a cake – e.g. blowing – it just needs to be left to cool so there is no point in using an activity.

> **TIP:** Analyze the process in terms of what is a task and what is an event.

Use of text annotations to make the model unambiguous

Let's discuss one more topic – ambiguity. Look once again at the *Make cake* process. For someone who doesn't have the recipe, it is not necessarily obvious what the task *Mix ingredients* means exactly.

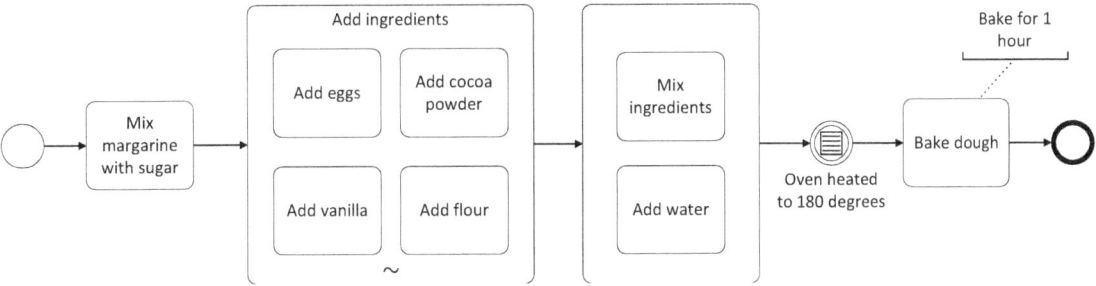

Figure 15: Make cake process ambiguity

At first glance, as the Ad-Hoc subprocess is named *Add ingredients*, it may be understood that the ingredients added in the previous subprocess are those to be mixed. This is, in fact, wrong as the margarine and sugar are also mixed within the *Mix ingredients* task.

> **TIP:** Use text annotations to explain the meaning of the terms or words used, so that the process is unambiguous for everyone.

To make this unambiguous, we could rename the task *Mix ingredients* to *Mix margarine with sugar, eggs, flour, vanilla, …* or use a text annotation:

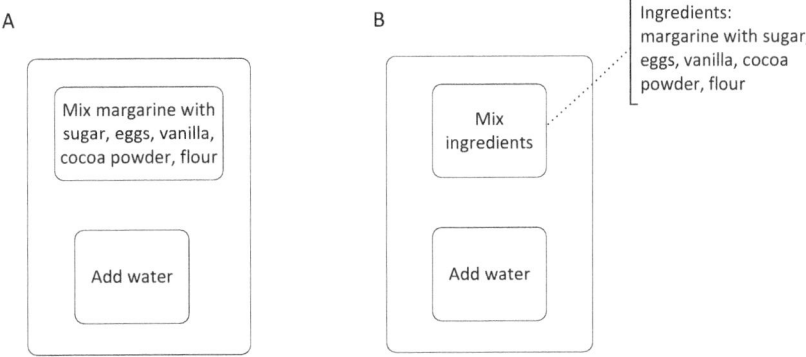

Figure 16: Achieving unambiguity: A – rename task; B – use text annotation

1.2. Make cake process

THEORY: Text annotations

A text annotation provides additional information for the reader. Importantly, it doesn't influence the flow.

$$\left[\;\text{Text}\right.$$

A text annotation should be associated with one of BPMN flow object elements. You can include any information that is important for the process flow or for the process reader.

We discussed the explicitness of the process. So what about the amount of each ingredient in our *Bake chocolate cake process*? The model lacks information on how much of each ingredient should be used.

The easiest way that may come to mind is to communicate the amount of each ingredient within the task names: e.g. 'Add 2 eggs.' In a non-executable process, this is an acceptable solution. However, the goal of the BPMN flow elements is to show the process flow, not to obscure readability with too much information that does not have a direct influence on the process flow.

> **TIP:** There are no strict rules on how to name tasks. It is recommended to start with the basic form of the verb, as the task should describe what action is performed.

To communicate the ingredient amounts, we may also use **text annotation**, which might be a better solution taking into account process readability.

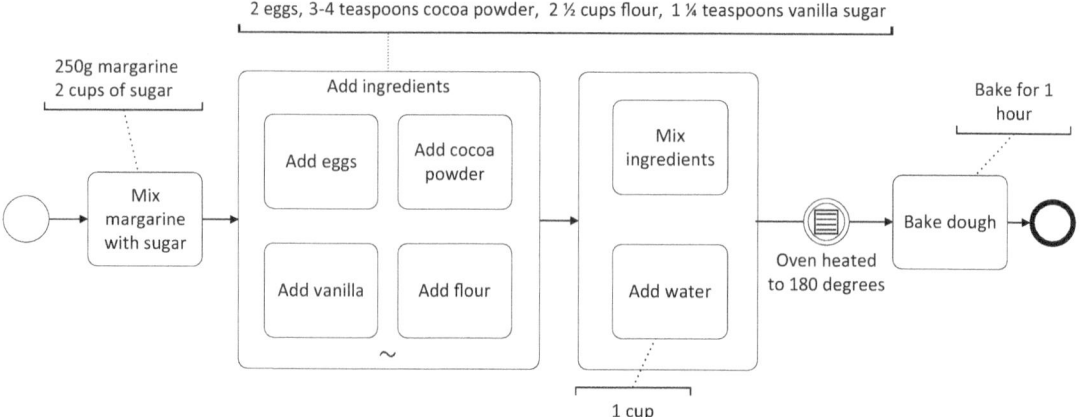

Figure 17: Make cake process with information about ingredient amounts

1.3. Make cream process

Let's model the second subprocess: *Make cream*.

Part of the recipe describes the cream preparation: *Dissolve 2 teaspoons of gelatin in 3 tablespoons of water. Pour the sugar into boiling water, and boil to dissolve the sugar. Pour the hot syrup onto the egg whites while whipping. At the end, add the dissolved gelatin, a pinch of salt and the vanilla sugar.*

Identify tasks and subprocesses within the top-level process

Now let's try to identify all activities and initially classify which are tasks and which can be organized within subprocesses. Here are recipe fragments and their analysis:
- *Dissolve 2 teaspoons of gelatin in 3 tablespoons of water*. This is one undivided activity – task *Dissolve gelatin*.
- *Pour the sugar into boiling water, and boil to dissolve the sugar*. We have at least two activities that need to be performed to achieve one goal – prepare syrup: dissolve and boil. We may model them directly within the top-level process if the whole number of steps won't be too great or we can organize them within a subprocess *Prepare syrup*.
- *Pour the hot syrup onto the egg whites while whipping. At the end, add the dissolved gelatin, a pinch of salt and the vanilla sugar.* We have four activities related to adding ingredients that we may organize within a subprocess *Add ingredients*. Another undivided activity is whip.

TIP: Include within a subprocess a consistent part of the flow that leads to a certain result or can be conceptually separate from the parent process.

Below is the first version of the top-level model (Figure 18). We may also consider to model *Dissolve gelatin* and *Prepare syrup* activities:
- between an AND-Split and an AND-Join
- within an Ad-Hoc subprocess.

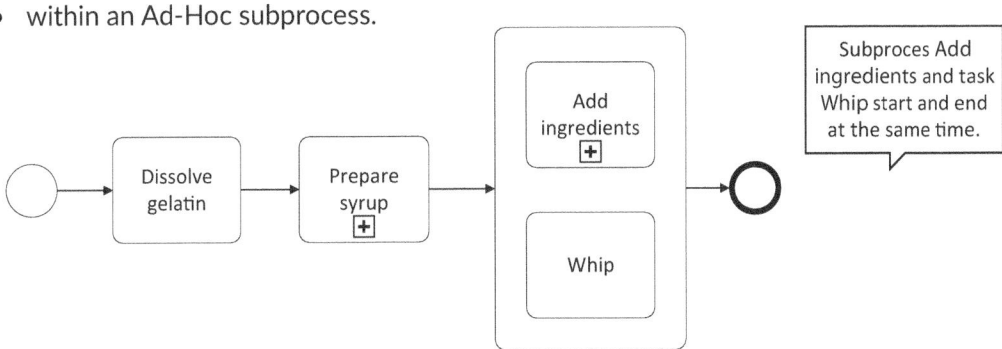

Figure 18: Make cream top-level process

To show that when we add all ingredients we need to whip at the same time, we use a **parallel box**. Task *Whip* and subprocess *Add ingredients* are modeled within the parallel box. The parallel box mechanism is applicable to any combination of parallel activities – both tasks and subprocesses. To show it in a more compact way, we recommend to always use collapsed subprocesses.

> **TIP:** Activities without incoming flows start when their parent process is instantiated. This rule is applicable to tasks and subprocesses.

Activity interrupted by other activity

Let's analyze the process of preparing syrup. The fragment of recipe that describes how to prepare a syrup is really short: *Pour sugar into boiling water, and boil to dissolve the sugar*. Everyone knows what to do reading this fragment so a first step can simply distinguish two tasks.

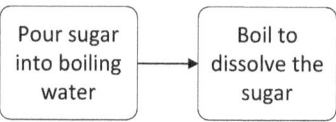

Figure 19: Prepare syrup subprocess – version A

But is such an approach correct? I'm sure that part of the flow (Figure 19) is clear for everyone and we may leave it as it is. Still, not all activities are explicitly presented, and based on this simple example we can practice how to extract all needed elements and model unambiguous flows.

> **TIP:** Create unambiguous models which do not leave room for various interpretations.

Before we pour sugar into boiling water we need to boil the water first – this fact seems to be obvious but is not presented explicitly in version A (Figure 19). Then we continue boiling till the sugar is dissolved.

Let's add an activity responsible for boiling the water and interpret this approach (Figure 20): we boil water, then end this task; next pour sugar (which means that we aren't boiling the water at this point); then boil the water till the sugar is dissolved. In real life, we just boil the water all the time till the sugar is dissolved. What could be improved?
  1. The task boil should be continuous, not broken up
  2. The task boil has an additional restriction that we can model using separate BPMN elements

1.3. Make cream process

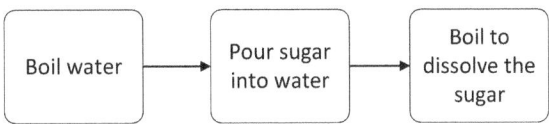

Figure 20: Prepare syrup subprocess – version B

TIP: Is there an activity that is interrupted by other tasks? This is a signal that an intermediate event attached to the boundary of the activity may be a good solution.

In the next three sample solutions (Figure 22), we use a non-interrupting conditional event that indicates that when the water starts boiling, we pour the sugar and continue this activity.

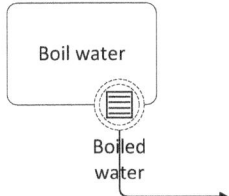

Figure 21: Example of non-interrupting conditional event

The information about dissolving sugar is shown differently:
- Version C – using an interrupting conditional event *Sugar dissolved* that when it is met, terminates the task *Boil water*
- Version D – using an additional task *Dissolve sugar*
- Version E – using text annotation, we leave the decision on when to stop boiling to the performer.

1.3. Make cream process

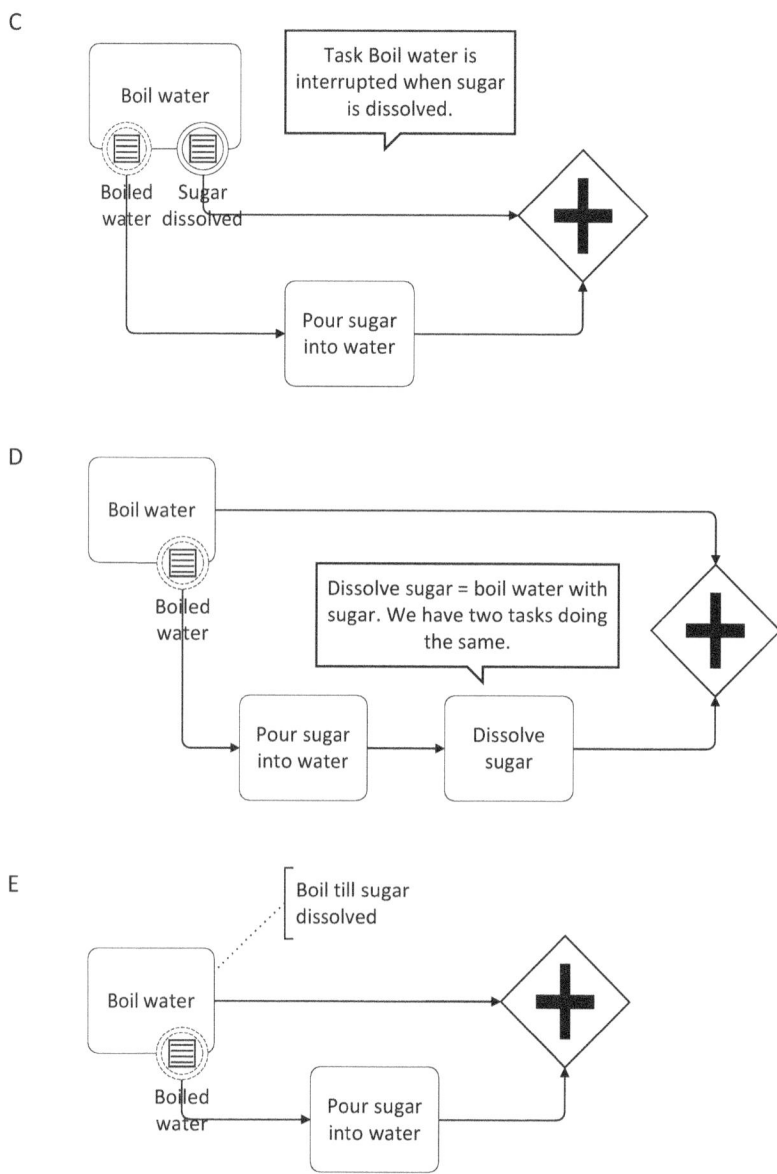

Figure 22: Prepare syrup subprocess – versions C, D, E

THEORY: Conditional event

A conditional event communicates what happens when a defined condition becomes *true*.

The condition relates to a process's internal variables or to external environment variables. It can be specified in any manner that is logical and understandable: x + y = 10, employee_num > 10, number of participants is bigger than 20, etc.

A conditional intermediate event is used in a sequence flow when some condition must be met so the process may go further.

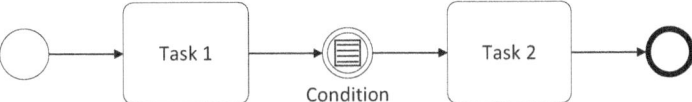

A conditional intermediate event attached to the boundary of an activity is used to activate an exception flow. The event can be triggered only if the activity is active. The activity itself can be interrupted or not. This is interpreted as follows:

During execution of Task 1, if *Condition* becomes *true*, Task 1 is interrupted (cancelled) and the process is continued only through the exception flow to Task 3.

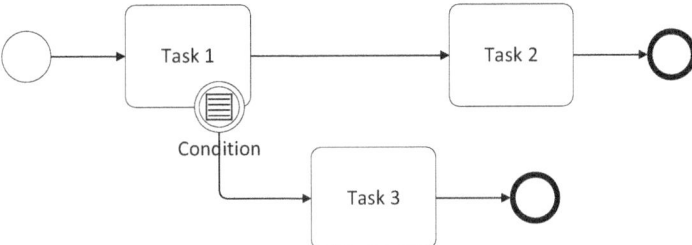

During execution of Task 4, if *Condition* becomes *true*, the conditional event fires an exception flow and the process goes to Task 6. Task 4 is still active so after it ends, the process goes to Task 5.

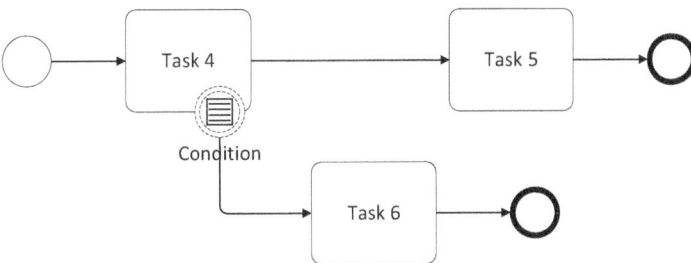

A conditional event can also be used to start a process: it fires when the condition becomes *true*. In this case, however, the start event condition can only reflect external variables. It cannot specify process variables because the process instance simply doesn't exist yet. For example, you can define a condition like 'outside temperature < 25C,' or 'number of employers in company is over 20,' but a condition related to the process itself, for example 'process data changes state,' is forbidden.

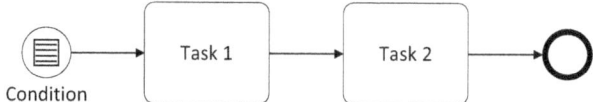

A conditional start event can be also used as a trigger for an event subprocess. It may be defined as an interrupting or non-interrupting start event. Read more about event subprocesses in Section 2.1. **THEORY: Event subprocess.**

The conditional event is a trigger event; that's why you cannot use it to end a process. BPMN doesn't define a conditional end event element.

Let's analyze the second collapsed subprocess *Add ingredients*. Our intention is to show that the order of adding ingredients is important, so we use a sequence flow to show the order of tasks. The task *Pour syrup on egg whites* has an additional input requirement: syrup is hot. As before, the most common ways to model this in non-executable processes are:
- include the condition within the task name: Pour hot syrup on egg whites
- use text annotations
- use a conditional intermediate event: *Syrup is hot* within the sequence flow as an event directly preceding this task.

Just remember that this information should be included in the process (Figure 23).

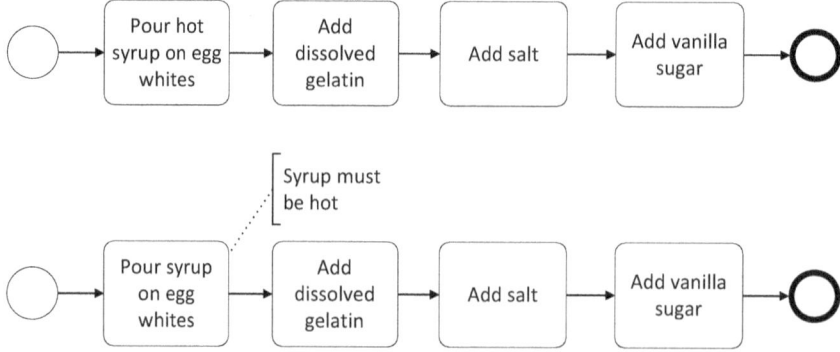

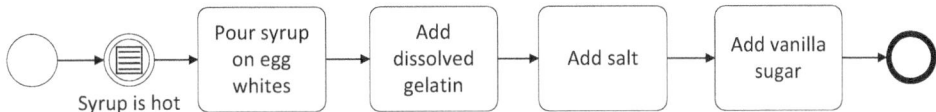

Figure 23: Add ingredients subprocess with input requirement for task Pour syrup – three versions

1.4. Data flow

In many models, we also want to include information about what data and information are needed to perform some activity and what data are produced as a result of some particular step or the whole process.

BPMN defines special elements responsible for data modeling. In BPMN diagrams we can model what physical objects and information are used or produced during execution of an activity or the whole process. So the **data flows** are about how to model the flow of needed data and objects within a process.

Modeling data flows is not so obvious and can lead to some mistakes. Using the bake a cake process, we will practice how to model (and how *not* to model) data objects within a process. Let's start from the theory.

THEORY: Data flow elements

BPMN provides the elements needed to model data flows: data objects, data inputs, data outputs, data stores.

A **data object** represents information or a physical object and is used to show how data are processed during process execution. Its lifecycle depends on the lifecycle of the parent process, which means that the data object exists only as long as the parent process is active. When the process is finished, the data instance is no longer available.

Data input and **data output**, in contrast to a data object, refer to the whole process. Their lifecycle is not tied to the parent process lifecycle. We use data input to indicate what data are needed before the process begins, and data output to indicate what data are a result

of the process execution. These types of elements exist respectively before the process begins and after the process ends.

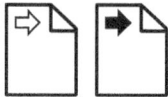

Use the **data collection marker** to indicate the collection of data.

To show the flow of the data, we use **data association** and link data objects with related activities or events.

A **data store** is used within the process to enable storage, update and retrieval of data that are used while the process is executed and may exist after the process ends.

You can also use properties and messages to include information about the data flow. Unlike data objects and messages, properties are not visible on the diagram.

We know the theory – now let's do some practice. Let's analyze data modeling rules based on the *Make cake* process (Figure 24).

1.4. Data flow

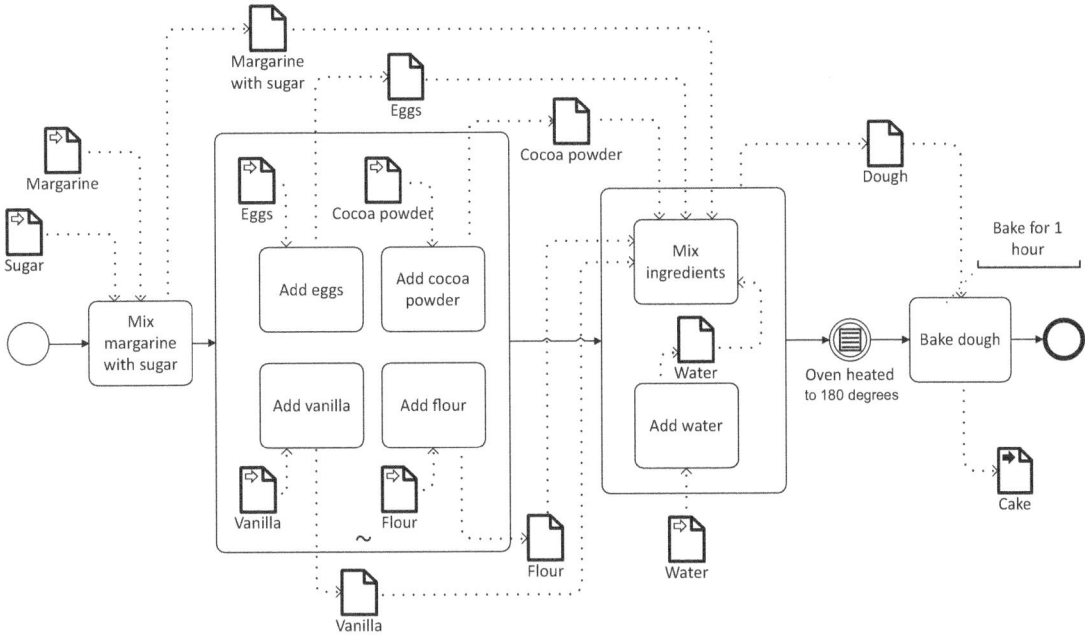

Figure 24: Data flow of Make cake process

We use data inputs to show what ingredients are added. The interpretation goes as follows: data exists (ingredients are prepared) before the process begins, and these data items are required to start performing the particular activity.

To show what ingredients are mixed in the *Mix ingredients* we used data association and data objects as inputs and outputs for the task. This means that the result of one activity is used as input to another (ingredients added to the pot are next mixed together).

Data object modeling rules
- A data object can be associated with a task or a subprocess (e.g. dough).
- Data objects can be modeled as inputs and outputs of activities that are executed within the same or different subprocesses within the same process (e.g. flour, eggs, water).
- Data objects with the same name within the process represent the same data.
- You must not model data input and data output directly associated with a subprocess! See the diagram below.

1.4. Data flow

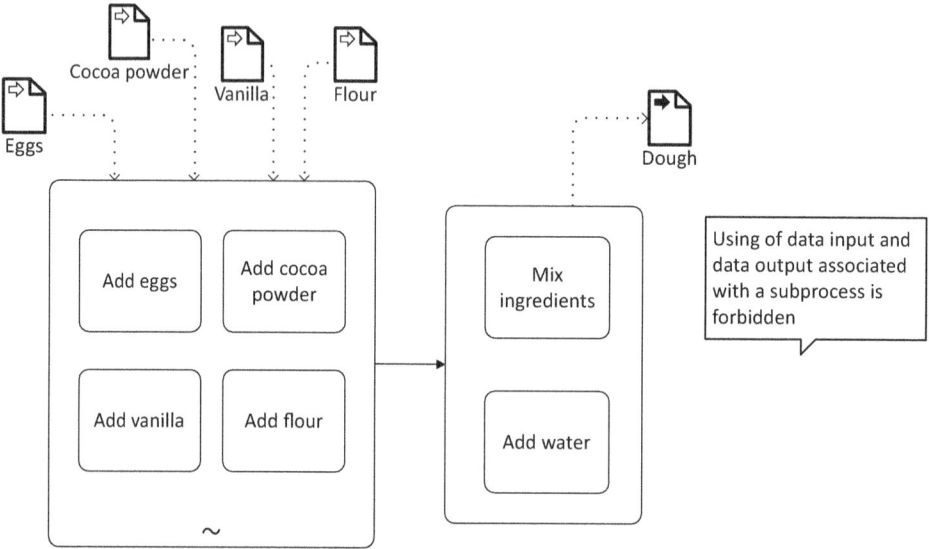

Figure 25: Use of Data inputs and Data outputs associated with a subprocess is forbidden

- You may use a data objects as input and output associated with a subprocess. Look at the top-level process example. We have deliberately changed the name of the task *Decorate cake with cream* to *Decorate cake* as the data flow shows what items are used in this task (Figure 26).
- For data object, data input and data output you can define a state [*state*] (Figure 26).

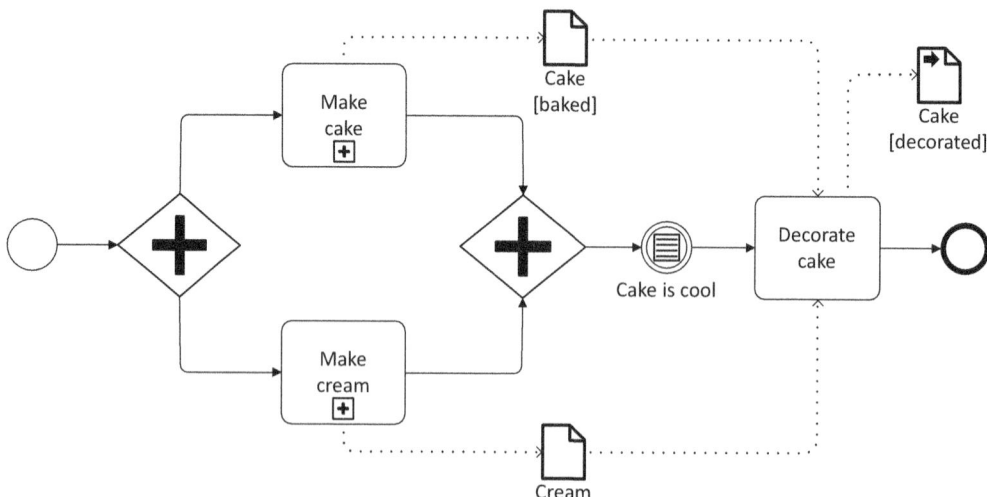

Figure 26: Make chocolate cake top-level process with data flow

Example 2: Scrum

In this example we will be working with processes describing the Scrum framework. Process descriptions are prepared based on *The Scrum Guide* [2]. Process scope is adapted to the learning outcomes and does not cover all aspects that may arise in the Scrum framework and software development.

Learning outcomes

Based on this example we discuss and learn:
- Tasks and subprocesses markers
- The difference between loop and multi-instance activities
- How to model public and private business processes
- The differences between private executable and private non-executable business processes
- How to organize and present processes on different levels
- How to identify process participants and avoid mixing them with roles/users within process participants
- Message flow modeling rules and message event theory
- Exclusive gateways
- Event subprocesses and boundary events – theory, when to use them and what are the differences
- How you can organize processes using lanes
- How to model collaborative activities
- Main issues related to Collaboration

2.1. Scrum process

Let's start with an overview of Scrum, which is an incremental framework for managing a team working on a software development. It consists of iterations called Sprints during which a team delivers a software product increment.

All Sprints are organized as follows:
- The Sprint starts with a Sprint Planning meeting in which the team determines the goal for the coming sprint. Development of a new Increment starts after the Planning Meeting.
- Every day of the Sprint at the same time, the Development Team has a 15-min long meeting called the Daily Scrum or Stand-up, to plan their development work and make commitments to each other.
- At the end of the Sprint, two meetings take place. The first is a Sprint Review meeting in which the team presents what was done in the Sprint.
- The final meeting is a Retrospective Meeting in which the team reviews its work and how to improve it during the next sprint.

People directly involved in the software product development belong to the Scrum team; the roles are as follows:
- The Product Owner is responsible for building and managing the Product Backlog.
- The Development Team is a self-organized team that drives the sprint to deliver a software product increment and manage the Sprint Backlog.
- The Scrum Master in general supports the team in Scrum implementation and facilitates Scrum meetings.

The two main Sprint artifacts are:
- The Product Backlog: a list of all items (functionalities etc.) needed for the software product.
- The Sprint Backlog: a list of product backlog items covering the functionality that is to be delivered at the end of the Sprint – called increment. The Increment consists of "done" Product Backlog items.

Multi-instance process

Let's analyze the above description in the context of developing a process model. In general, Scrum consists of Sprints, which are always carried out one by one. The top-level process has a *Take Sprint* subprocess with a **multi-instance marker** for sequential instances.

> **TIP:** When an activity is performed many times with different data, use the multi-instance marker.

The marker means that a subprocess is performed iteratively. In each iteration a new instance of the subprocess is created. This is required for the *Take Sprint* subprocess as in every sprint, we use a different set of backlog items and produce a different Increment.

Figure 27: Top-level scrum process

BPMN specifies two types of markers indicating that a subprocess is performed iteratively. See the theory section that follows for more information.

THEORY: Loop subprocess characteristics

BPMN distinguishes two types of markers that are used to show that a subprocess is repetitively executed.

The **loop marker** is used when the task has a looping behavior. It this case there is one task instance that iteratively executes some activity till a looping condition is *true*.

The **multi-instance marker** also indicates that a subprocess may be performed many times. However in this case every execution creates a new subprocess instance. This means that in every iteration, the subprocess may use and produce a different data set. Subprocess can be performed sequentially or in parallel.

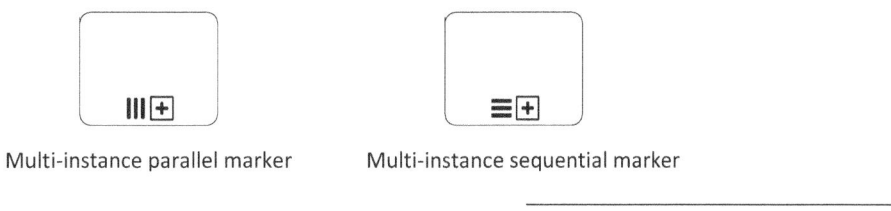

Multi-instance parallel marker   Multi-instance sequential marker

2.1. Scrum process

Let's now model the *Take Sprint* process showing how the Sprint is organized. In the Sprint we can distinguish four types of meetings, which take place at different times but always in a specific order.

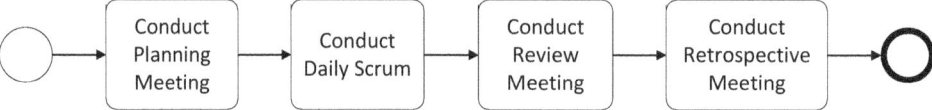

Figure 28: Scrum subprocess with order of scrum meetings

We now have two more issues to resolve and model. First we should include one more activity – the development. Second our model should show that the Daily Scrum is conducted many times within the Sprint.

Let's start with the first issue. The main activity within Scrum is development that leads to producing an Increment. According to the Scrum description, development starts after the Planning Meeting. However, we don't have exact information on when development of an Increment ends. Can it be performed till the end of the sprint or should it be finished before the Review Meeting in which the team presents the results of their work?

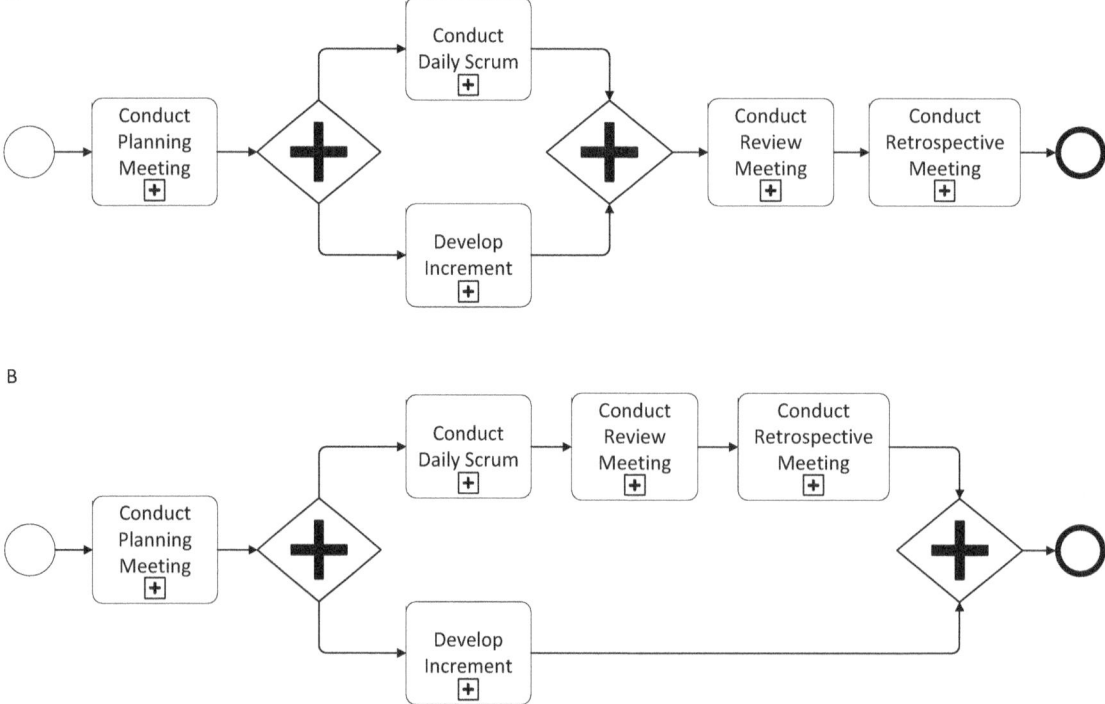

Figure 29: Develop Increment subprocess – two versions

46

2.1. Scrum process

In the first diagram (Figure 29A), development finishes before the Review Meeting, and the Review and Retrospective meetings are modeled as the last activities in the Sprint. The adopted solution results from the description "At the end of the Sprint, there is a Sprint Review Meeting in which the team presents what was done in the Sprint." and the official Scrum framework graphic. In the second diagram (Figure 29B) we assume that some work related to the Increment development can be performed between and after Review and Retrospective meetings (e.g. testing). This seems to be a more natural approach as not every Scrum Team needs to plan Review and Retrospective meetings in the last hours of a Sprint.

For the purposes of the example, we assume that the development ends before the Review Meeting (Figure 30). In this solution, development and daily Scrum activities are independent and both are executed after the Planning Meeting and should end before the Review Meeting.

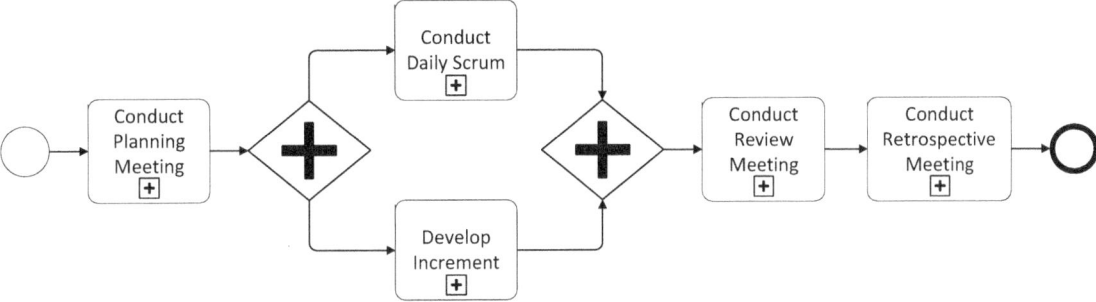

Figure 30: Sprint process with Daily Scrum meeting and development performed independently

Subprocess called within execution of another activity

The second issue is related to the Daily Scrum. In our current model (Figure 30), a Daily Scrum starts after the Planning Meeting and it is executed only once. What we want to achieve is to show that the Daily Scrum meeting is conducted on a daily basis during the time the Development Team work on developing an Increment. Or, in other words, that the Daily Scrum is part of the Development. We may resolve this case in two ways – using an **event subprocess** or using a **boundary event**. Let's go through the event subprocess theory first.

> **TIP:** If an activity may be performed many times during execution of another activity, use a non-interrupting event subprocess or a non-interrupting boundary event.

THEORY: Event subprocess

An event subprocess, in contrast to the standard subprocess, is triggered by an event and is not a part of the standard sequence flow.

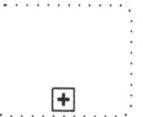

Because an event subprocess starts only if a specific event occurs, it has no incoming and outgoing flows.

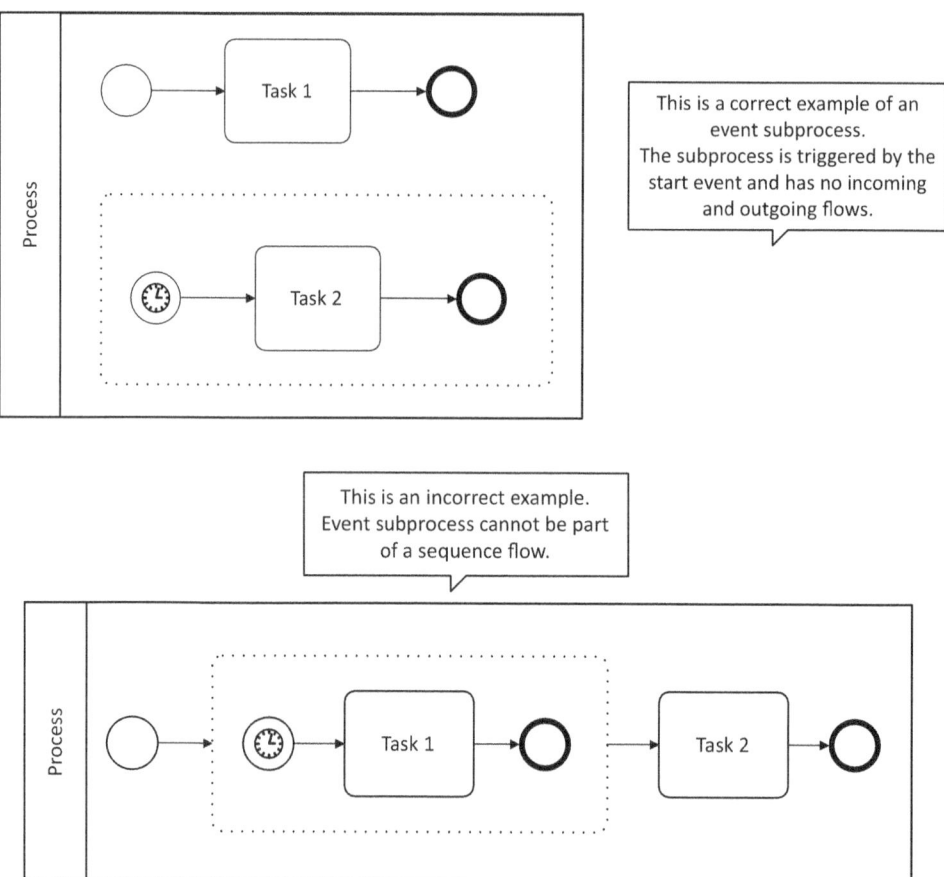

We can use an event subprocess within both top-level processes and subprocesses.

2.1. Scrum process

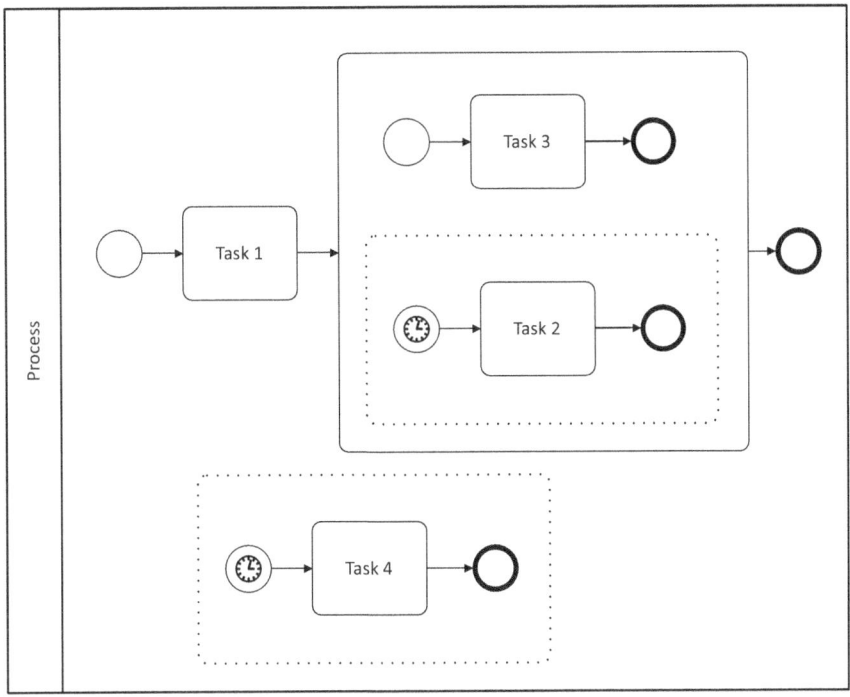

In standard subprocesses, start and end events are optional, and the subprocess may have many start events.

For an event subprocess, the rules are different. Event subprocess MUST start with a trigger, so a start event and thus an end event are obligatory. What's more, there can be only ONE start event (one trigger for one event subprocess).

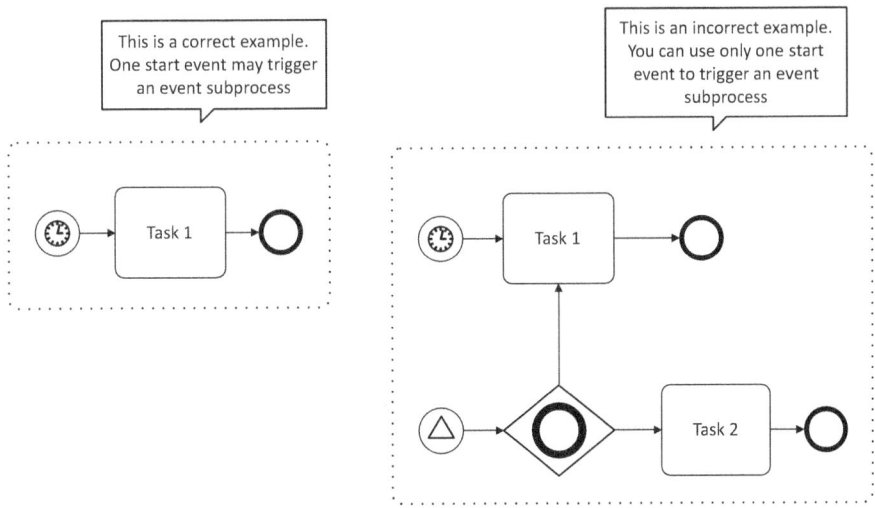

49

An Event subprocess starts with one of the following start events. Other types are not allowed.

Event Type	Interrupting	Non-Interrupting
Message	✉	✉
Timer	⏲	⏲
Error	⚡	
Escalation	▲	▲
Compensation	⏪	
Conditional	🗏	🗏
Signal	△	△
Multiple	⬠	⬠
Parallel Multiple	⊕	⊕

Most of above start events are interrupting. If an event subprocess starts with an **interrupting event**, it cancels the process within which it's fired. If a **non-interrupting** event is used, both the event subprocess and the process within which it is fired are active.

This rule also results in the fact that a non-interrupting event subprocess can be triggered many times, while an interrupting event subprocess can only trigger once as it terminates the parent process.

An event subprocess cannot have boundary events. This is a very important rule that is often broken as standard subprocesses and tasks may have boundary events.

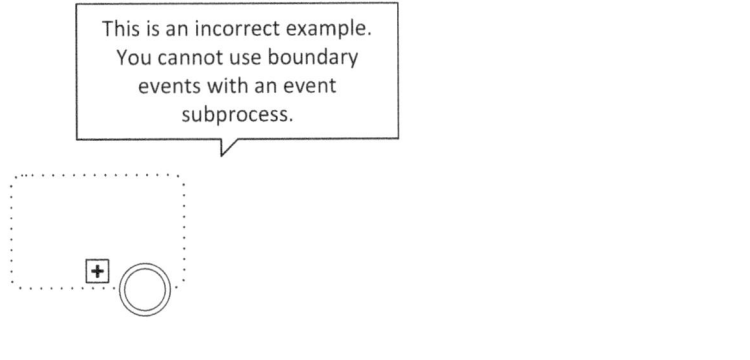

Let's go back to our example. To show that the Daily Scrum is repeated daily, we model the *Conduct Daily Scrum* activity within an event subprocess. The meeting is held daily at some specific hour so the trigger that fires the event process is a non-interrupting timer event (Figure 31).

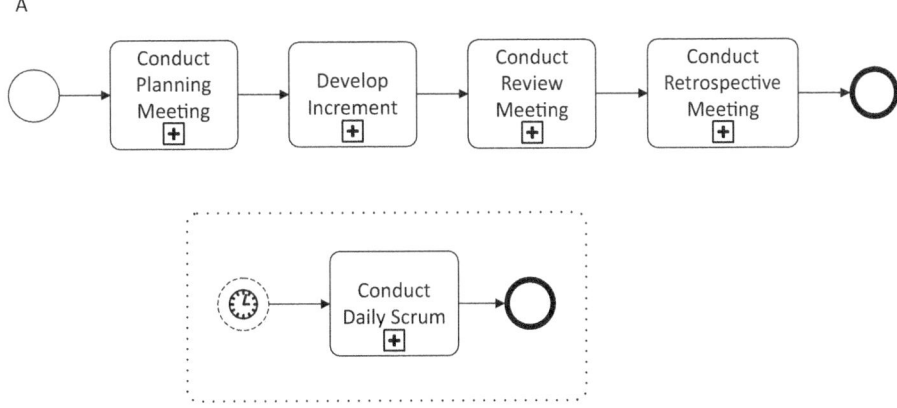

2.1. Scrum process

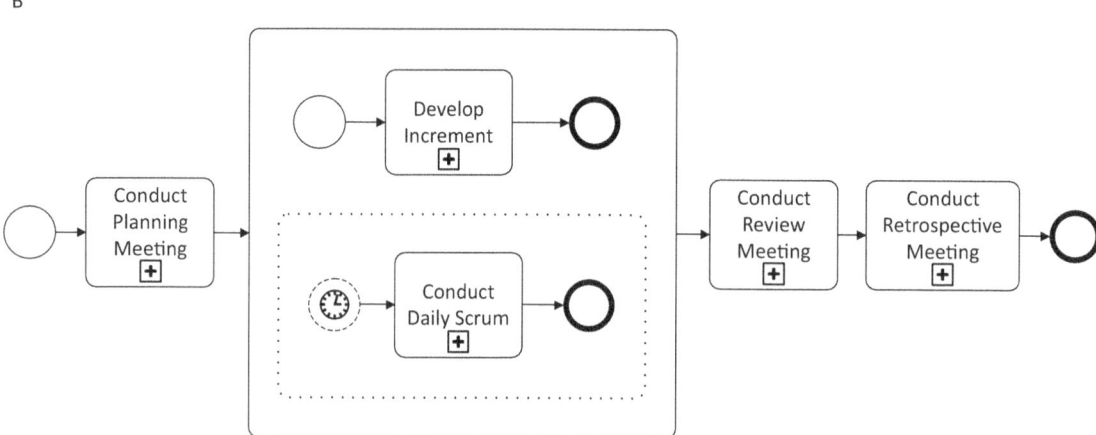

Figure 31: Conduct Daily Scrum subprocess within an event subprocess – two versions

In diagram A (Figure 31), the event subprocess is modeled within the *Take Scrum* process and fires from the top level. This means that an event may occur at any time when the *Take Scrum* process is active. In diagram B (Figure 31), the subprocess is modeled within a newly introduced subprocess (without name) and may be triggered only when this process is active. We modeled it in such way as to show that Daily Scrum meetings are organized while the Development Team work on an Increment development.

> **TIP:** Model an event subprocess only within a process during which the subprocess start event may occur.

Which approach is better? All meetings are held at a certain time; using solution A we can't be sure that Daily Scrum won't overlap with Planning, Review or Retrospective meetings. Using approach B we are sure that Daily Scrum, like development, can only be held after planning and before review meetings, which we previously assumed.

Introducing subprocesses and process levels

Let's now discuss the issue of introducing new processes and presenting process levels (Figure 32).

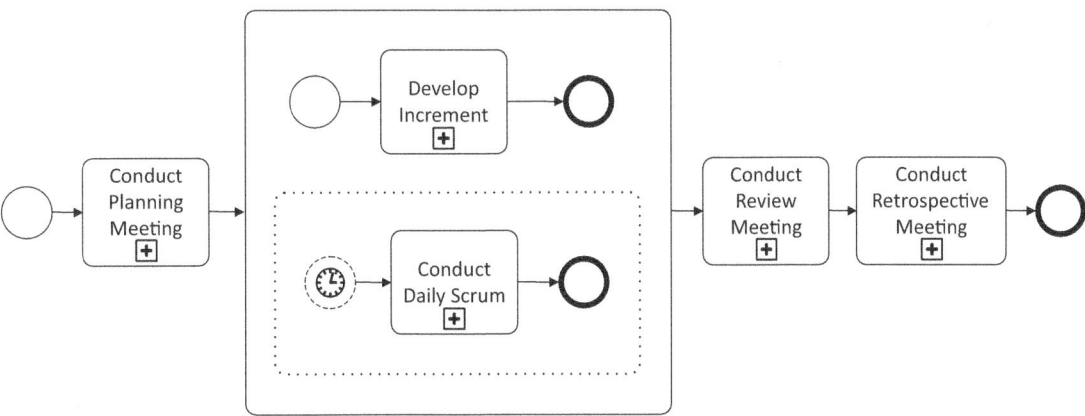

Figure 32: Take Sprint process

As we already discussed, every process level should be modeled separately to make the process easier to analyze and read. Sometimes we deliberately want to show some specific subprocess expanded. This typically relates to parallel boxes and event subprocess but can also relate to standard subprocesses that are provided to restrict some specific behavior. In such cases, when we don't show the process collapsed at any level, not giving a name to the subprocesses is acceptable (but still recommended). If at some level the newly introduced process is shown as collapsed, the title is required.

Look what happens if we now go back to the top-level view of the *Take Sprint* subprocess with collapsed child-level subprocesses: the newly introduced subprocess serving as a grouping container has no title (Figure 33).

2.1. Scrum process

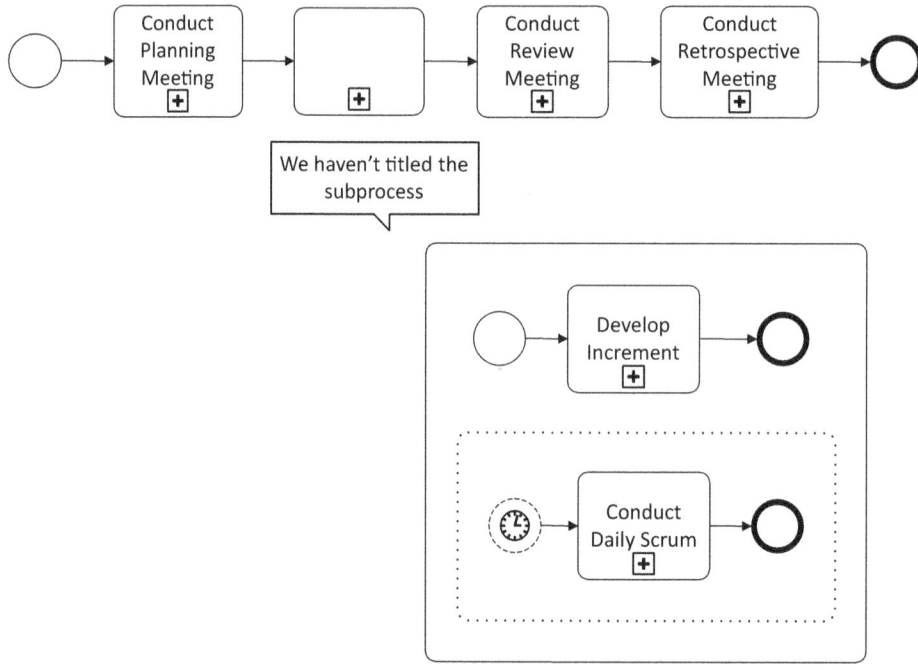

Figure 33: Top-level view of Take Sprint process – newly introduced standard subprocess has no title

To solve this issue we may rearrange subprocesses. Look at the proposal in Figure 34. Conduct Daily Scrum is 'part' of Increment development so it can be included directly within the *Develop Increment* process. In this example we won't analyze how the *Develop Increment* process is performed and what elements it consists of. There are a number of approaches and methods of organizing work within a development team, and we are not going to discuss them here. For the purposes of the example, we just provide one activity, Develop Software, which we assume consists of all the needed steps leading to developing the Increment.

2.1. Scrum process

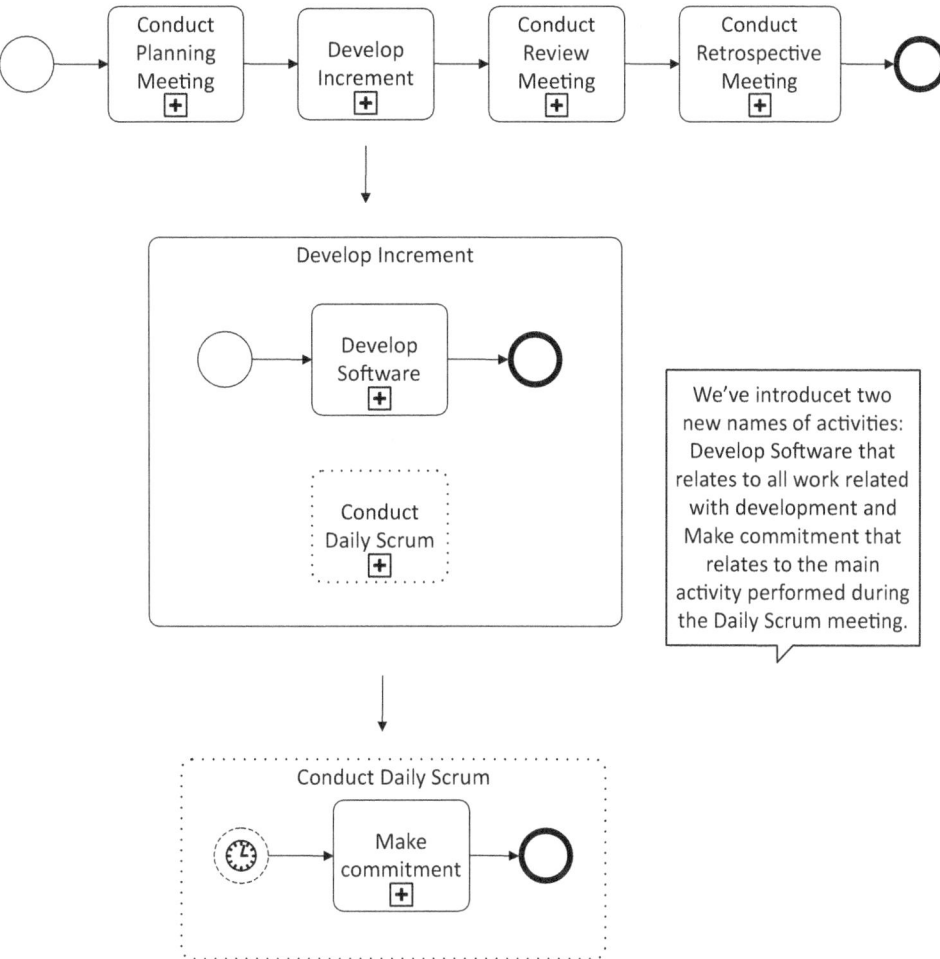

Figure 34: Naming of newly added subprocesses.

Boundary event

An alternative to the event subprocess is usage of the boundary event. Let's look at the theory of boundary events.

THEORY: Boundary event

A boundary event is an intermediate trigger event attached to the boundary of an activity that fires an exceptional flow.

Only intermediate events can be attached to an activity boundary. Start events and end events are not allowed. Why? You cannot start a new process when executing some activity within the current process, or end the whole process in such a way.

The boundary event is always a trigger event. During execution of a task or a subprocess, some event may occur and somehow influence the process flow. However, an executed activity itself cannot throw any events. Throw events are used only within a sequence flow and understood as one of the process steps.

A boundary event can be interrupting or non-interrupting. For any type of event used as a boundary event, the rules are the same. An interrupting boundary event interrupts the parent activity to which it's attached. When an interrupting event is fired, the parent activity is immediately cancelled. Non-interrupting events do not influence parent activity performance; this means that if the event is triggered and fires the exceptional flow, the activity it's attached to is still active.

The list of events that can be attached to the activity boundary:

Event Type	Interrupting	Non-Interrupting
Message	✉	✉
Timer	⏲	⏲
Error	⚡	
Escalation	▲	▲
Cancel	✖	
Compensation	⏮	
Conditional	▤	▤
Signal	△	△

2.1. Scrum process

Event Type	Interrupting	Non-Interrupting
Multiple	⬠	⬠
Parallel Multiple	⊕	⊕

We may resolve the issue related to the iterative performance of the *Conduct Daily Scrum* subprocess using a timer intermediate non-interrupting trigger event attached to the boundary of the *Develop Increment* subprocess. In this case, the *Conduct Daily Scrum* subprocess is modeled in an exceptional flow that is fired by the timer event every day while the *Develop Increment* subprocess is active.

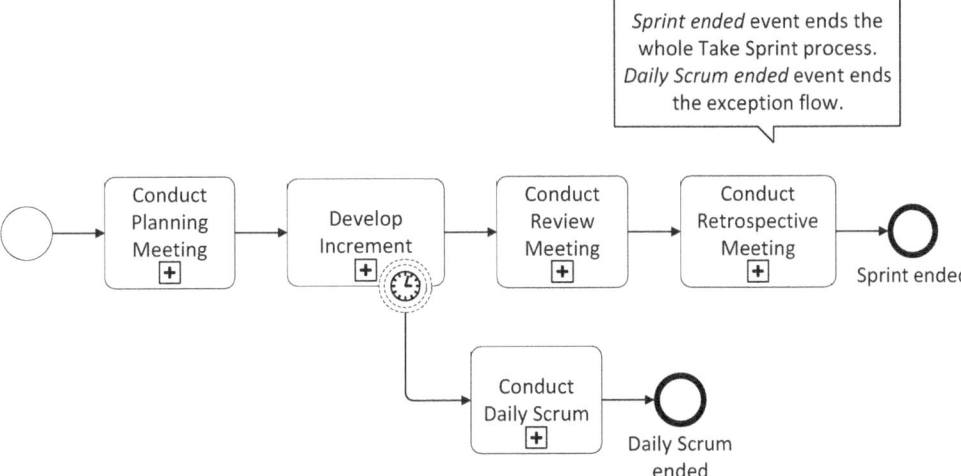

Figure 35: Conduct Daily Scrum subprocess within exceptional flow

In this version, the *Conduct Daily Scrum* subprocess is directly seen from the top-level view of the *Take Sprint* process. As we also don't need to introduce additional subprocesses, it's seems to be the simplest version. However in this approach, the *Conduct Daily Scrum* subprocess is fully contained by the *Take Sprint* process, not *Develop Increment*, which means that it doesn't have access to Develop Increment variables, e.g. data objects. At this level we don't know if this is necessary, and to be honest, in non-executable business processes readers usually do not pay attention to this. Still, this is a very important difference between an event subprocess and a boundary event. If you want the activity fired during the execution of another activity be contained completely by this activity, model it as an event subprocess within this activity.

For the purpose of a further example, we use both solution alternatives to discuss other interesting BPMN modeling patterns.

2.1. Scrum process

Process participant

So far we've modeled non-executable **private** business processes. A private process is the basic process from the author's point of view that shows all the process details. So far, processes have been shown without information about who is executing the given process. In BPMN, processes can be modeled within special containers – **pools** – that represent the process participant.

THEORY: Pool

A pool is a graphical container of a process that you can title any way you want to. A pool may represent a team, person, system, organization or any other participant that performs activities within a process. Using pools is optional. The pool is dedicated to one whole process. You cannot use one Pool for many processes or include part of a process within a Pool.

All the process elements must be drawn inside the Pool. The only BPMN element that can cross the Pool boundary is a **message flow**. We discuss message flows in Section 2.5.

THEORY: Message flow

Below is an example of *Take Sprint* subprocess modeled within a pool that indicates the Scrum Team (Figure 36). This means that the Scrum Team participates in the process.

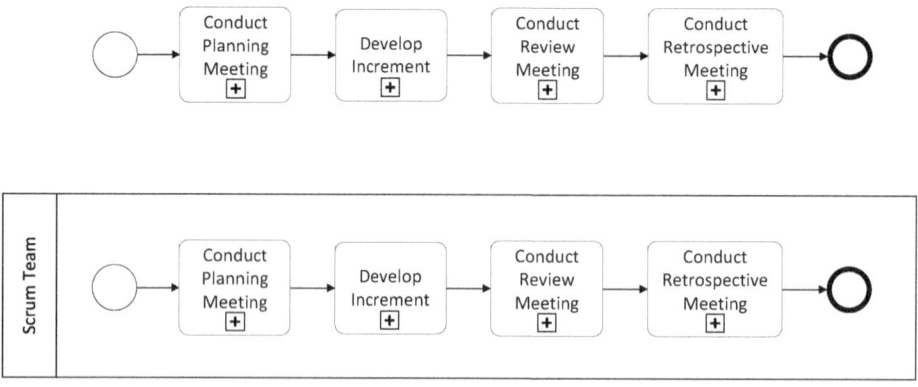

Figure 36: Private process without pool and private process within a pool

2.2. Planning Meeting

We have a top-level model of the sprint; let's try to model particular child-level processes related to meetings. Based on these processes we will learn how to model private and public processes and collaboration.

2.2. Planning Meeting

Process description

The Planning Meeting is divided into two parts. The first part of the meeting is dedicated to determining what will be done in the Sprint. At the start, the Product Owner (PO) discusses objectives and product backlog items related to the goal. Next the Scrum Team collaborates on understanding the work. As a result of the discussion, the Development Team selects Product Backlog items for the Sprint. Based on the selected items, the Scrum Team sets up the Sprint Goal. The second part of the meeting focuses on determining the plan for delivering an Increment. Knowing the goal and having selected the product backlog items, the Development Team creates the plan for how to deliver an Increment. The result of this activity is a Sprint Backlog. If the Development Team thinks it has too much or too little work for a Sprint, it may renegotiate selected items with the PO.

What activities can we distinguish in the process?
- Discuss Product Backlog items
- Collaborate on work
- Select Product Backlog items
- Set up Sprint goal
- Determine delivery plan
- Renegotiate selected items

We will model all the above activities as tasks, as we have a brief process description and we don't have information on exactly how each activity is performed. Could it be divided into smaller tasks? To indicate that activities consist of other smaller tasks, you may use collapsed subprocesses.

In the first part of the meeting, activities are sequential (Figure 37).

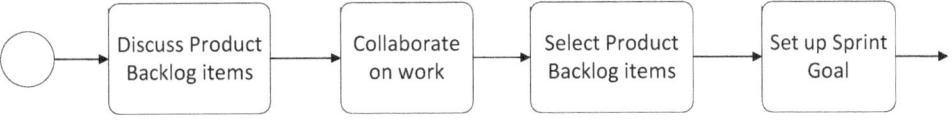

Figure 37: First part of the planning meeting process

Decision point

In the second part of the meeting, the Development Team determines the plan for delivering Product Backlog items and renegotiates items with the PO if necessary. To model a decision point (do we have too much or too little work?), we use the **exclusive gateway** with condition: too much or too little work. Each of the outgoing flows from the exclusive gateway contains one of the possible answers (Figure 38).

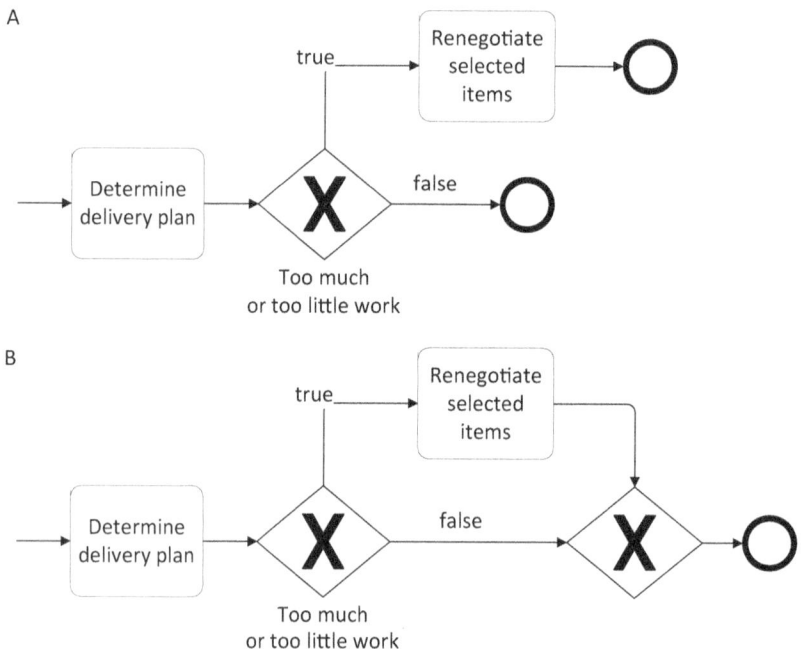

Figure 38: Exclusive gateway – alternative flows and different approaches to ending the process.

Number of end events in the process

We have two solutions that differ in the way the process ends (Figure 38). We can use two end events or merge alternative paths into one and finish the process with one end event.

In our case, regardless of whether the Product Backlog items are renegotiated with the PO, the process finishes with a defined Sprint Backlog, which is a delivery plan tied to the team capacity. We don't want to underline the fact that items were negotiated – it's not important from our point of view. Separate end events are also not supported by the next *Take sprint* process steps.

2.2. Planning Meeting

We don't have differences in the top-level flow regardless of which event ends the *Planning meeting* subprocess. That's why we decide to use solution B.

TIP: If a process finishes with different conditions depending on which path the flow took, use separate end events to indicate these differences. Each event should be named differently.

TIP: If the process always finishes with the same conditions, use one end event.

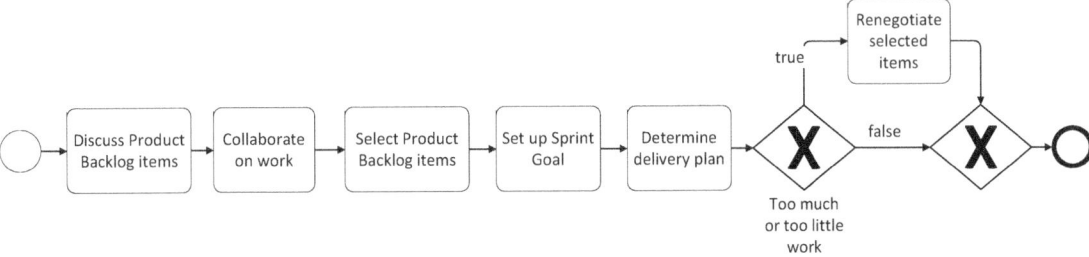

Figure 39: Conduct Planning meeting process

THEORY: Exclusive gateway

The Exclusive gateway is a decision point that branches the flow into alternative paths. On each outgoing path we define a condition that is a possible answer for the condition defined /question asked on the exclusive gateway. The gateway behavior is analogous to a logical XOR: only one path can meet the condition and can be chosen.

The Exclusive gateway is modeled with or without a marker. The decision is up to the modeler; however, it is important to be consistent within the whole diagram.

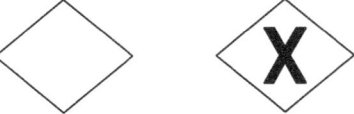

All outgoing paths from an exclusive gateway should include all the possible answers to the question asked on the gateway. If not, an exception is thrown. To be sure that all possibilities have been handled, you can use an outgoing default flow.

2.2. Planning Meeting

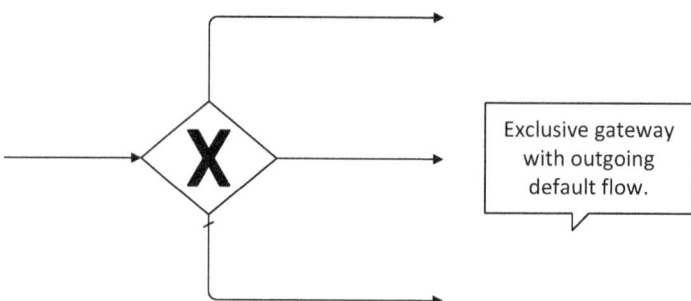

If the gateway is used to merge paths, the path that arrives, goes through the gateway and continues the flow. It is not a synchronization point! Each incoming path is routed to the outgoing path without synchronization.

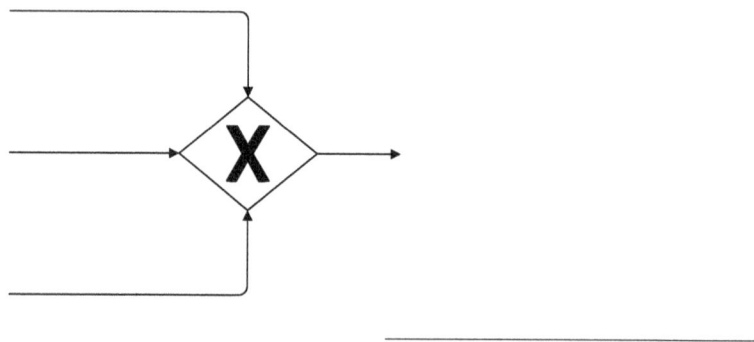

Process organization

Very often in processes we need to additionally categorize activities to show, for example, by which department, system or role the activity is performed. BPMN provides the possibility to group and categorize activities within a pool.

The next thing we can do in this exercise is to categorize *Planning Meeting* process activities within Scrum Team roles. Our model will explicitly show which role performs each activity. To categorize activities within a pool we use **lanes**.

2.2. Planning Meeting

THEORY: Lanes

Lanes may represent people, systems, positions in organizations, departments, or any other concepts that categorize activities within a pool. The most important thing about lanes is that their meaning is up to the author. The author decides if and how to categorize activities.

Lanes are modeled within a pool. The pool represents process participants whereas lanes additionally categorize activities.

There are no restrictions on the number of lanes within a pool. You can also model nested lanes.

Activities and events must be drawn within one lane. You must not draw an event or activity between two lanes on the lane boundary.

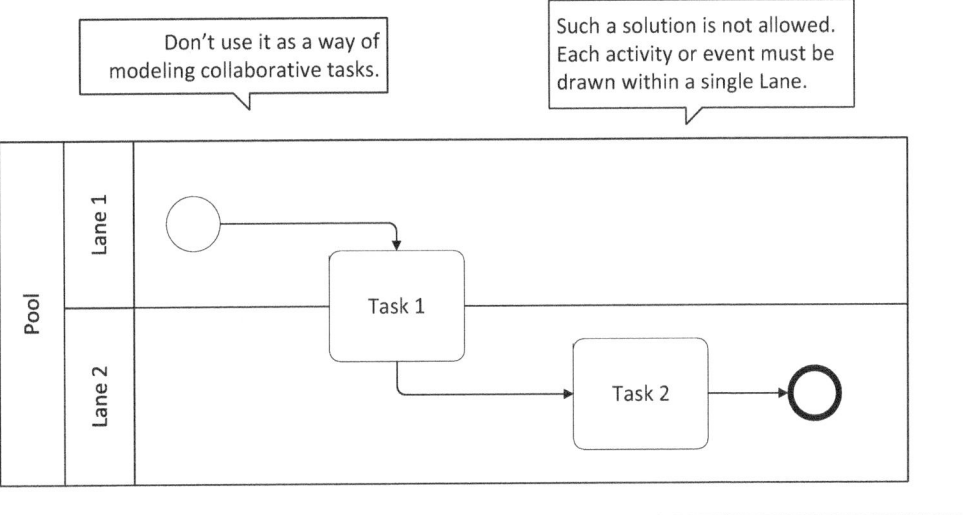

2.2. Planning Meeting

In the *Planning Meeting* process example, the individual steps are performed by people with different roles. In the process we can distinguish activities performed by the Product Owner (PO), the Development Team or the whole Scrum Team. There are no activities performed only by the Scrum Master.

Let's model the *Conduct Planning Meeting* process with categorization of Scrum Team roles. The pool indicates the Scrum Team. Analyzing once again the process description and our final model, we get:

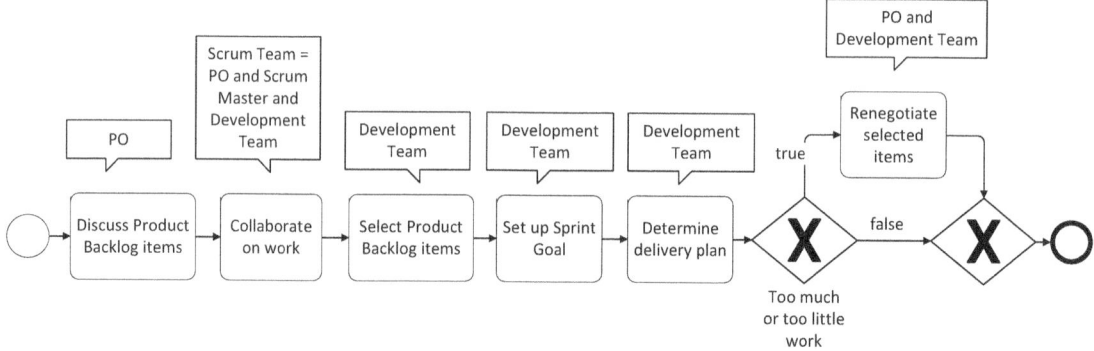

Figure 40: Analysis of which roles perform each task

Collaborative activities

In the *Conduct Planning meeting* process, there are tasks that are performed by many roles at the same time: e.g. the task *Renegotiate selected items*. Organizing such tasks between lanes is not so obvious. Each activity must be in only one lane and must not cross a lane boundary / be between two lanes. You cannot model one big activity that is between two or more lanes.

So how we can model collaborative activities that, according to our process organization, are performed within more than one Lane at the same time? Below we discuss different approaches to this issue.

Let's first model the *Conduct Planning meeting* process with categorization of basic Scrum Team roles. We will use lanes:
- PO
- Development Team
- Scrum Master.

2.2. Planning Meeting

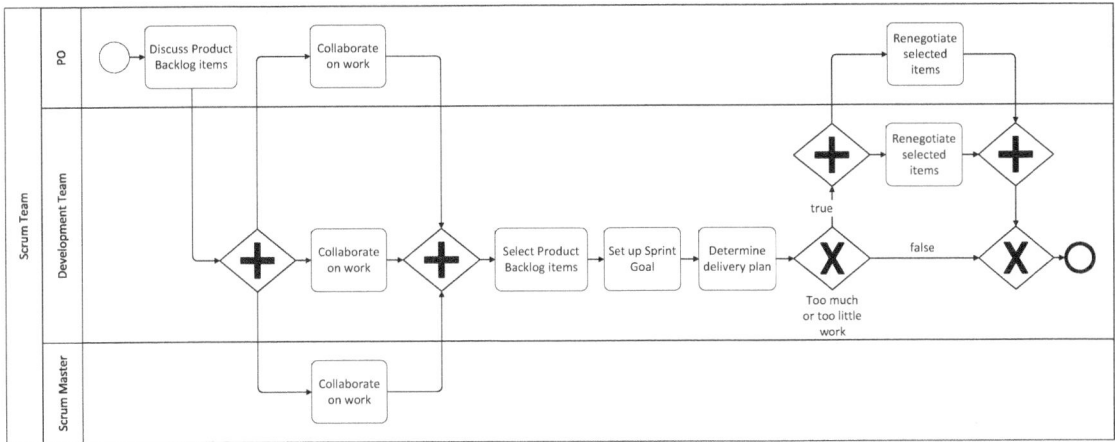

Figure 41: Collaborative tasks copied and modeled within an AND gateway for every related Lane

In this solution (Figure 41), tasks that are performed by more than one role are 'copied' and modeled independently within AND gateways. In this approach we explicitly show that a collaborative task is performed by different roles. What's more, it doesn't change our categorization, and we have three lanes indicating scrum roles.

Such a solution is commonly used in simple non-executable processes where the number of lines is quite small. When reading a model, we usually interpret activities with the same name as being the same activity. However, this is wrong from a semantic point of view. Tasks or subprocesses with the same name are not necessarily exactly the same activity.

Imagine you have many more users in the process and many more tasks performed by multiple roles. Readability and optimization of such diagrams becomes really hard.

Another approach is to separately model lanes for all combinations of roles that perform the same activity. The strength of this solution is that collaborative activities are not duplicated and are shown only once on the diagram. Remember that the meaning of lanes is up to you, and you can categorize flow elements in any way.

For the *Conduct Planning meeting* process, we can use the following Lanes:
- PO
- Development Team (DT)
- Scrum Master (SM)
- Scrum Team = PO, DT, SM (this is the pool)
- PO + DT

2.2. Planning Meeting

The task *Collaborate on work* is modeled directly in the pool without using lanes, as in this example pool means Scrum Team. We don't have any activity that is performed only by the Scrum Master so such a Lane is not needed (Figure 42).

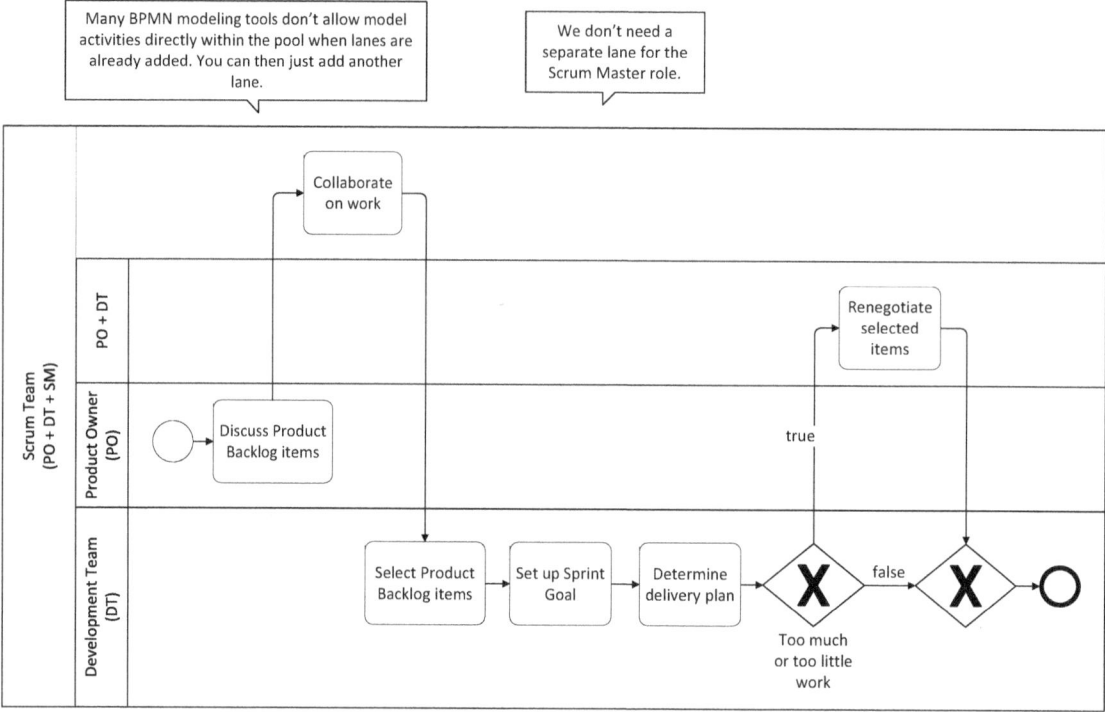

Figure 42: Lanes represent all possible combinations of collaborative activities

Again, imagine that you have many more roles and activities that are performed collaboratively by a mix of roles. The number of lanes can increase significantly, which spoils readability. The advantage is that a collaborative activity is modeled once. Another good point is that it's consistent with BPMN semantics, and it's much easier to introduce changes in the model than in the first approach.

Another solution is the use of a Collaboration, which represents, as its name indicates, collaboration between two or more participants. In a Collaboration, every Participant is represented by a separate Pool, and interactions between participants are modeled using message flows. We will discuss and practice Collaborations in Section 2.5. **BPMN Collaboration**.

2.3. Daily Scrum

Process description:

The Daily Scrum is a Development Team internal meeting that lasts 15 min. During the meeting, each Development Team member answers three questions:
1. What did you do yesterday?
2. What will you do today?
3. Are there any impediments in your way?

The time of the meeting should be the same each day. In our exercise, let's assume it's 09:30. We've already modeled the basic behavior of the Conduct Daily Scrum process. In Section 2.1. Introducing subprocesses, the solutions were to model the Daily Scrum meeting within the exception flow from the Develop Increment subprocess or as an event subprocess. In both cases the timer event is non-interrupting, so the parent process Develop Increment is not cancelled (Figure 43).

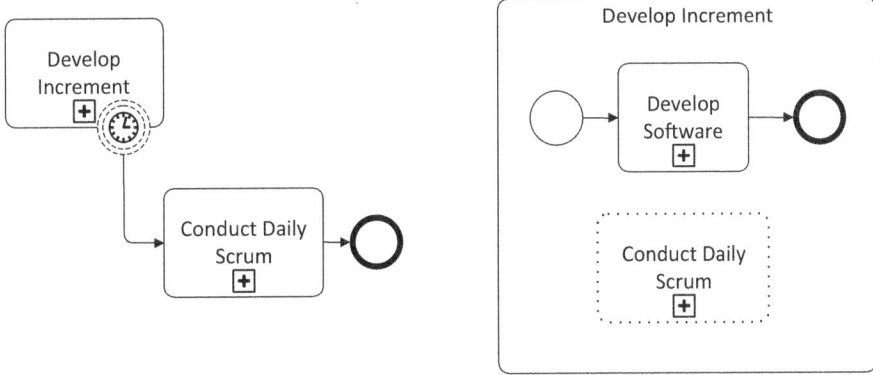

Figure 43: Conduct Daily Scrum activity as subprocess within exception flow and as event subprocess within Develop Increment subprocess

Both solutions represent the correct flow of the process. The interpretation from the business point of view is as follows: as long as the team is working on developing an increment, Daily Scrum meetings take place each day. Once the team finishes developing the Increment, the daily scrum is no longer arranged.

Activity deadline

In Scrum, all meetings have a specific timeframe that should not be exceeded. In our examples we introduce the deadline for the Daily Scrum meeting; however, the approach we present below can be used in other cases.

2.3. Daily Scrum

If we want to model a deadline for an activity, no matter whether it's modeled within a normal or exception flow, we use an interrupting timer event attached to the boundary of the activity. Let's practice this based on the Daily Scrum, which is a 15 min time-boxed meeting.

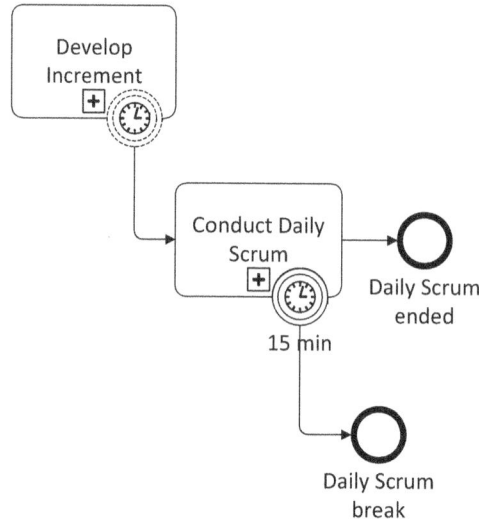

Figure 44: Activity within exception flow with deadline modeled using interrupting boundary timer event

Event subprocess deadline

Another thing that's worth discussing is modeling deadlines for event subprocesses (Figure 45).

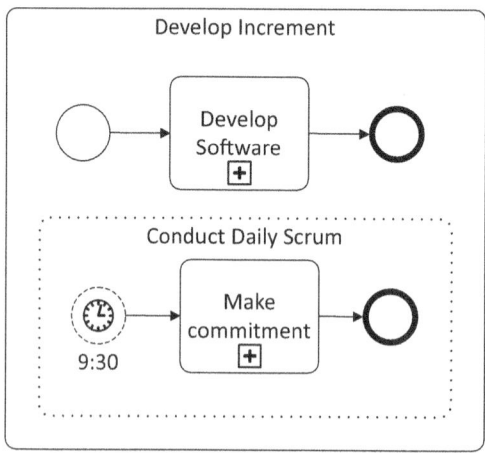

Figure 45: Conduct Daily Scrum as event subprocess

2.3. Daily Scrum

A very important rule related to event subprocesses is that you mustn't use boundary events attached to the event subprocess boundary.

TIP: You cannot attach any event to an event subprocess boundary.

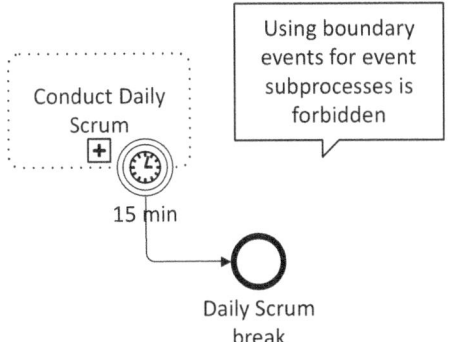

Figure 46: Example of wrong usage of intermediate boundary event

We cannot directly set the deadline for the *Conduct Daily Scrum* event subprocess, but we may do this for its activity, the *Make commitment* subprocess (Figure 47). If the timer event fires, it immediately terminates the *Make commitment* subprocess. The *Make commitment* subprocess is the only activity in the *Conduct Daily Scrum* event subprocess. If the only activity is cancelled because of an interrupting boundary event, the whole *Conduct Daily Scrum* subprocess is also cancelled as there is no active flow any more. This is a way to get around the rule saying that events cannot be attached to an event subprocess boundary.

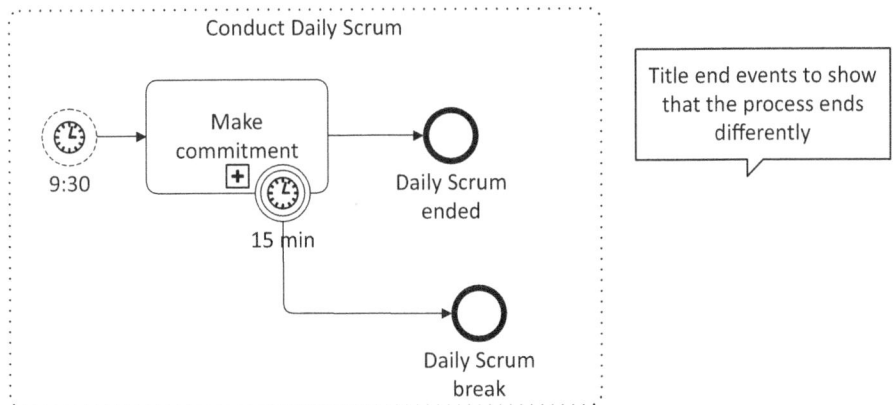

Figure 47: Using timer event as a deadline

2.3. Daily Scrum

> **TIP:** Event subprocesses should start with one start event but may finish with multiple end events.

In order not to mix both approaches, from here we will only use the model in which the *Conduct Daily Scrum* subprocess is modeled as an event subprocess.

Loop vs. multi-instance subprocess

Let's now analyze the course of the meeting in detail. The whole Development Team takes part in the meeting. During the meeting, every team member answers three questions one by one. So the subprocess *Make commitments* is repeated for every team member. This is a signal that a loop or multi-instance marker should be used (Figure 48). We've already discussed these markers previously in Section **2.1. THEORY: Loop subprocess characteristics.**

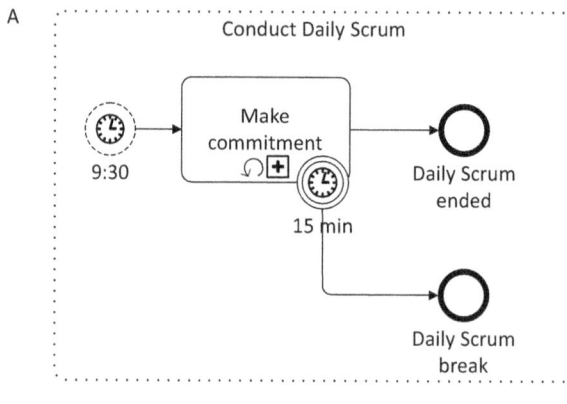

Firgure 48: Make commitment subprocess with different markers: A - loop marker, B - multi-instance marker

The interpretation of diagram A is as follows: Subprocess *Make commitment* loops while all Development Team members make commitments to other team members.

Diagram B may be interpreted as follows. The *Make commitment* subprocess is instantiated for every Development Team member present at the meeting. The activities are performed sequentially.

So what's the difference, and which approach is better? The questions that can help you make the decision on which marker use are:
- Do we use a different data set for each performance of the *Make commitment activity*?
- Do we produce a different data set for each performance of the activity?
- Whether the activity is performed automatically?

We may interpret each member's answers as independent output (so use solution B) or the answers of all members as one meeting feedback (use solution A).

The loop marker is usually used to describe an automatic behavior so we recommend to use solution B.

Sequential tasks vs. multi-instance task

We know that every member answers three questions in sequence. The most natural interpretation is to use three different tasks – a task for every question – in a given order using a sequence flow:

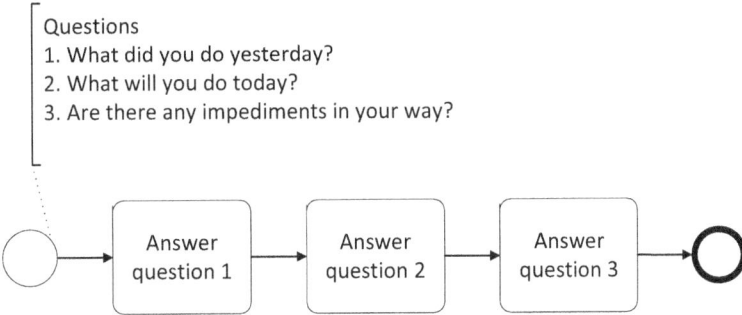

Figure 49: Sequential tasks

In above diagram the team member performs the same task three times: answer question. The things that change are the question and the answer.

> **TIP:** If the same activity is performed sequentially or in parallel with a different data set, use a multi-instance marker.

2.3. Daily Scrum

We exactly know the inputs, the outputs and the number of instances (three questions and three instances of the task). So another solution is to use a multi-instance task (Figure 50).

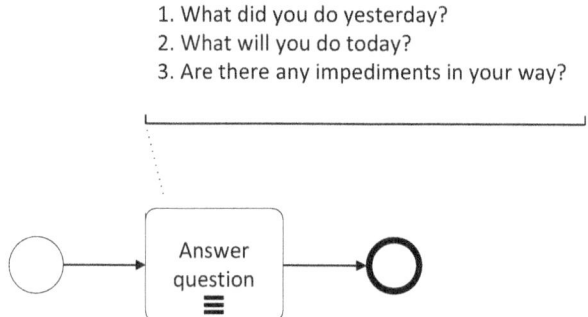

Figure 50: Multi-instance task

Both models – using sequence tasks or a multi-instance task marker – are logically and semantically correct.

THEORY: Loop task characteristics

BPMN distinguishes two types of task markers that allow model looping behavior.

The loop marker means that the task is executed iteratively until a looping condition is true. There is one task instance that performs some activity iteratively. It is usually used to describe an automatic behavior.

The multi-instance marker also indicates that a task is performed many times. However in this case every execution creates a new task instance. This means that for every iteration, the task may use and produce a different data set. Tasks can be performed sequentially or in parallel.

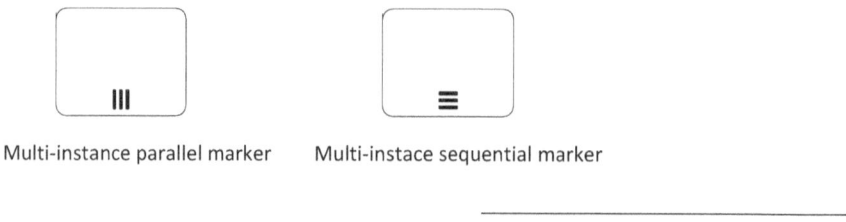

Multi-instance parallel marker   Multi-instace sequential marker

2.4. Review Meeting

Process description

The goal of the meeting is to review the sprint and revise the Product Backlog. Attendees are the Scrum Team and stakeholders invited by the PO. First, the PO presents which items have been completed and which are incomplete. Next, the Development Team discusses the sprint: they demonstrate done items and answer stakeholders' questions. In the next part of the meeting, the PO reviews the Product Backlog. The whole group discusses presented Product Backlog items; this results in revision of the Product Backlog. Output of the meeting: revised Product Backlog.

We can distinguish the following activities:
- Present Sprint items (PO)
- Demonstrate completed items (Dev Team)
- Answer questions (Dev Team)
- Review Product Backlog (PO)
- Discuss Product Backlog items (all)

Figure 51 shows the first version of the process model. Let's discuss each step in more detail.

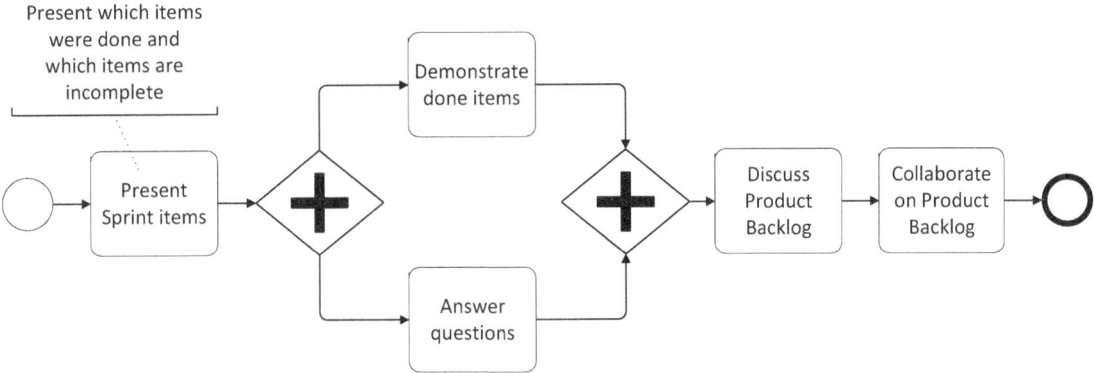

Figure 51: Review meeting process

The process starts with presenting the current sprint state. In the above solution, we model it as one task. If you want to show that the PO presents complete and incomplete items separately as this is important from your point of view, you may use two separate tasks or a collapsed sub-process that contains two tasks (Figure 52).

2.4. Review Meeting

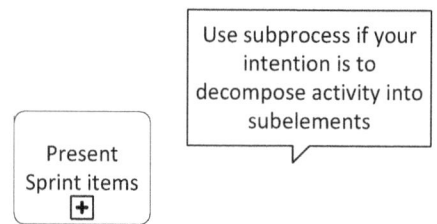

Figure 52: Subprocess containing smaller elements

The next part of the meeting is conducted by the Development Team, who perform two basic activities: demonstrating completed items and answering stakeholders' questions. In our above solution (Figure 51), we use AND-split and AND-Join to show that these activities are independent and may be performed at the same time – for example, during the demonstration, the team answers questions. To indicate that completed items are presented one by one, a multi-instance marker may be used.

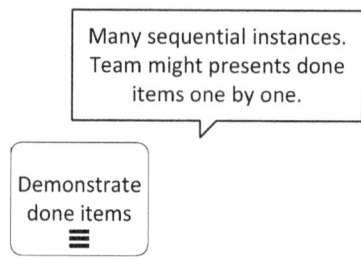

Figure 53: Multi-instance task

Let's now analyze in more detail the task *Answer questions* that is modelled between AND gateways. The Development Team answers a question if it's asked by a stakeholder. Unlike the task *Demonstrate done items*, occurrence of this task depends on stakeholder behavior. So there might be no, one or many questions asked during presentation/discussion.

Our present model doesn't represent such a situation as on the diagram, the task *Answer question* is always performed and is executed only once (Figure 51).

> **TIP:** An interrupting event may occur zero or one time; a non-interrupting event may occur zero, one or multiple times.

We've previously discussed the problem of some activity occurring many times during execution of another process, when occurrence of the activity depends on some external events that are not within the process flow. To solve such a modelling issue, we use a non-interrupting event subprocess.

Message event and process participants

We model the *Answer question* task within the event subprocess as triggered by a non-interrupting start event, since questions may be asked many times. The type of event is *message*, as the event subprocess is triggered every time a question arrives from a stakeholder.

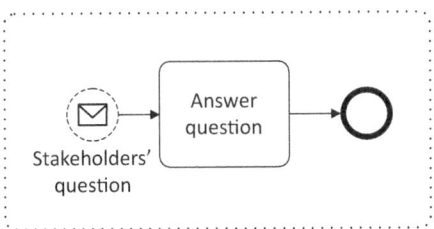

Figure 54: Event subprocess triggered by non-interrupting message event

In our process, a stakeholder represents another process participants as his/her behavior influences the *Review meeting* process and cannot be directly predicted. We don't know how many (if any) questions stakeholders will ask. Another reason why we interpret the stakeholder as a different process participant than the Scrum Team is that a message event cannot be sent/caught within the same pool, and every process participant is represented by a separate pool.

THEORY: Message event

A message event represents a message that arrives from or is sent to other Participant. By message we may understand any content forwarded between Participants: order, question, questionnaire, form, etc. That's why messages are also used to model data flows.

Messages cannot be forwarded within a process because the process represents one Participant.

This rule also applies to different lanes. You cannot send a message between different lanes that are within one pool. Lanes are used to categorize activities within the process so no matter how many lanes you have, they all represent one process participant – the pool.

2.4. Review Meeting

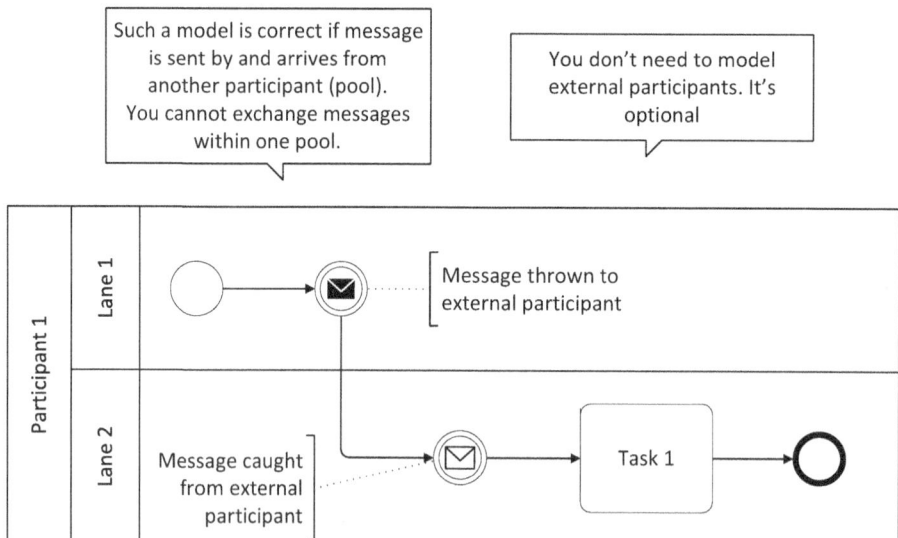

Within a sequence flow, a message event can be modeled as a start, intermediate or end event. BPMN additionally distinguishes two types of messages: catch and throw.

A catch event means that the process waits till the message arrives, so the process can go further. A message start event is a catch.

A throw event indicates a place in the process where the process sends a message to an external Participant. Once the message is sent, the process continues or ends. A message end event is a throw.

A message intermediate event can be either a catch or a throw.

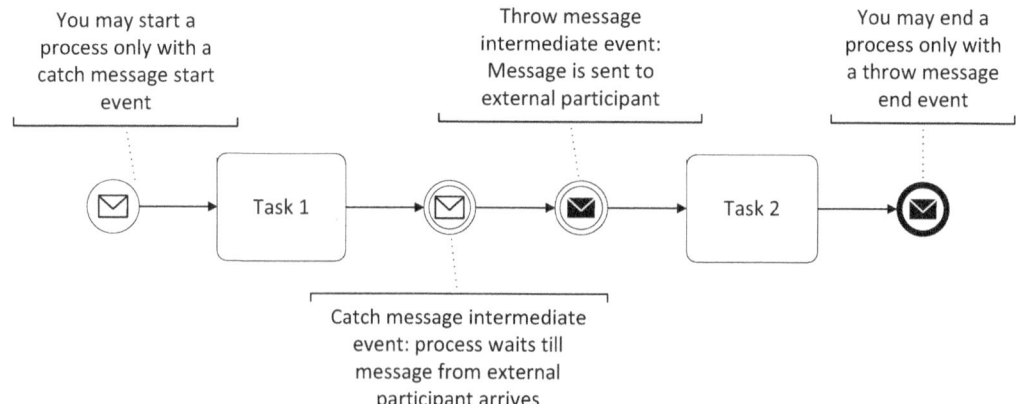

An intermediate message event can also be attached to the boundary of an activity. It is used to activate an exception flow after a message arrives. Only a catch message event may be used. Like in other boundary events, the message event may interrupt or not interrupt the execution of the parent activity. It's interpreted as follows:

– when *Message A* arrives, *Task 1* is interrupted (cancelled), and the process continues only through an exception flow to *Task 3*

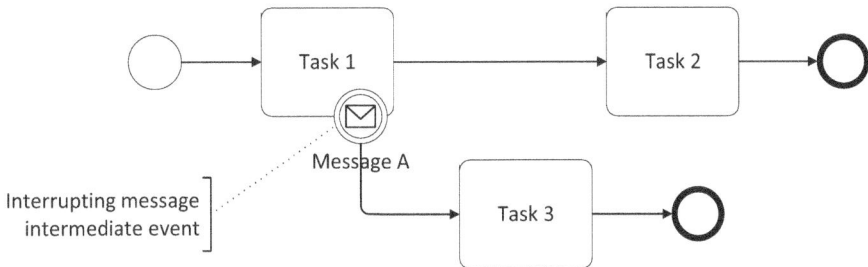

– when *Message B* arrives, the process goes through an exception flow to *Task 6*. Remember that in this case, *Subprocess 4* is still active, so after it ends, the process goes to *Task 5*.

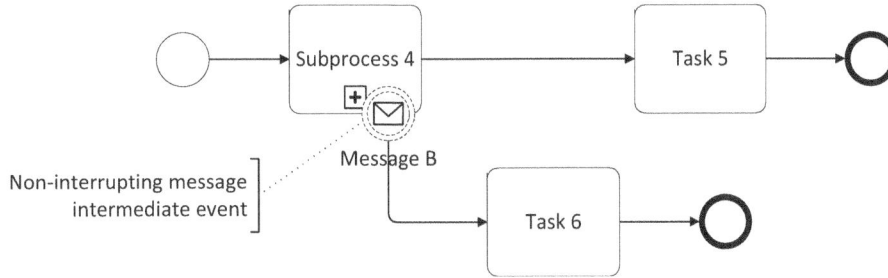

A message start event can be used to trigger an event subprocess. We can also distinguish interrupting and non-interrupting message start events in this case.

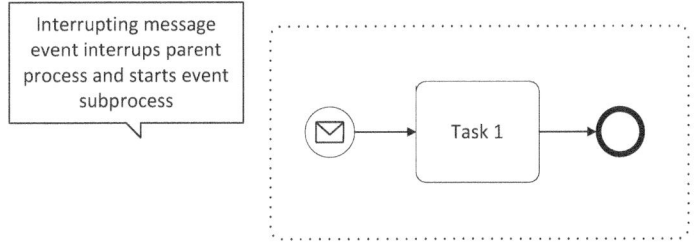

2.4. Review Meeting

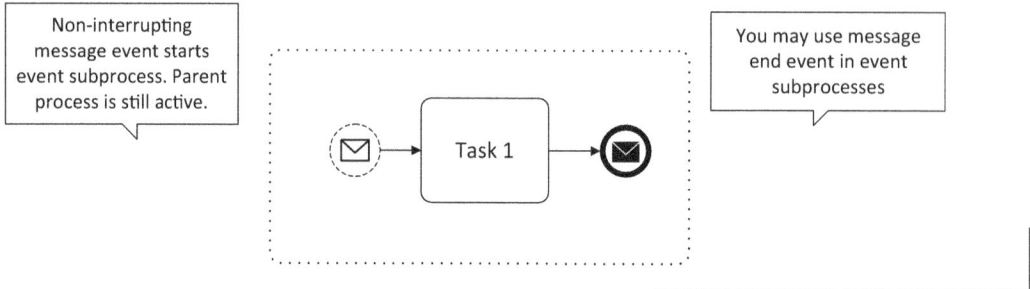

Catch events in the process

Let's go back to our *Answer question* activity modeled within an event subprocess. As previously discussed, we always need to decide at what point in the parent process execution we may catch the event. In other words, within which process / subprocess our event subprocess should be modeled.

> **TIP:** If an event subprocess can only be triggered in a certain part of the process, use a sub-process to narrow down the period in which the event can be triggered.

If we want to allow questions from stakeholders to be asked during the whole review meeting, an event subprocess should be placed within the *Review meeting* process (Figure 55).

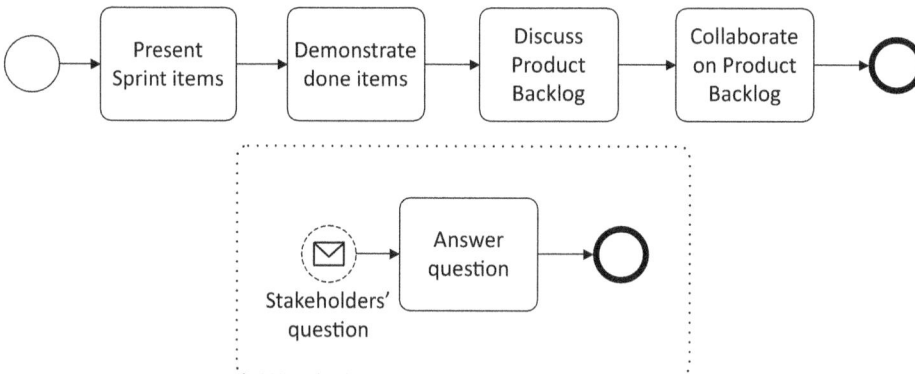

Figure 55: Event subprocess may be triggered during execution of the whole process

This approach seems to make sense; however according to the process description, questions are asked only during the Development Team presentation.

If we intend to narrow down the period in which stakeholders can ask questions to the meeting part in which the Development Team presents done items, we need to separate out this part of the process so that the event subprocess can be triggered only during the demonstration of done items (Figure 56).

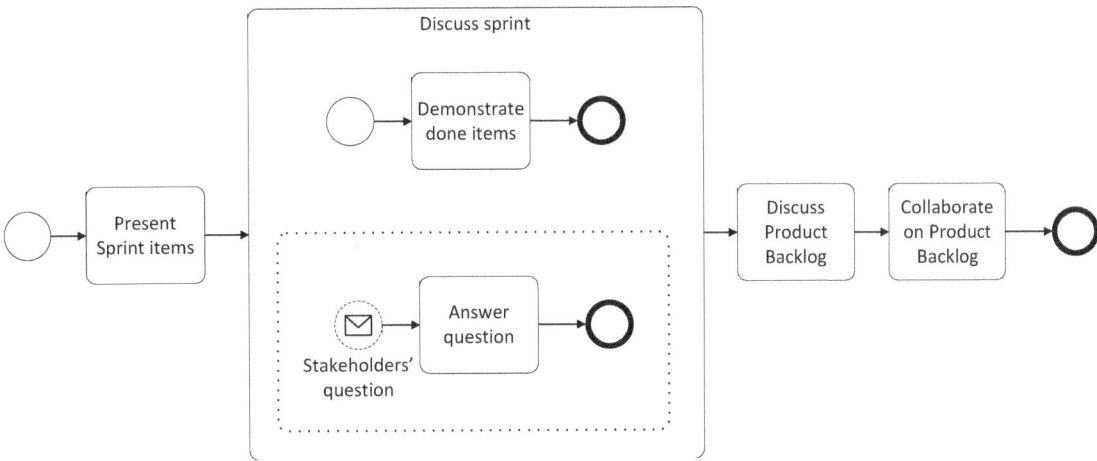

Figure 56: Additional subprocess Discuss sprint is provided to narrow down the part of the process in which the event subprocess may be triggered.

Event subprocess vs. boundary event

We've already discussed that the modeling issue related to triggering activities while executing another activity can be resolved in two ways: using an event subprocess or using an event attached to the activity boundary. The difference between these two approaches is in the process that handles the additional flow and has access to subprocess variables.

We can resolve the issue related to triggering *Answer question* activity in two ways. Using an event subprocess, as before (Figure 57A), or using a boundary event (Figure 57B). Notice that in the second model, a boundary event is attached to the *Discuss sprint* process that includes only one task. In such a case, there is no need to use the additional container (*Discuss sprint* process). We may remove it without changing the process logic (Figure 57C).

2.4. Review Meeting

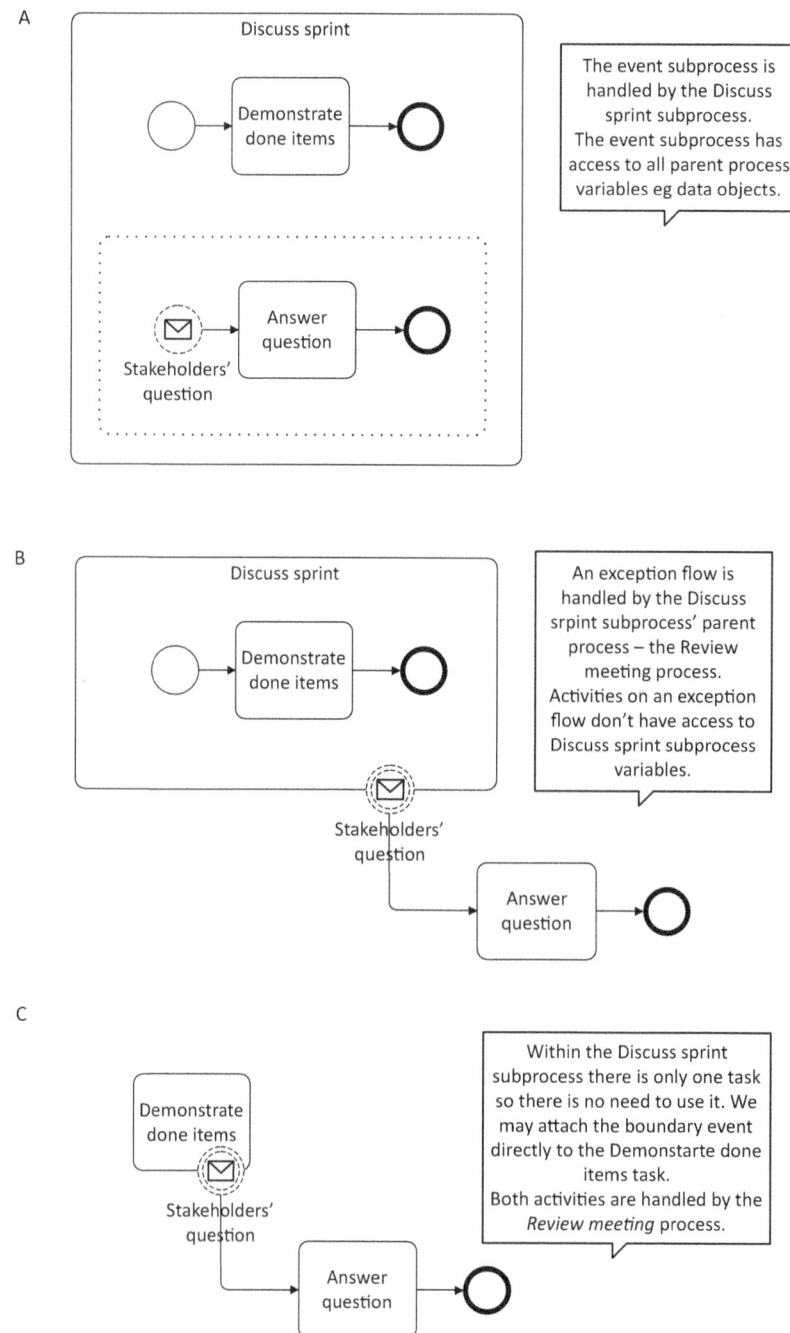

Figure 57: Answer question task handled by the Discuss sprint subprocess (A) and Review meeting process (B, C)

Our current model looks as in Figure 58.

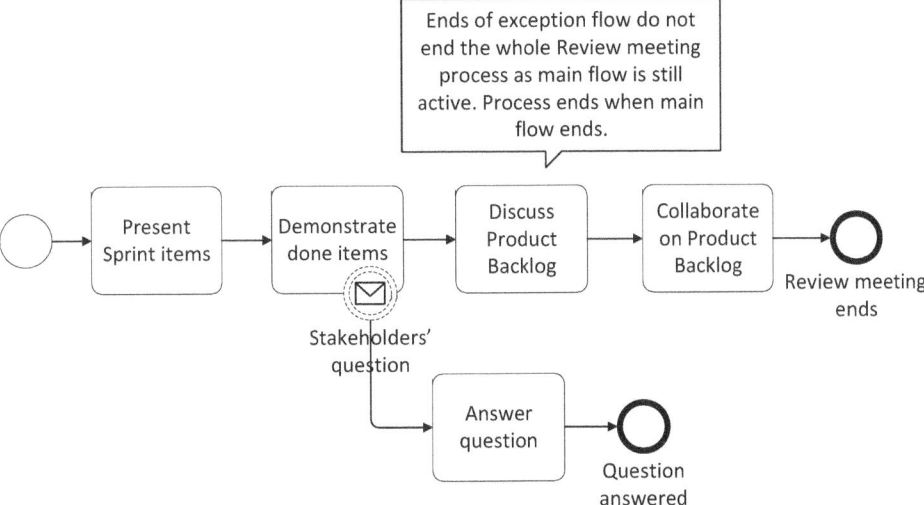

Figure 58: Review meeting process

Explicit goals of activities

Let's analyze the rest of the *Review meeting* process. After the team demonstrates Product Backlog done items, the PO discusses the current Product Backlog, based on which the whole team collaborate.

> **TIP:** Create diagrams in a way so that someone who does not know the description of the process is able to understand it by reading the model.

According to the meeting description, "The whole group collaborates on presented Product Backlog items, which results in revision of the Product Backlog." In the first version we called the task *Collaborate on Product Backlog*. However, this name doesn't necessarily make it clear for readers. To explicitly show that the goal of collaboration is Product Backlog revision, we may:

- clearly title the task: Revise Product Backlog
- use text annotation
- associate the task with data input.

While the approaches are different, the objective of each is to show explicitly what is the purpose of the activity. First of all, the name of the activity should convey what is being done and what its purpose is. If, however, you decide that this information is too complex to provide through the activity name, use text annotation to provide additional needed explanations or data objects.

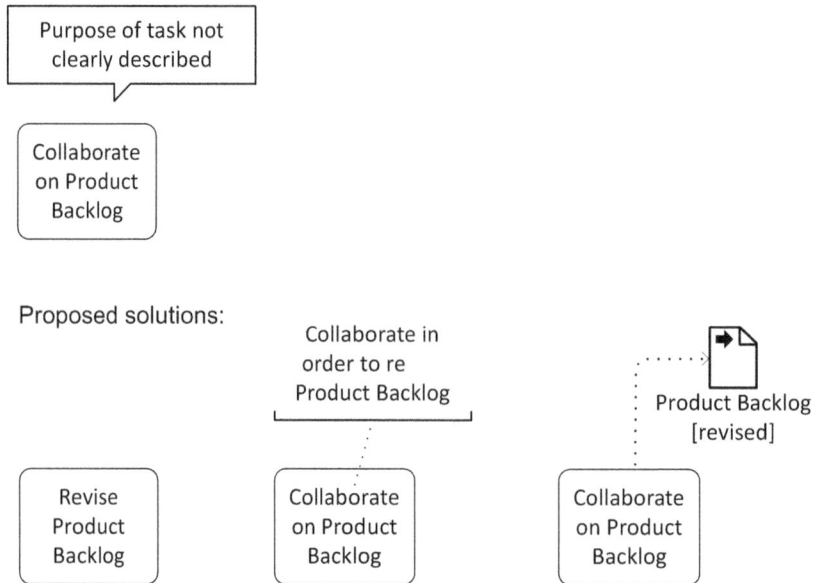

Figure 59: Ways of explicitly showing the activity purpose

In the remainder of the example, we will use the new task name: Revise Product Backlog.

2.5. BPMN Collaboration

If we want to explicitly model interactions between our process and other process participants that we understand as external participants, we can use **collaboration**. Collaboration is a common way to show interaction between collaborating participants. Using collaboration we can solve issues related to sending/receiving messages between participants and instancing a process/subprocess many times by one of participants. Let's first go through the theory.

THEORY: Collaboration

Collaboration represents interaction between two or more participants. Every participant represents an **independent** process.

The main process from the modeler's point of view is called the internal process. Other participants collaborating with the internal process are represented by external processes. As we already learned, a process can be modeled within a pool. In collaboration this is the required way to show external process participants. An internal process can be modeled without using a pool.

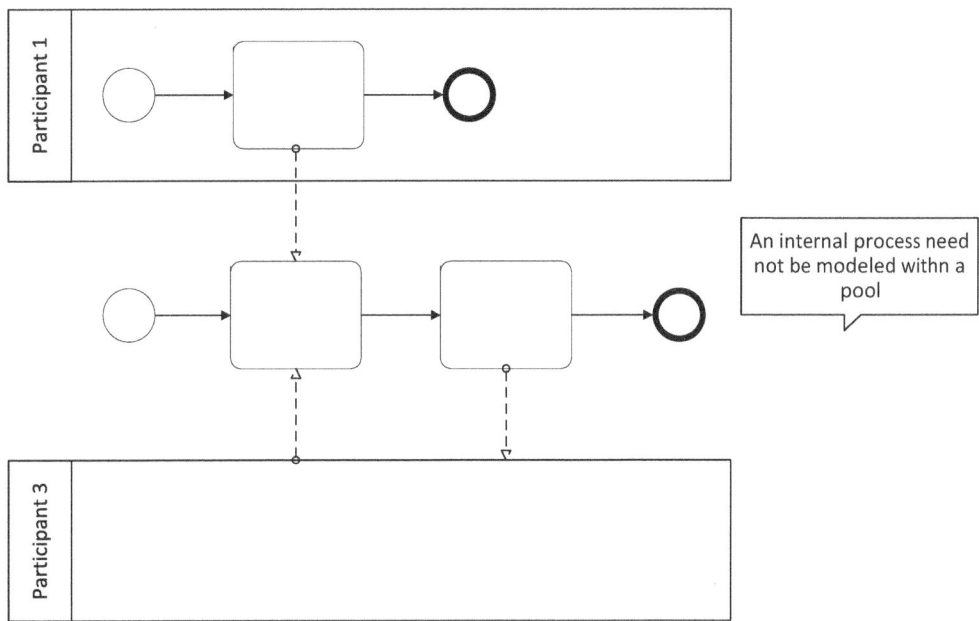

An internal process need not be modeled withn a pool

A pool may be modeled as a **white box** that shows the process details or as a **black box** without any elements inside (as an 'empty white box'). When we want to show commu-

2.5. BPMN Collaboration

nication between our process and an external process and the information on how the external process looks is not relevant or unknown, we may use a black box pool. If the process on the external user side is known and important from our point of view, we can present it as white box pool.

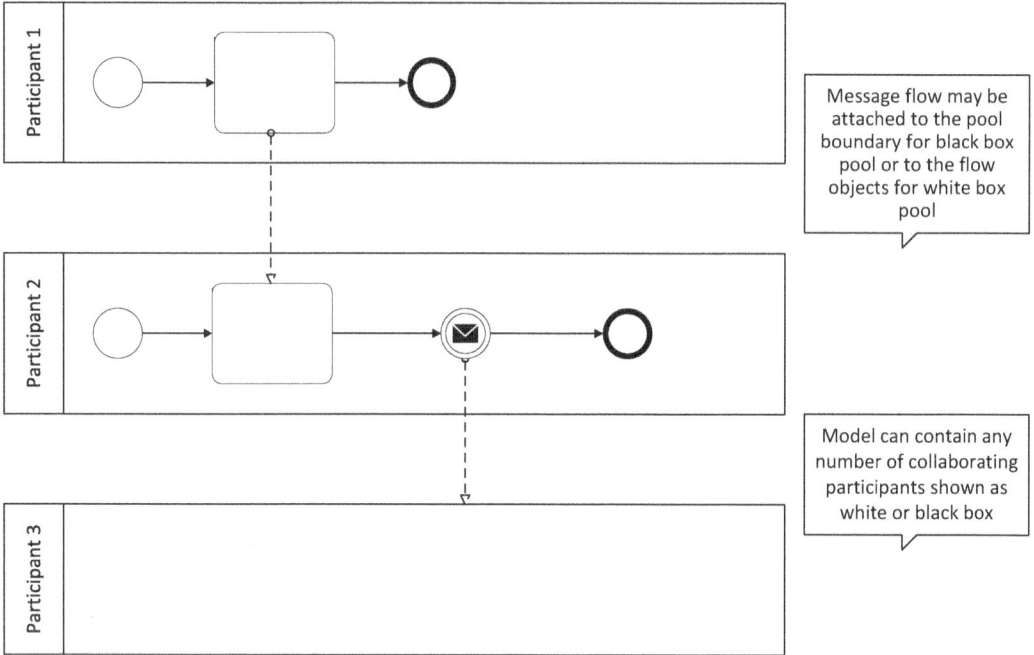

In a collaboration, we may show interactions between any combination of participants (white and black box pools). Interactions between participants are modeled using **message flows**. A message flow is the only BPMN element that can cross Pool boundaries. The whole process needs to be included within one pool.

Collaboration is closely related to message flow, so let's also go through the modeling rules and theory of the message flow.

THEORY: Message flow

A message flow is used to show associations between two or more participants, where by participants we mean pools.

A message flow connects elements from different pools; you cannot use it to associate elements within the same pool.

A message flow can connect activities, events and pool boundaries; the BPMN objects that can be connected using message flows are:
- message event: start, intermediate and end
- task boundary
- subprocess boundary
- pool boundary

If you include external participants in the diagram, connect the message flow to the pool boundary (if it's black box) or pool activity / event (if it's white box).

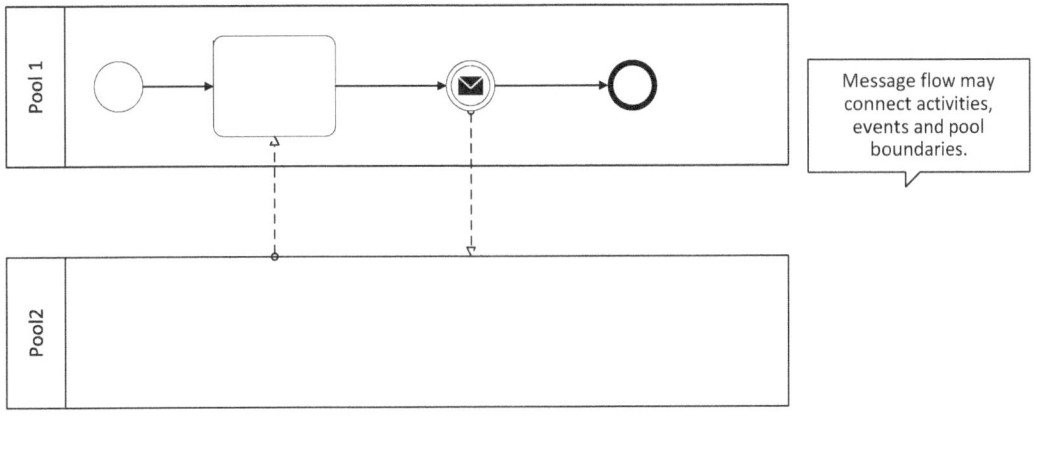

Review meeting process – collaborative or not?

Collaboration is usually used to show how your internal process influences and is influenced by other participants. Sometimes, even if your intention is not to model Collaboration, it turns out that some activities or events within the process do not depend on the process flow, and you cannot directly predict when and/or how something happen. In this case you also need to model your process as if it were collaborating with an external participant. Still, explicitly modeling external participants is optional. Let's practice these issues.

Based on the *Review meeting* process example, we will learn and practice how to model Collaboration. The process looks as follows (Figure 60).

2.5. BPMN Collaboration

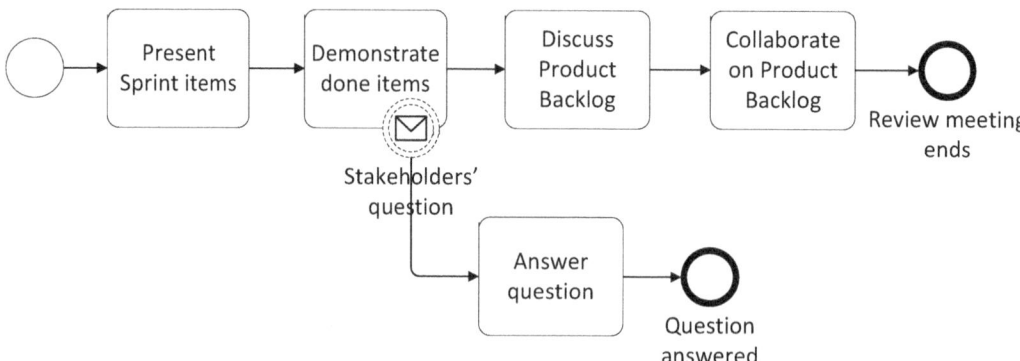

Figure 60: Review meeting process

We want to model collaboration and organize the internal process elements within meeting participants with different roles who take part in the meeting: PO (Product Owner), Development Team and Stakeholders.

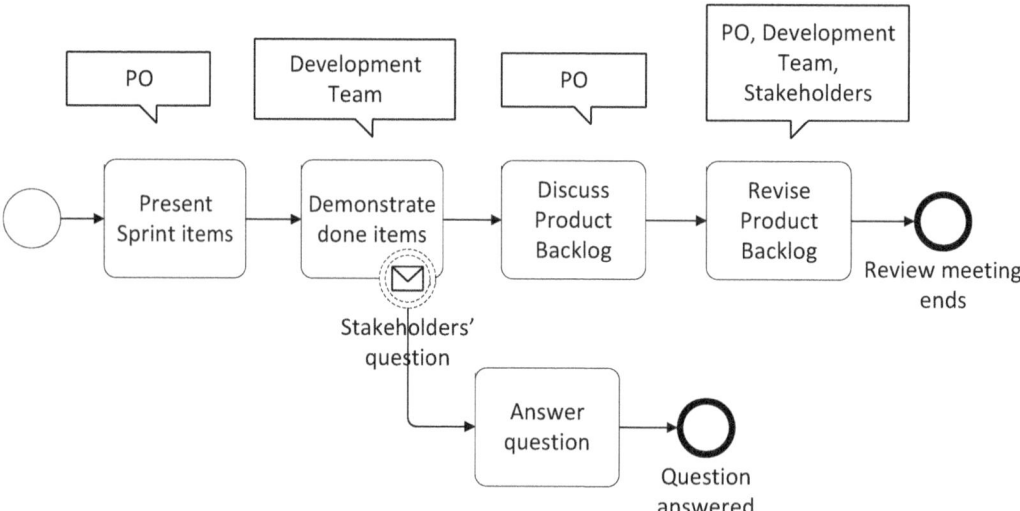

Figure 61: Analysis of which roles perform each task

Based on the above analysis, we model a first version of internal process (Figure 62). Look what happens if we include all the defined roles within a pool without analyzing first what the interaction with external processes looks like and who/what can be considered as external and internal participants in the *Review meeting* process.

2.5. BPMN Collaboration

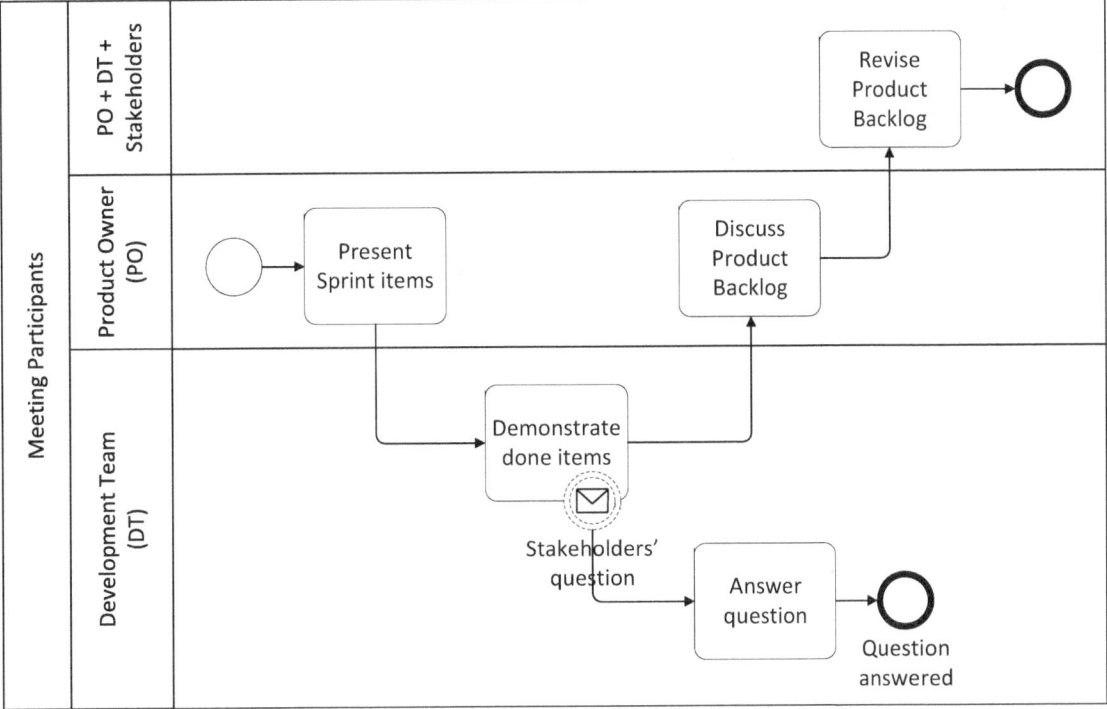

Figure 62: Review meeting process directly organized within lanes – first version

We called the pool *Meeting Participants* because the meeting attendees are not only the Scrum Team but also the Stakeholders. Stakeholders, PO and DT are jointly represented by one lane as they all take part in the *Revise Product Backlog* activity. The *Demonstrate done items* task and its exception flow are performed by the Development Team, so it's modeled within a lane that indicates this role. We also have a lane dedicated to the PO and two activities within it performed by this role.

What's wrong with this process? The first thing is that we have used different participants than in the *Review meeting* parent process *Take sprint*. In the *Take Sprint process*, the pool indicates the Scrum Team. Here the process participants are different and represent not only the Scrum Team but also Stakeholders: Meeting Participants.

Another error is related to the message event and process organization. The Demonstrate done items task contains a message catch event that may be thrown by a Stakeholder. In our diagram (Figure 62), however, one of lanes indicates Stakeholders + PO + DT. Because of this process organization, we confuse the reader.

> **TIP:** If some performer is modeled as a participant (pool), don't indicate them in a lane in another process within the same diagram.

The most important reason the model is wrong follows from the BPMN modeling rules. A message event can be forwarded only between different pools. Here, because of a wrong definition of a process participant – *Meeting Participants*, which means both Scrum Team and Stakeholders – we cannot forward messages between them.

Identifying external process participants

Sometimes it's just impossible to include the whole process behavior within one pool. Exclude external participants from your process when:
- someone/something sends a message to an internal process participant
- someone/something receives a message sent by an internal process participant
- someone/something may trigger an internal process or subprocess many times

By process participant we mean any object or item that performs activities and fires events in the process (system, role, company, person, device etc.).

Going back to our case, we may exclude Stakeholders from the internal *Review meeting* process. The exclusion includes and influences the pool and lane. Remember that if you exclude an additional external Participant from the internal process, you don't need to necessarily model it. Including external process participants within a diagram is optional.

So the solution is to rename the lane that indicates Stakeholders + PO + DT and model the process only from the Scrum Team perspective. Look at Figure 63: the pool represents the Scrum Team, and the Stakeholders are not included in the diagram. To provide the information that Stakeholders also take part in the *Revise Product Backlog* task, we use text annotation.

2.5. BPMN Collaboration

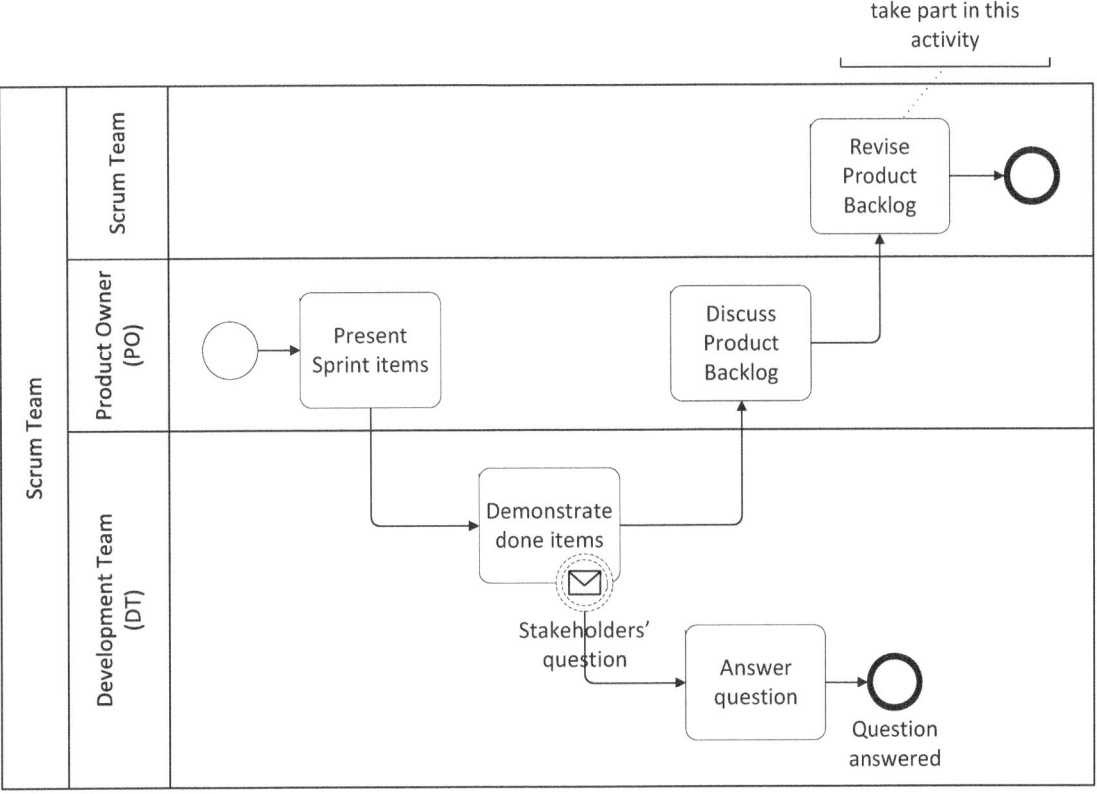

Figure 63: : Review meeting process organized within lanes without Stakeholders

The current diagram represents the correct internal *Review meeting* process. Let's now add an external participant – Stakeholder – to show how it collaborates with the Scrum Team.

Review meeting collaboration

Let's practice the Collaboration model. We model Scrum Team and Stakeholder as separate pools. This means that the Stakeholder represents another independent process. The Stakeholder collaborates with our main (internal) process. The internal process is performed by the Scrum Team, the external process by the Stakeholder.

2.5. BPMN Collaboration

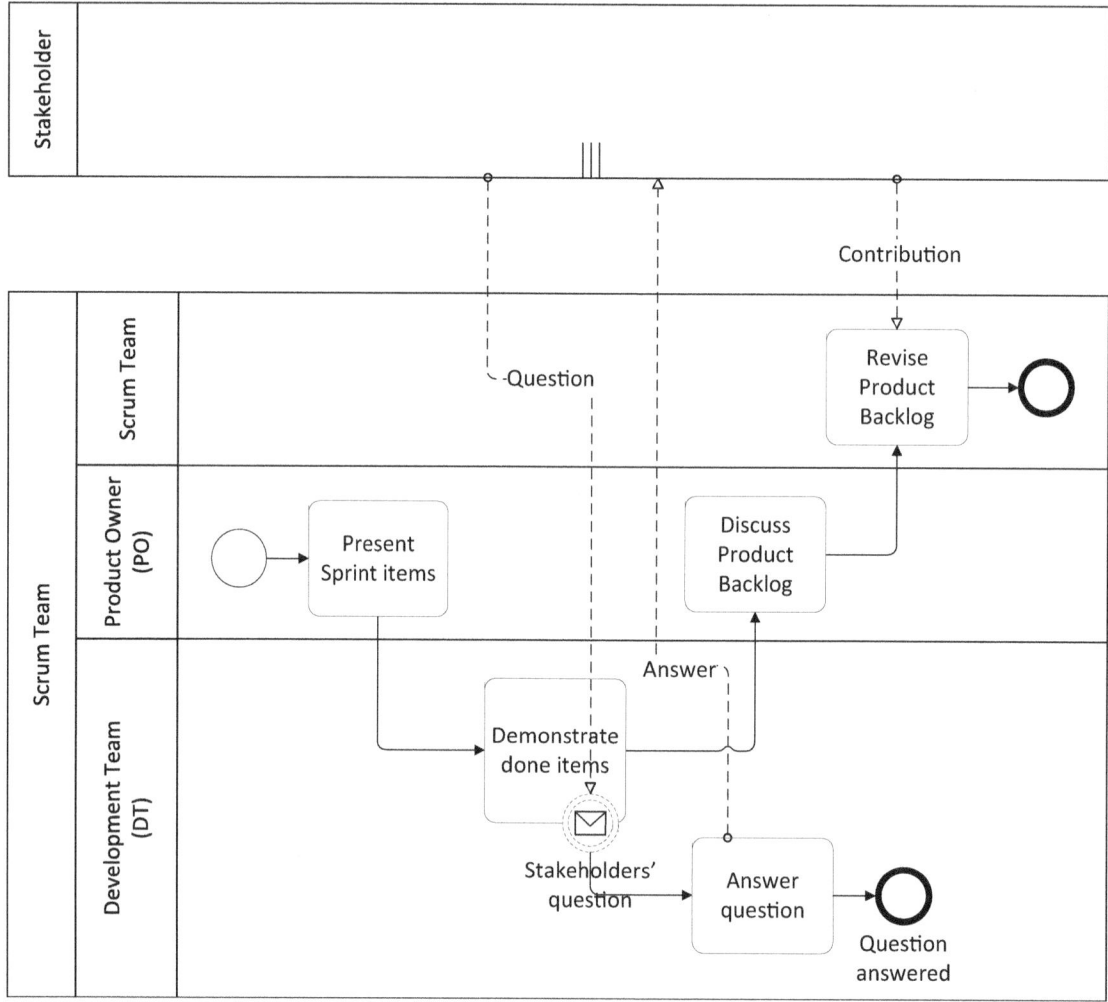

Figure 64: Review meeting modeled in Collaboration

From the meeting description, we know that Stakeholders take part in the meeting. They may ask questions during sprint demonstration by the Development Team. They also take an active part in the Product Backlog revision (task *Revise Product Backlog*) and may contribute to the discussion. We use **message flows** to show these collaboration points.

> **TIP:** Naming message flows is optional.

Multiplicity of Participant

Notice that we use a **multi-instance marker** for the Stakeholder pool. In BPMN this is the only marker we can use with pools. It is used to specify that there are multiple Participant instances. In our case, many Stakeholders may participate in the meeting; each of them may ask questions and contribute to the Product Backlog revision independently of other Stakeholders.

When and how use Message flows

We know that Stakeholders take part in the whole meeting. They are the recipients of presentations presented by the PO (*Present sprint items* task) and Development Team (*Demonstrate done items*). Let's look once again at our previous solution. Knowing Stakeholders take part in the whole meeting, we associated Stakeholders only with a message event and two tasks: *Answer question* and *Revise product backlog*.

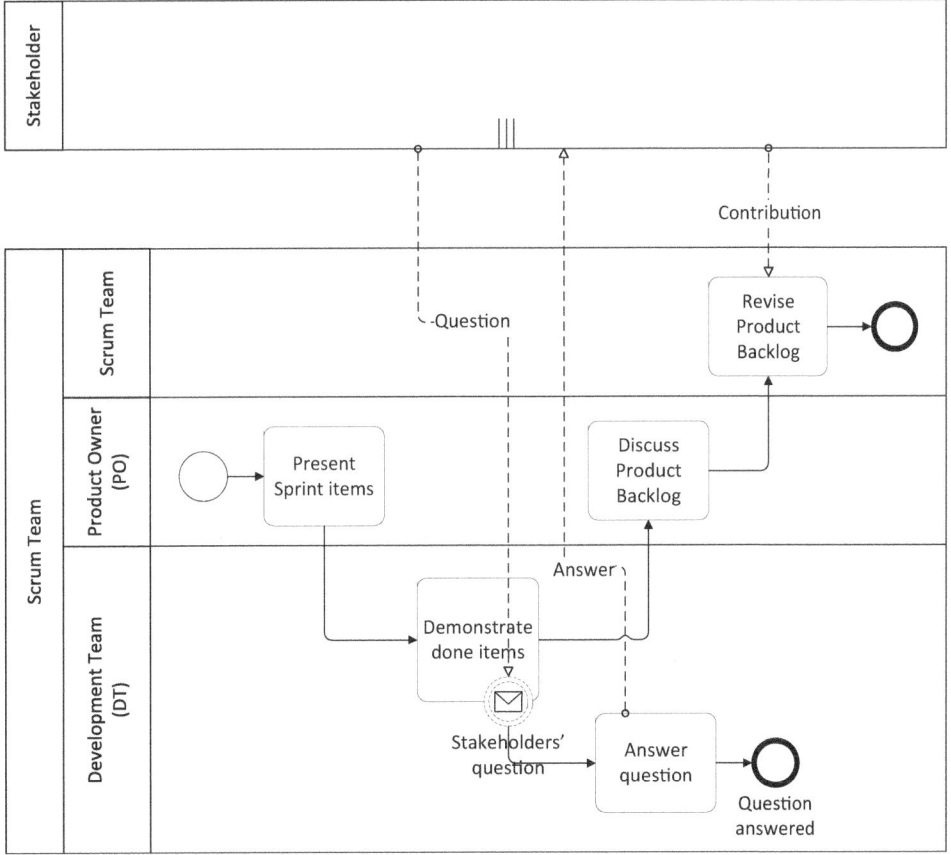

Figure 65: Collaboration with message flows – first version

2.5. BPMN Collaboration

The above diagram doesn't show that Stakeholders are recipients of the PO presentation and Development team demonstration. According to the BPMN specification, message flows are used to show the flow of messages between participants, and the message represents the content of participants' communication.

If we assume that Stakeholders listen to all the discussions and presented information, we may model message flow from all the activities included in the internal process (Figure 66).

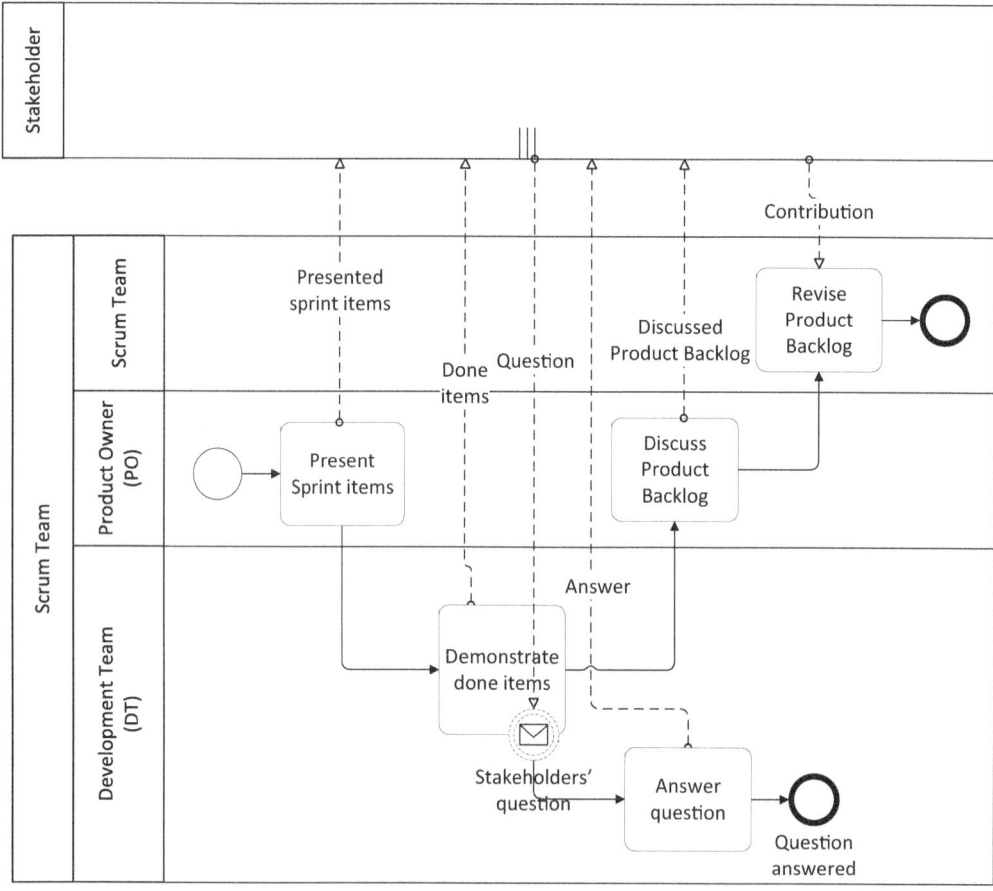

Figure 66: Collaboration with message flows – second version

Is such an approach correct? Yes – both from a BPMN technical point of view and the process flow logic, you can model the collaboration in this way.

> **TIP:** Use message flow to indicate relevant interactions between participants that actually affect the process flow.

While modeling collaboration, use message flow to indicate relevant interactions between participants that actually affect the process flow. What constitutes a relevant interaction? It is one that:

- Is relevant from the internal process point of view.
- Is modeled using an explicit element of the process that enforces communication – e.g. a catch/throw message. In our example, it's receiving a question from a Stakeholder.
- Has influence on activity execution results. In our example, Stakeholders' contributions may have an influence on Product Backlog revision.

Black box or white box?

In the example solution, we've modeled the Stakeholder as a black box. External participants can also be modeled as white boxes.

Before you decide to model an external process as a white box that contains all the processes details, answer these questions:

1. Is the course of the process important from the internal process point of view?
2. Do you have enough information to model the process fully and correctly?

If the answer to one of these questions is NO, don't waste time and do not obscure the model with unnecessary information that may only lead to misinterpretations.

If answer to both questions is YES, you may include process details on the diagram.

In more complex cases, it can also be a good approach to switch process context and separately create models in which external participant processes are treated as the internal one.

2.6. Retrospective meeting

Let's model the last meeting within the Scrum process example: Retrospective meeting.

Process description

In the meeting, the Scrum Team discusses what went well during the sprint and identifies needed improvements. At least one process improvement should be contained in the next Sprint Backlog.

The sample solution for the *Retrospective meeting* process is presented below. We model tasks *Discuss sprint* and *Identify improvements* as independent activities. Using text annotation we indicate that sprint discussion focuses on what went well. We don't know how exactly *Discuss sprint* or *Identify improvements* activities are performed. Do they consist of smaller activities? Usually during the meeting each team member writes/says what he/she liked during the sprint; however, this is not part of our sample process description.

The process is modeled within a pool indicating the Scrum Team. We don't use any lanes as all activities are performed by the Scrum Team.

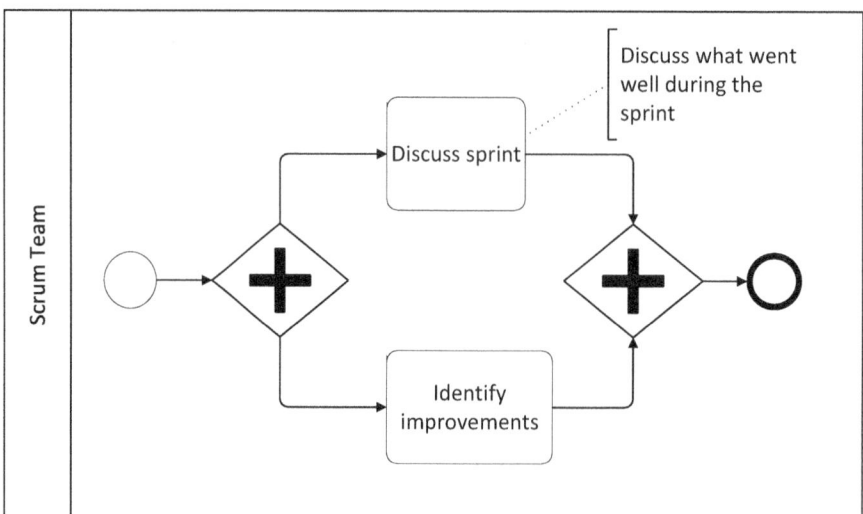

Figure 67: Retrospective meeting process

We can also use a **collection data output** element for improvements that are identified as a result of the *Identify improvements* task and are an output of the whole meeting.

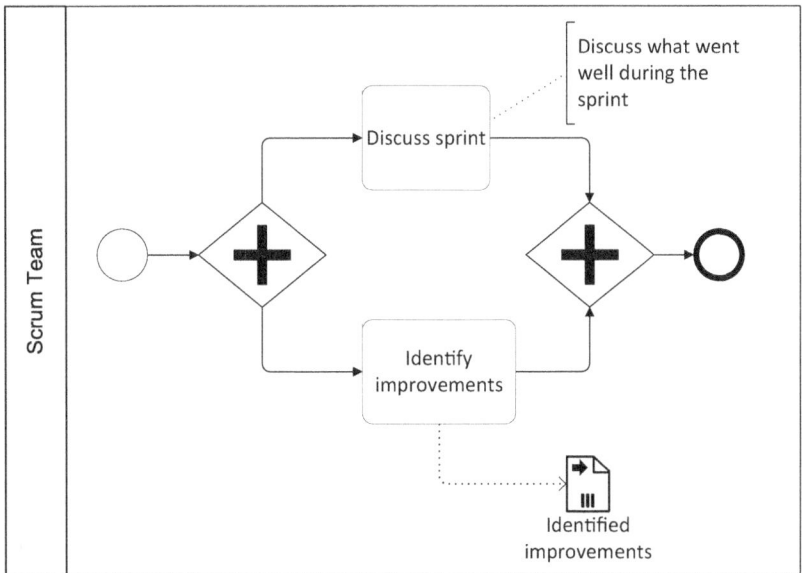

Figure 68: Retrospective meeting process with data flow

2.7. Process levels models

Let's once again sum up all models created within the *Scrum* process using pool notation.

We started with the top-level Scrum process that consists of the *Take Sprint* subprocess performed iteratively. Next we created the detailed *Take Sprint* process that consists of a set of meetings and *Increment development* activity. On the next level, we analyzed in more detail every child-level subprocess of the *Take Sprint* process and created process models.

What conclusions we can put forward?
- The top-level process and its child-level subprocess at any level are modeled within the same pool.
- Every process level can be organized in different ways using different lanes. It's good if at every level, lane names are consistent; still, sometimes you simply don't need to use some lane or it's better to organize a particular child-level flow in other way. Process organization is up to the modeler.
- When modeling some process, always show collapsed subprocesses and then model them separately. The exceptions are event subprocess and parallel boxes: these can be shown as expanded to facilitate understanding of the parent process.
- The way a child-level process ends (number of end events and their states that indicate pro-

2.7. Process levels models

cess state) should be consistent with its parent process flow. In other words, if the subprocess ends with two or more end events, these differences should be handled by the parent process. An exclusive gateway can be used to handle different subprocess end states.
- Maintain the transparency of the process: if the process contains many activities, group some of them that have some common subgoal within the subprocess.

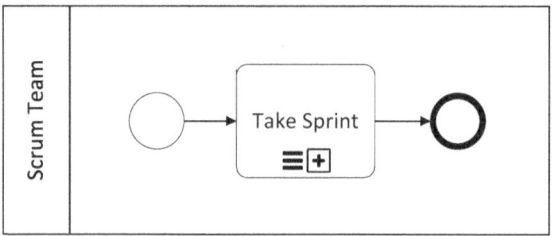

Figure 69: Top-level Scrum process

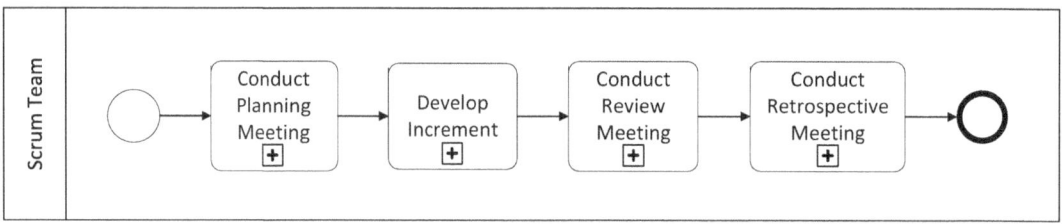

Figure 70: Take Sprint process – high level view with collapsed subprocesses

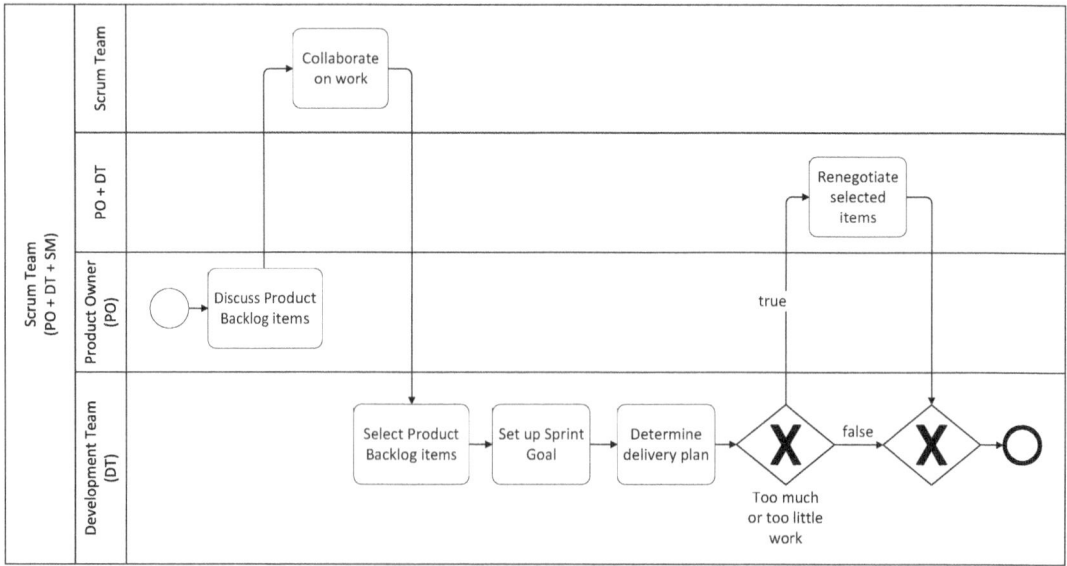

Figure 71: Conduct Planning meeting process

2.7. Process levels models

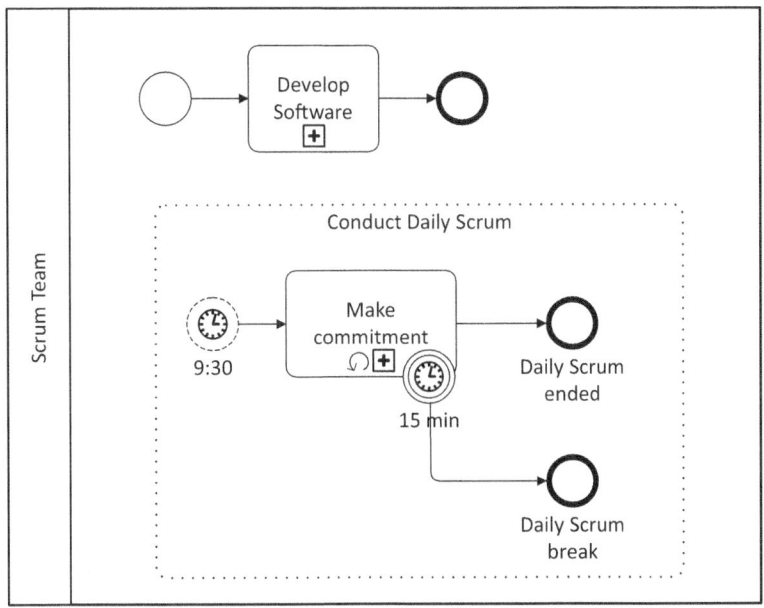

Figure 72: Develop Increment process and Conduct Daily Scrum event subprocess

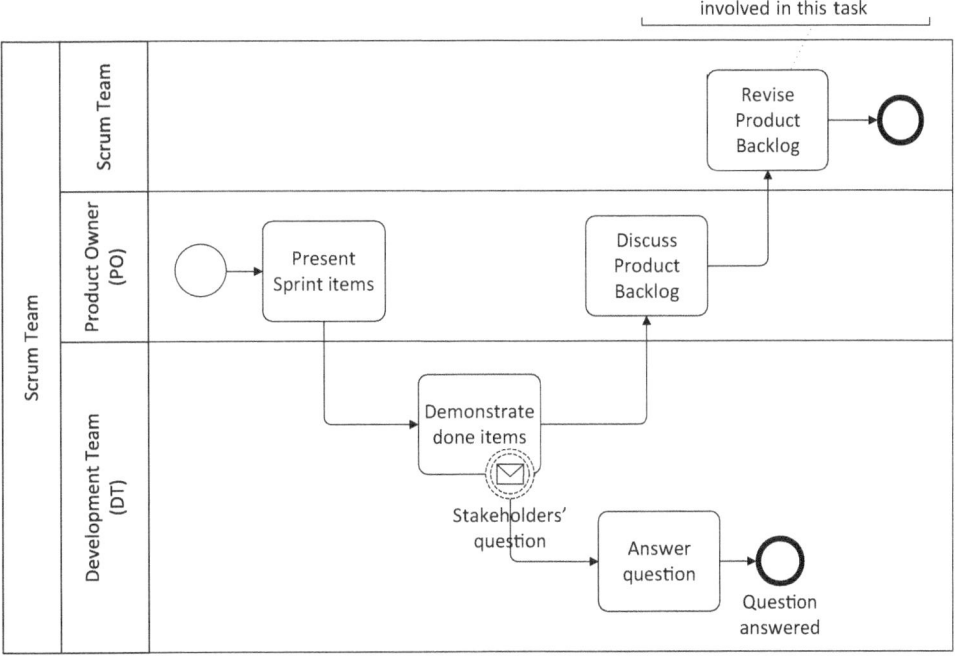

Figure 73: Conduct Review meeting process

97

2.7. Process levels models

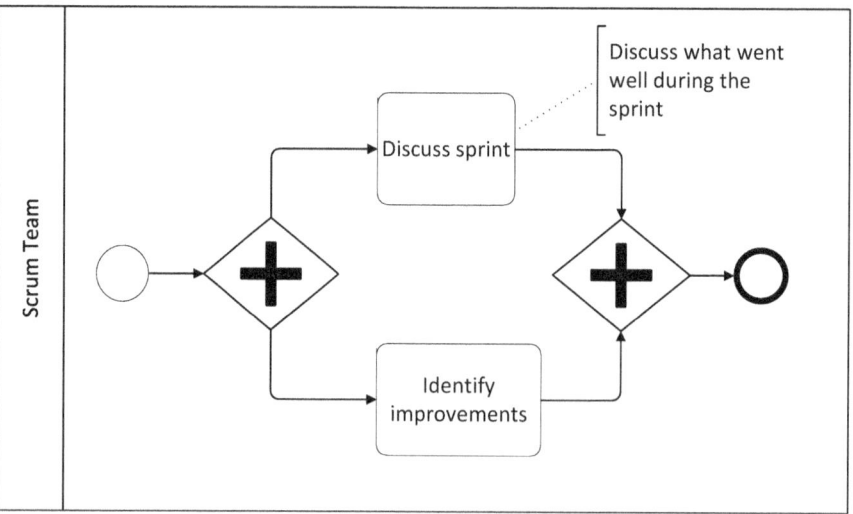

Figure 74: Conduct Retrospective meeting

Example 3:
Library

A library is an organization in which we may define a number of processes like registering a library card, ordering new books for the library collection, and many more. In this example we model the sample process of borrowing books from the library. The library uses an IT system to manage book borrowing. We don't impose any input requirements and assume that anyone can borrow a book.

Learning outcomes

By the end of this example you will be able to:
- Analyze a process from the high level perspective
- Start creating a model of a top-level process
- Identify top-level activities and starting and ending top-level process points
- Define transition conditions between top-level elements
- Know when to use event-based gateways
- Use terminate end event
- Use compensation – both in theory and practice
- Use a call activity
- Model Collaboration
- Understand end events – their effect and usage within a process

3.1. Borrow book process

Process description

A customer can order a book using an online account or directly in the library. Customers may only order available books. If the desired book is already borrowed or ordered, the customer can reserve it; the customer receives an email notification that he/she has ordered/reserved the book.

For a reserved book, the status of the book changes to 'ordered' at the point when the borrowed book is returned to the library or in the event that a customer who previously ordered it cancels the order. After that, the process follows that for an ordered book. A book can be reserved by only one customer at a given time. A customer may also cancel an order or reservation from his/her account or at the library; an email with information about the cancellation is sent to the customer.

An ordered book is prepared for borrowing by a library worker, and when it's ready, the customer receives an email notification that the book can be picked up. From this time, the customer has three business days to pick up the book from the library. If the customer cancels his/her order or does not pick up the book, the book is returned to the collection. If the ordered book has not been borrowed within three business days, the order is cancelled.

When picked up, a library worker provides the book for the customer who comes into the library, the book's status changes to 'borrowed,' the system sets up a borrowing period and the customer gets an email notification about the period of borrowing. Information about the due time is visible in the system for all customers.

Library books can be borrowed for a period of 31 days. The library system sends reminders to customers, 7 days and 1 day before the end of the borrowing period, informing them of the end date. The library charges its customers for overdue books. Every two weeks from the time the book becomes overdue, the system sends a message to the customer about the retention and the fee owing.

A customer may renew a borrowed book a maximum of three times. Renewal can be done only if the book is not reserved by another customer and the customer doesn't have outstanding fees for any borrowed books. Renewals must be made not later than on the day the book's borrowing period ends. The system informs the customer whether the book has been renewed or not.

At the time of return, a library employee checks the state of the book and is authorized to charge an appropriate fine if it is damaged. Information about the fine being charged is sent to the customer's email.

3.1. Borrow book process

We start with developing the top-level *Borrow book* process. In the two previous examples, identification of basic activities that were included within a top-level process was quite easy. In the Bake cake example, we just distinguished two main cake elements as they were presented in the recipe. In the Scrum example, its description and separate subprocesses descriptions directly indicated the basic components from which we developed the top-level process and subprocesses.

In contrast to the two previous examples, the borrow book process is quite involved, and specifying the course of the top-level process is not so obvious. We know that the top-level process should show the basic steps of the process and their sequence. The number of process elements shouldn't be large. These requirements are not so easy to meet. A top-level model influences other subprocesses so it really needs to be carefully considered and modeled adequately. We not only consider the basic process steps, but also alternative scenarios and possible starts and ends of the process.

The following tips can be really helpful for analyzing a process in the context of a top-level model.

Define top-level process elements

To model a top-level process, try first to answer the following questions:
1. What are the process goals?
2. Who or what are the process participants? Which of these is the internal process participant? (From what point of view is the process to be modeled?)
3. What is the scope of the process?
4. How can the process start and end?
5. What are the basic steps of the process and the transition conditions between them?

Goals

From the customer's perspective, the main goal is to borrow a book; from the library's perspective, the goal is good performance of the book borrowing service in accordance with the library's terms.

Process Participants

One of the basic things that gives us a better understanding of the process is identification of the process participants.

3.1. Borrow book process

Reading the borrow book process description, we can distinguish two main process participants: the library and the library customer. Within a library we can additionally distinguish activities performed by the system and by the library workers; however, this is related to the organization of the internal process. We will return to this issue when we discuss Collaboration (Section **3.6. Collaboration - advanced**).

The scope of this exercise is to analyze and model the process from the Library's perspective.
Internal participant: Library
External participant: Customer

A customer is a process participant that triggers and influences the course of the internal process. In our example we consider his/her actions as external message events.

Scope

The process describes the book borrowing service starting from book ordering till the book is returned back to the library.

Start events

The process starts when a customer wants to borrow a book. Depending on the status of the book, the first possible activity is to order or reserve the book. This is our interpretation of the process. In our solution we use one start point and we include different paths depending on all possible book statuses:
- Borrow book

We can also look at the start points of the process from other perspectives. In the process description, a customer can either order a book from a library or using the online library system. Imagine you are logged in to the library system to order a needed book. Only if the book is available can you click on 'order' to start the process. The same applies with a reservation. If you see the book is already borrowed or ordered, you can reserve it. The 'reserve' book action starts the Borrow book process. We can define two start events – *Order book and Reserve book* – that directly lead to the referenced activities.

It is your decision which to choose based on what information is more important to the reader and how you wish to present the process.

End events

In the basic scenario, the process ends with the return of the book.
- Book returned

The process may also end when:
- the customer cannot order a book;
- the customer cancels their order;
- the customer cancels their reservation;
- the customer doesn't collect the ordered book from the library within a specified time.

If alternative flows end the process with the same conditions, we can consider one end event. In our example, if we are not going to present within a process end state what is the reason for cancelling book order (book not collected by a customer, customer cancelled book order), below scenarios leads to the same process end event – *Order cancelled*:
- the customer cancels their order;
- the customer doesn't collect the ordered book from the library within a specified time.

Identifying all alternative end points can be really hard at the beginning; however, it's really helpful when modeling the lower level processes. You know how the subprocess starts and in what statuses it should end. We will go back to this discussion later in the example. The decision on whether to include all possible endings within the top-level model belongs to the modeler.

In Section **3.2. THEORY: End events – their effect and usage within a process,** we present additional information on how to model such cases.

Basic steps

So how to divide the process into smaller pieces? The general advice is: the top-level process should show the order of the basic steps and at the same time should contain only a small number of activities (plus required gateways and events).

This can be quite hard. You could, for example, start to list all steps in the order they occur, or start from a very high view and try to divide it into smaller parts. The decisions on how to organize the process and how much to specialize the activities are up to you.

3.1. Borrow book process

Let's define the basic steps of the *Borrow book process*:
- Order book – subprocess containing everything that relates to ordering a book
- Reserve book – subprocess containing everything that relates to reserving a book
- Manage book order – subprocess containing everything that happens after a book is ordered till it's picked up from the library
- Manage borrowed book – subprocess containing everything that happens when a book is borrowed by a customer
- Return book – all activities needed to return a book to the library.

TIP: If you are not able to correctly model all dependencies between parts of the top-level process because of too much detail, or you think a process contains too many elements, use a more general view that contains elements and relations you are sure of. You can always model and analyze these details within the lower-level processes.

We have specified the basic steps of the process. We also know start and end points of the process that are consistent with those presented on the diagram. Based on this information, we model a first version of the top-level process (Figure 75). As previously discussed, we start the process with a message event as an external process participant – the customer – triggers the process. The process is modeled from the Library's point of view.

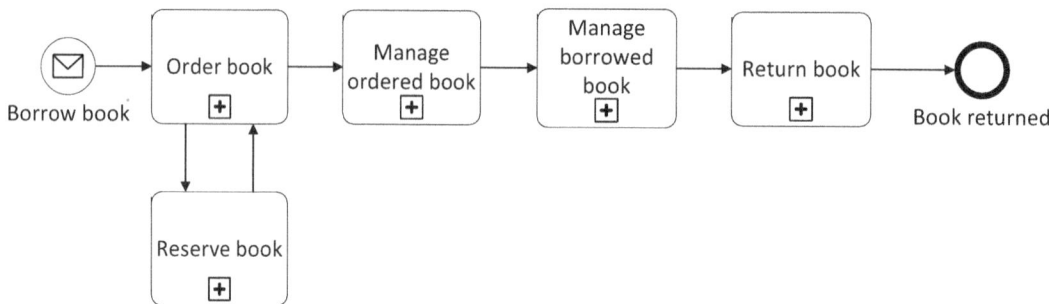

Figure 75: Top-level Borrow book process – first version

Our current diagram presents the 'basic simple' flow between subprocesses that we distinguished from the *Borrow book* process. The process shows the main activities and their sequence. However, this is not a completely correct process because it doesn't explicitly show when we can go from the *Order book* subprocess to *Reserve book* subprocess and when to *Manage ordered book* subprocess.

TIP: If there are two or more outgoing paths from a subprocess, show in what situation we choose each of the paths.

What can we do to improve the process? The two most common approaches are:
- Include one process within another; in this way, we get a clear sequence flow between two processes in the top-level view. The disadvantage is that we 'hide' a step that we previously considered significant.
- Analyze the transition conditions in more detail and define them explicitly. More complex transition details (such as alternative paths or gateways that branch or split flows) don't need to be included within the top-level process. However, if a subprocess has two or more outgoing flows, it's recommended to explicitly distinguish between them: i.e., to specify what is the subprocess end state that leads to the choice of each outgoing path.

Define transition conditions between top-level process elements

Let's try to define and explicitly model within the top-level process the detailed flow between top-level activities. We will also figure out when the process goes from the *Order book subprocess* to the *Reserve book* subprocess and when it goes to the Manage book subprocess. This requires more effort at the beginning, but it gives you and your readers a better understanding of the process flow. What you need to do is to analyze what conditions should be met/under what circumstances the flow may move from one top-level activity to another.

> **TIP:** If the process is about processing some data/object, you can define data/object statuses to explicitly determine transition conditions between process steps.

What's important at the beginning of the process we consider a book that is not managed by the customer for which we instantiate the *Borrow book* process. In other words, we assume that the customer has not yet reserved, ordered or borrowed the book. You can extend your model and handle checking if the book is already ordered, reserved or borrowed by the customer and what happens if any of the above is true.

- Book available – book is available, is not borrowed or reserved; customer can order book.
- Book reserved – book is reserved by another customer; no action is possible
- Book borrowed – book is borrowed by another customer and not reserved; customer can reserve book
- Book ordered – book is ordered by another customer and not yet collected; customer can reserve book

3.1. Borrow book process

Let's first consider transition conditions between the first two subprocesses: *Order book* and *Reserve book*. The customer may directly order the book only if it's available. A book already ordered by another customer can be reserved. If the book is already reserved, the customer can't take any action.

Activity performance dependent on conditions

To model the *Order book* subprocess, we must make the execution of the activity dependent on the book status. Let's discuss two possible solutions:

A. Always start the activity and then cancel it if necessary, depending on the occurrence of a given condition. In our case, the *Order book* subprocess would start immediately and then if the book status is or is changed to reserved/borrowed or ordered, the activity is cancelled (Figure 76).

B. Create separate flows that depend on the condition/status. So we start with checking the book status, and make the course of the process dependent on the current state of the book. Activities that can be performed when a book is in a given status are modeled within the relevant flow (Figure 77).

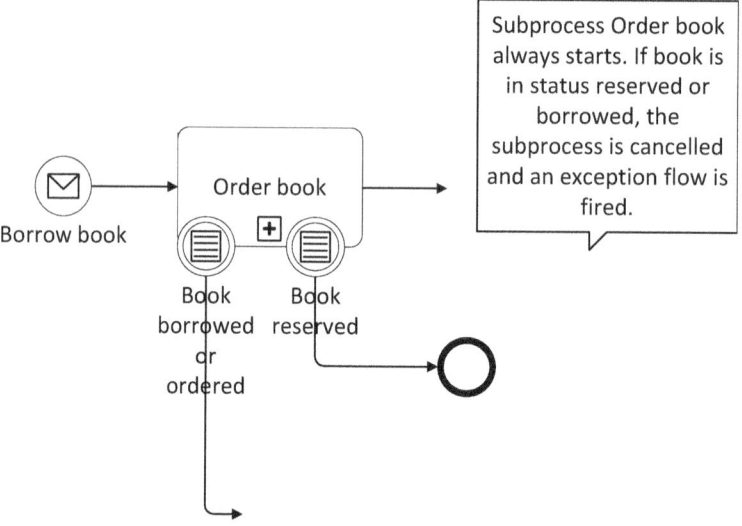

Figure 76: Order book subprocess performance dependent on book status – version A

106

3.1. Borrow book process

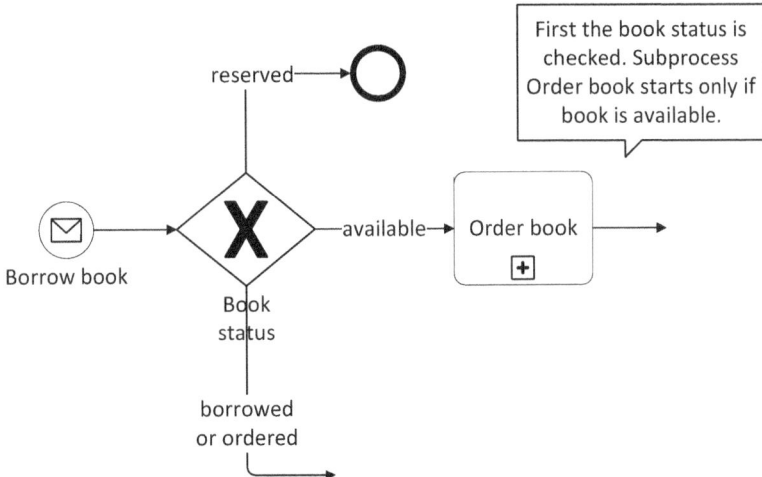

Figure 77: Order book subprocess performance dependent on book status – version B

In both versions A and B we make the *Order book* subprocess conditional on the status of the book. Activity cannot be completed (version A) or cannot start (version B) when the book is in a different status than *available*.

Wrong usage of exclusive gateway

Such behavior, when we need to check conditions to perform an activity, is very often modeled incorrectly. Modelers reverse the course of the process by first performing the activity and then checking the conditions. Look at diagrams in Figure 78. In both cases, regardless of the status of the book we order it anyway, which is incorrect behavior.

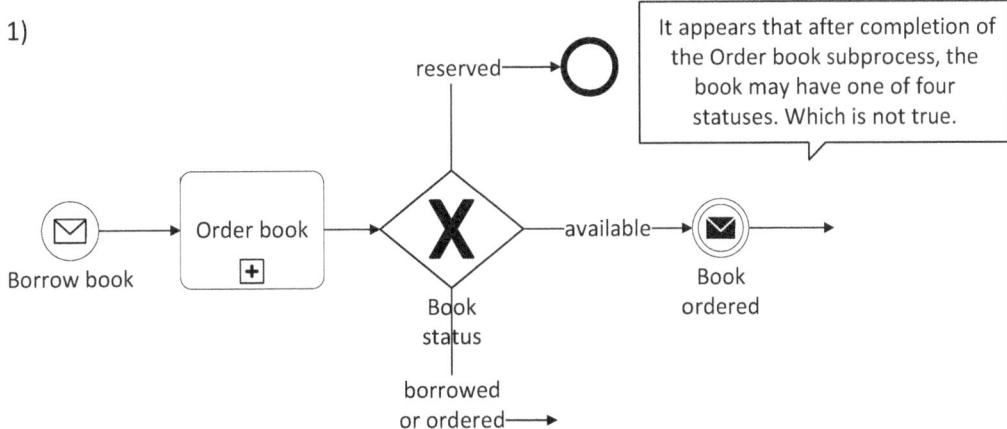

3.1. Borrow book process

2)

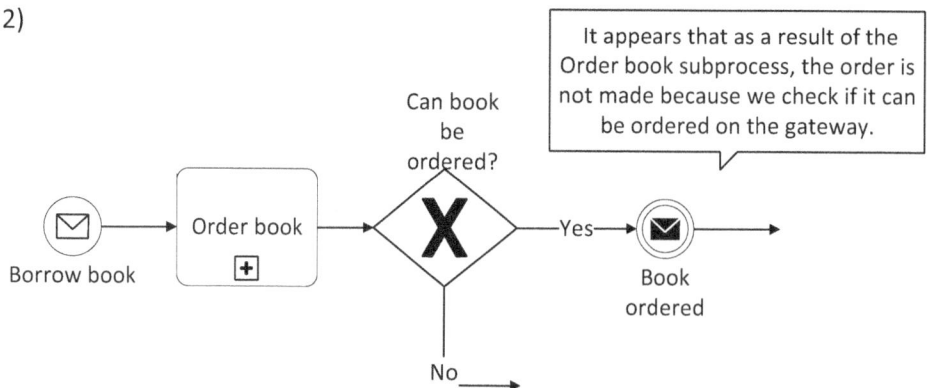

Figure 78: Activity performance dependent on condition – incorrect solutions

Model alternative process flows using exclusive gateway

In the remainder of the example we use version B (Figure 79) as the activity *Order book* cannot start when the book is in a status other than *available*. Let's discuss this process in more detail.

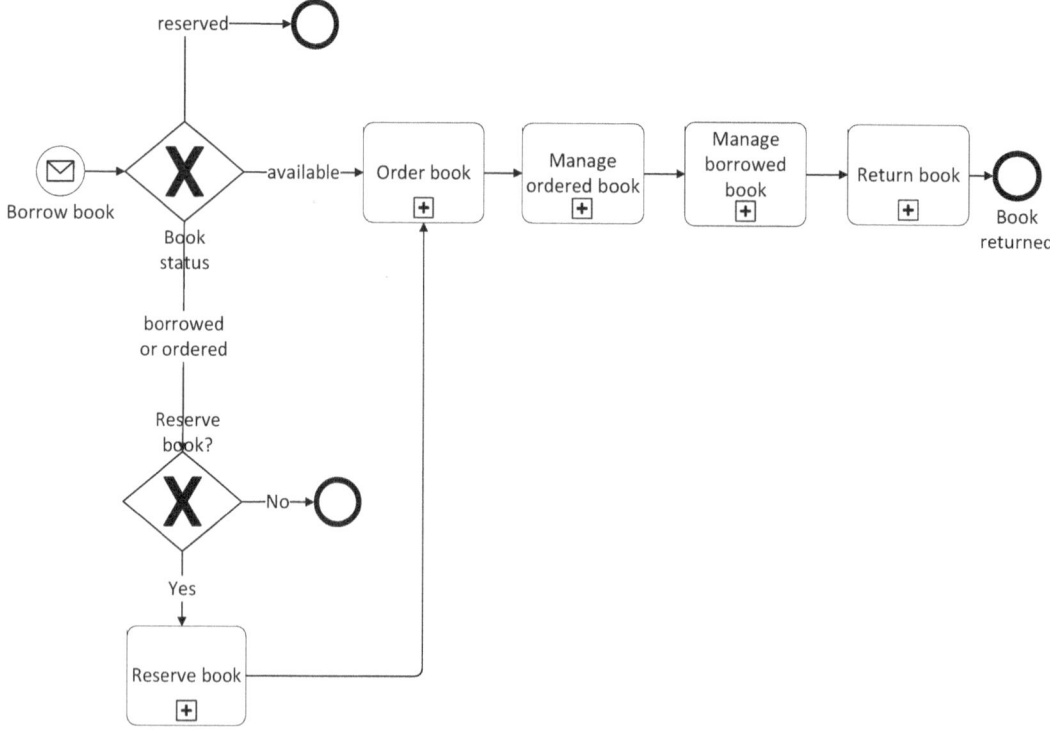

Figure 79: Top-level Borrow book process – second version

We know that if the book is in status 'reserved,' a customer can do nothing so the process ends. If the book is already borrowed or ordered, a customer may reserve it.

In the description of the process, we do not have direct statements that a customer may cease from reserving a book because the book is already ordered, or that we may decide to reserve an unavailable book. Much of the information in the borrow book process description is not straightforward and, as in real life processes, should always be subjected to a deeper analysis to ensure that all alternatives have been taken into account. In our exercise, as in real life, the customer decides if he/she wants to reserve an already borrowed/ordered book.

Reserving a book is optional, so we again use the **exclusive gateway** to model this decision point. If a customer doesn't want to reserve the book, the *Borrow book* process ends; otherwise, the flow continues to the *Reserve book* subprocess.

We have defined a top-level process taking into account possible decisions of the customer before ordering or reservation takes place. Such an approach gives the reader clear information on what are the possible transitions between the basic elements of the process.

Compared to the first version of the process, we have two more process endpoints, one of which – indicating that a customer doesn't want to reserve the book – wasn't listed during the earlier endpoint identification process. We also have direct information on why the process takes some path (Figure 80).

Let's also title the new end events so the reader knows exactly with what condition/state the *Borrow book* process may end.

Whether or not to end the process with two additional end states depends on you. Instead of two end events (*No action possible, Book not reserved*), you can, for example, use one end event for two new alternative paths: no action.

3.1. Borrow book process

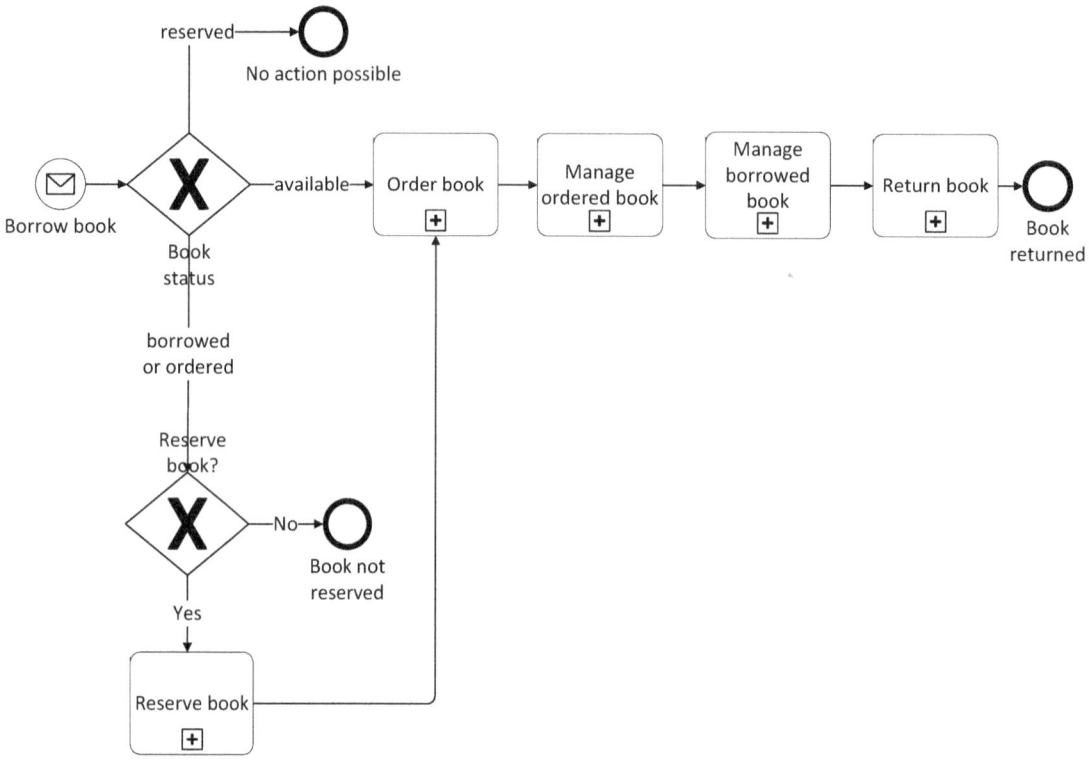

Figure 80: Top-level Borrow book process – second version with named end events

Including all possible process ends

Let's now try to include all possible process endpoints within the top-level process. We already included two more alternative scenarios with two different statuses of the process: *Book not reserved, No action possible*. We have a few situations that may end the *Borrow book* process differently than with the book returning. All of them have been previously identified:
- customer cannot order a book due to its status – this is already supported by our model
- customer cancels their order – not included
- customer cancels their reservation – not included
- customer doesn't collect the ordered book from the library within a specified time – not included

As we discussed previously, it's up to the modeler whether the top-level process shows all process endpoints. Remember that this is not mandatory. If including all or some other possible process endpoints within the top-level process requires a really big effort and deep analysis of child-level processes, it's better to not do this while modeling the top-level process as it may cause some inconsistencies. In a later part of the example, we will discuss what to do when we find out that within some lower level process there is the possibility to end the whole process instance that was not previously identified.

As part of this exercise, however, let's try to include all possible process endpoints within our top-level model. First we need to answer the question: within which activities can the process end in a particular way?
- customer cancels their order – *Order book* subprocess and *Manage ordered book* subprocess
- customer cancels their reservation – *Reserve book* subprocess
- customer doesn't collect the ordered book from the library within a specified time – *Manage ordered book* subprocess

As you can see, during execution of both the *Order book* and *Manage ordered* book subprocesses, the same event may occur and as a result end the whole process.

> **TIP:** If some event can occur during execution of two or more different activities, organize these activities within one subprocess.

This is a signal that these subprocesses can be organized within one subprocess so we will be able properly handle the same intermediate events. Let's join these two activities into one – *Manage book order* – so it will indicate from the top-level process that the subprocess contains all needed steps related to book ordering and other steps performed till the book is collected.

Below there is a model with all possible endpoints identified so far and with a *Manage order book* subprocess that joins two previously specified subprocesses: *Order book* and *Manage ordered book* (Figure 81). We present two versions:
- version A with separate end events indicating the separate process end states due to the ways a book order may be cancelled: order cancelled, and book not collected resulting in order cancellation (Figure 81). We additionally labelled exclusive gateways that handle different subprocess end states; however, this is not required.
- version B with a single end event related to book cancellation (Figure 82). In this version, inside the *Manage book order* subprocess we will join alternative paths: order cancelled or book not collected which results in order cancellation, and finish them with the same end event – *Order cancelled*.

3.1. Borrow book process

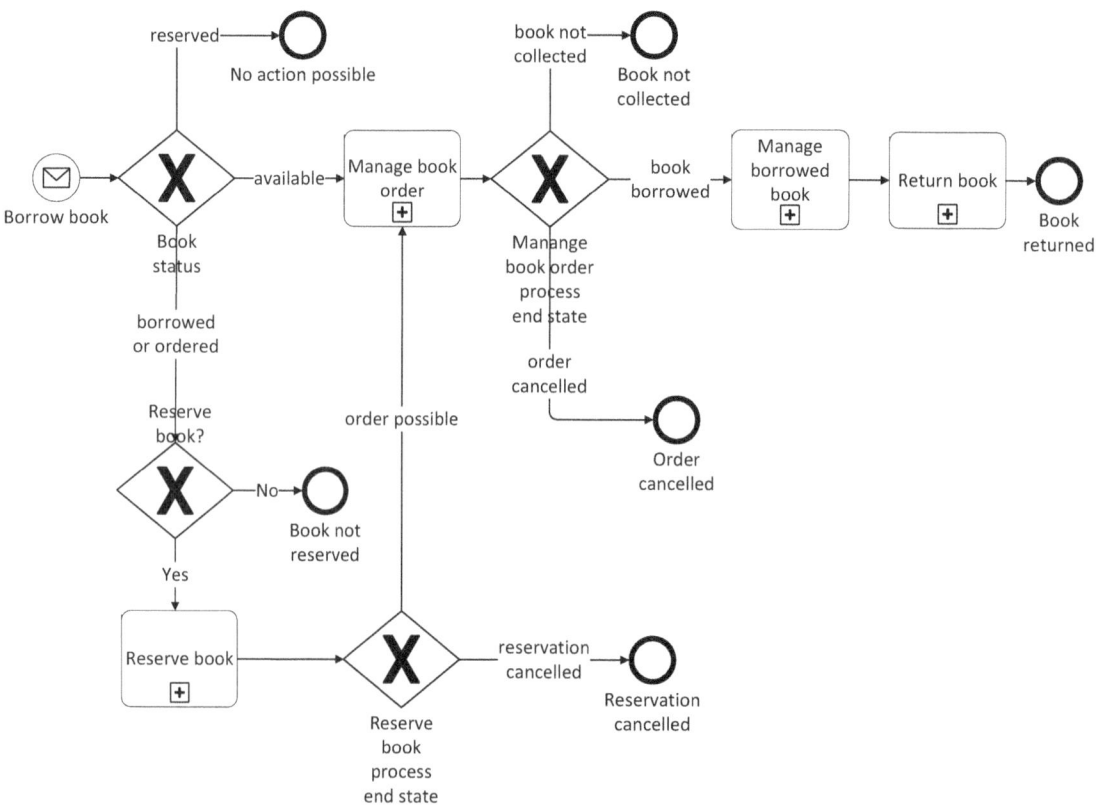

Figure 81: Top-level Borrow book process with all identified process endpoints – version A

3.1. Borrow book process

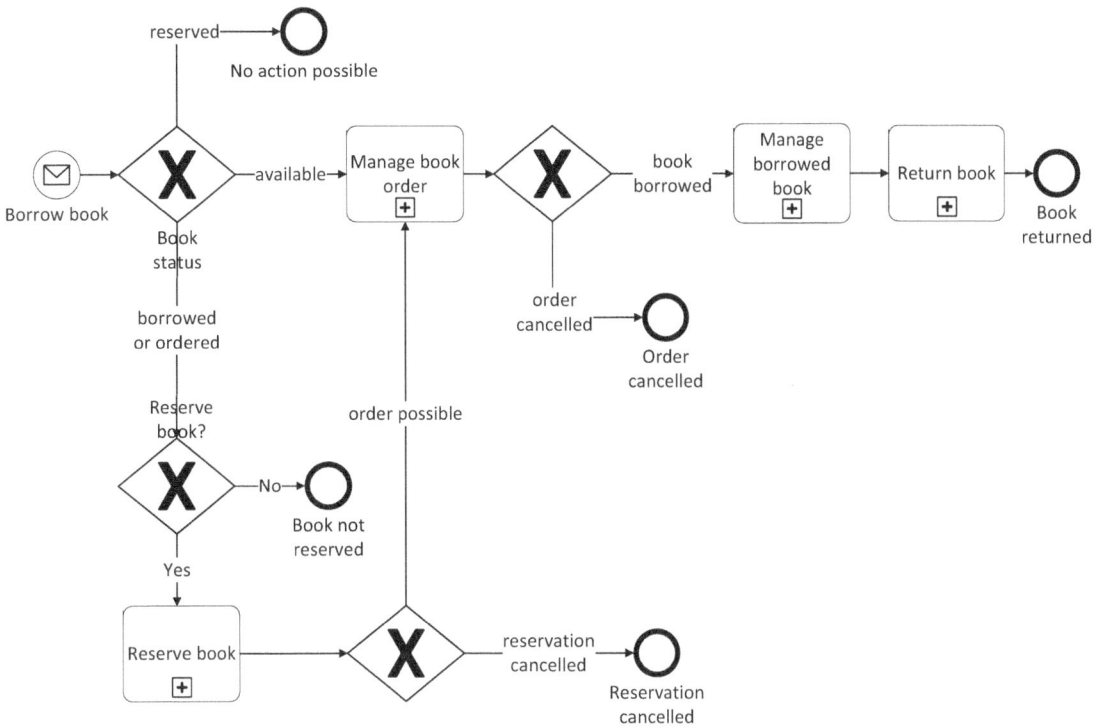

Figure 82: Top-level Borrow book process with all identified process endpoints – version B

What conclusions can we draw from the above considerations?
- The top-level process can be modeled at various levels of detail.
- You can show explicitly using gateways what conditions must be met so the flow goes from one subprocess to another or hide such details by modeling more general subprocesses.
- If a subprocess has two or more outgoing paths, indicate the condition for each path to be selected.
- You can hide or show all the alternative process endpoints. It's recommended to show at least one end event from the main scenario.

3.2. Reserve book process

Let's analyze in more detail the process of reserving a book. The process description that contains the part of the process related to book reservation goes as follows:

If the desired book is already borrowed or ordered, the customer can reserve it; the customer receives an email notification that he/she has ordered/reserved the book.

3.1. Borrow book process

For a reserved book, the status of the book changes to 'ordered' at the point when the borrowed book is returned to the library or in the event that a customer who previously ordered it cancels the order. After that, the process follows that for an ordered book. A book can be reserved by only one customer at a given time. A customer may also cancel an order or reservation from his/her account or at the library; an email with information about the cancellation is sent to the customer.

What can we learn from the description about the book reservation process? The process is triggered when a customer decides to reserve a book. The first activity is book reservation, and then an email confirming the action is sent. We also learn that a reserved book is automatically ordered when one of two events occurs:
- another customer returns the reserved book
- another customer cancels their book order.

The first decision is to decide to model these events within the *Reserve book* subprocess. They could be also modeled within the *Ordered book* subprocess. When modeling subprocesses, *you* decide their scope. The beginning and end of the subprocess should be consistent with what is happening at its entry and exit. The scope of the whole end-to-end process needs to be covered by its elements.

> To merge paths branched by an event-based gateway we use an exclusive gateway.
> The event-based gateway may only be used to branch a flow.

Figure 83: Reserve book process with event-based gateway

To model the situation where the process waits for one of several events, we use an **event-based gateway**. The behavior of the event-based gateway is similar to the exclusive gateway: only one branch can be picked up. The difference is that we don't define the condition at every outgoing flow but we insert intermediate catch events. The first caught event determines the further course of the process. In our case, occurrence of either of the events *Book returned* or *Order cancelled* causes the process to follow the same path. Still, they are different events, and we should include both in the model.

THEORY: Event-based gateways

BPMN specifies three types of event-based gateways: the event-based gateway that is used within a process flow and two types of event-based gateways to start a process.

 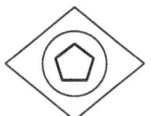 

Event-based gateway 　　Event-based gateway　　Parallel event-based gateway
　　　　　　　　　　　　　　to start a process　　　　　to start a process

The event-based gateway can be understood as an exclusive gateway driven by events. It indicates a point in the process at which the process waits on one of a number of events to occur. When the first relevant event occurs, the other outgoing paths are disabled. There are three important modeling rules related to event-based gateways. They are applicable to all three event-based gateway types.

1. Events that are included on outgoing paths from an event-based gateway must be catch events. Only a few types of catch intermediate events are valid: message, signal, timer, conditional and multiple. You cannot use the following intermediate events with the event-based gateway: error, cancel, compensation or link.

2. Another rule is related to use of a **receive task** type. You may use a receive task with the event-based gateway only if no catch message event is used and vice versa. Both elements cannot be used together within the same event-based gateway.

3.1. Borrow book process

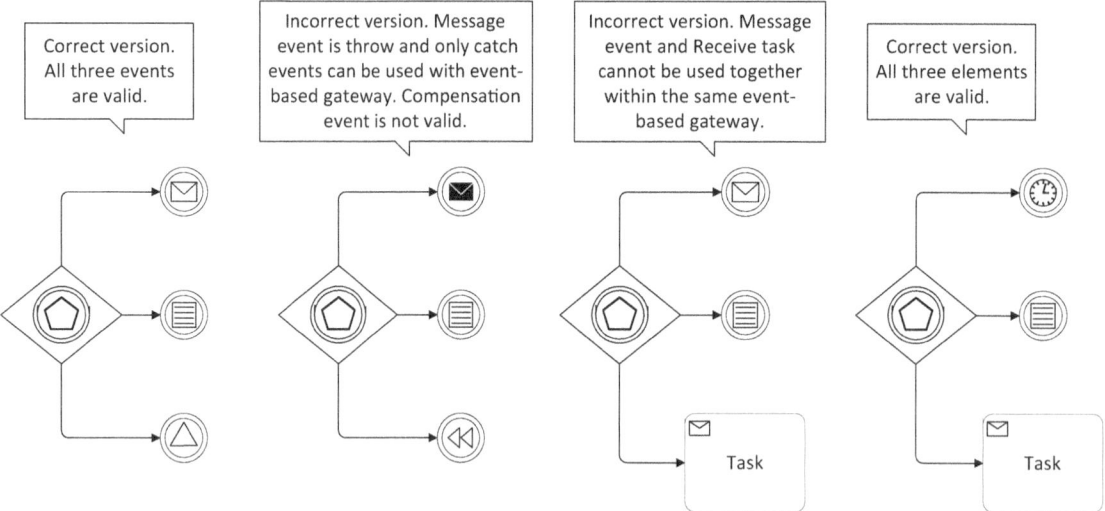

3. The final thing you should remember is that events or receive tasks that are the target of an event-based gateway cannot have other incoming flows.

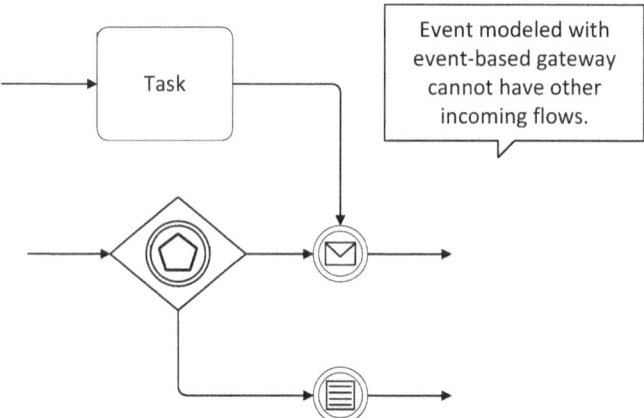

BPMN defines two types of event-based gateways that can be used to start a process. When there are several possible events that may independently start the process, use an event-based gateway to start the process. This is an exclusive event driven getaway that behaves like an event-based gateway but is used only at the beginning of the process.

A parallel event-based gateway to start a process is used, as its' name indicates, at the beginning of a process when two or more events can instantiate a process. The first occurring event starts the process; however, in contrast to the event-based gateway, the other outgoing paths can still be used. So when we expect that one of several events can start a process, and the rest of them should also occur even if the process is already instantiated, use a parallel event-based gateway to start the process.

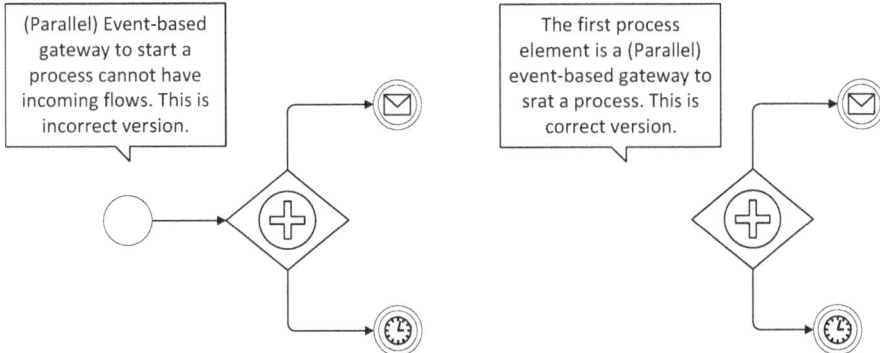

Event-based gateways to start a process cannot have any incoming flow. This means that you cannot use a start event as the first element of the process if the next element is a (parallel) event-based gateway to start the process. These types of gateways must be the first element in the process flow.

3.1. Borrow book process

If we define the two start points of the process that we discussed in the Section **3.1. Define top-level process elements**, we can use an event-based gateway to start the process (Figure 84).

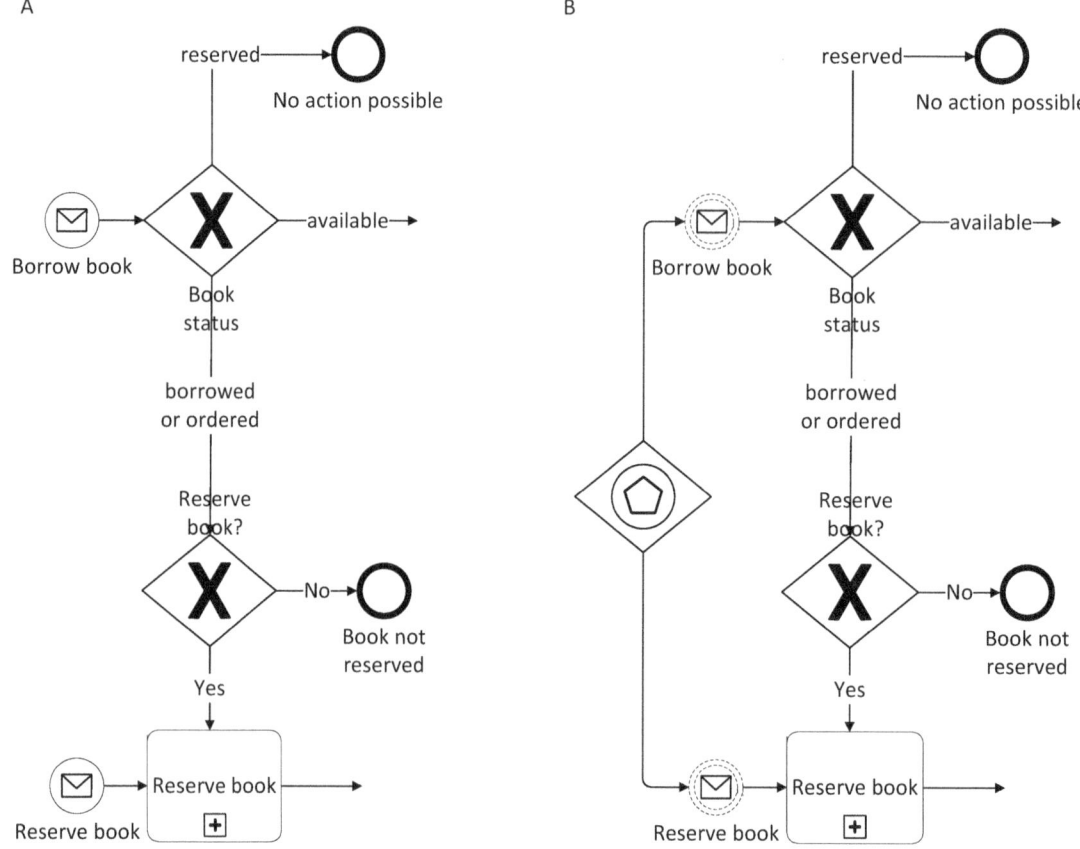

Figure 84: Two possible ways of start Borrow book process – version without (A) and with event-based-gateway to start the process (B)

We've already supported book order cancellation and book returning events within the *Reserve book* subprocess. But what about cancellation of a book reservation made by a customer who reserves a book?

Undo changes

Now we should add the possibility of cancelling the reservation. The first thing worth explaining is how we understand the cancel reservation activity. We interpret it as a change of book status from 'reserved' to it previous status. In other words, it simply undoes the activity that made the book status 'reserved.' But how we can cancel an activity that is already completed? The solution to this type of modeling problem is **compensation**, which is a mechanism for undoing already completed activities. Both boundary events and event subprocesses may only be fired when the parent activity is active. Compensation catch events are the only BPMN events that are fired for completed activities.

TIP: If you need to undo changes made by an already completed activity, use Compensation.

Look at the *Reserve book* process with added compensation in Figure 85. A **compensation intermediate event** is attached to the *Reserve book* task. This is a catch event that can be fired only if the task is completed. A compensation event is linked with a **compensation handler** – the *Cancel reservation* task – that is responsible for undoing the changes made by the task.

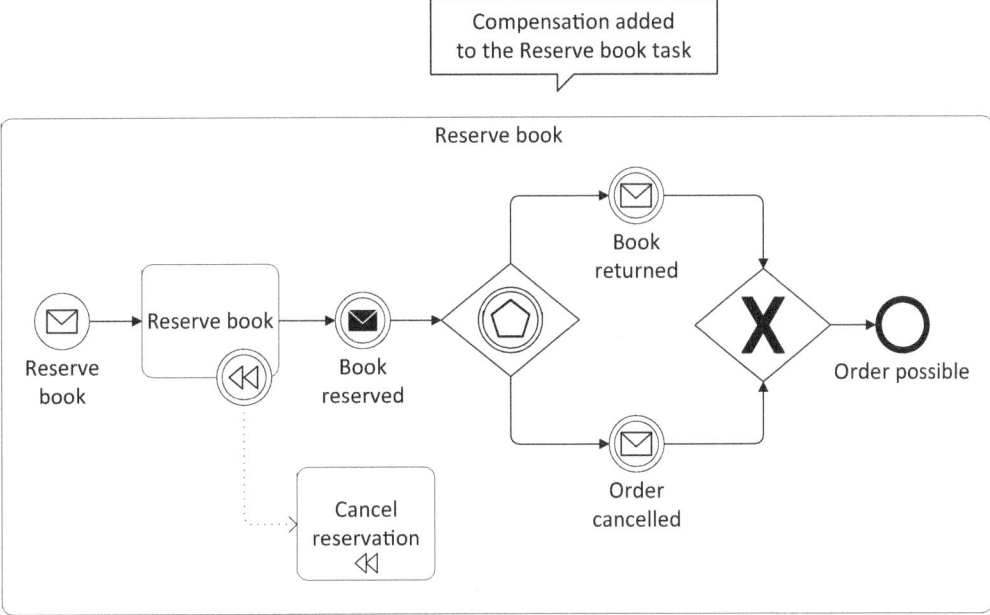

Figure 85: Reserve book process with Compensation

The compensation, like every event, needs to be triggered somehow. To trigger a compensation event attached to some activity, we need to fire a throw compensation event first. The throw compensation event must be included within the same process or a higher level process that has access to the catch compensation event. Let's now go through the compensation theory, and later in the example we will come back to the issue of throwing compensation for the *Reserve book* task.

3.1. Borrow book process

THEORY: Compensation

Compensation is a mechanism for undoing activity that is already completed.

To properly model compensation, we need to have a compensation trigger, a compensation catcher and a handler that performs the compensation. Let's discuss how we may model these elements step by step.

To start the compensation mechanism we first need to trigger the compensation. Compensation can be triggered by a **compensation end event** or by a **throw compensation intermediate event**.

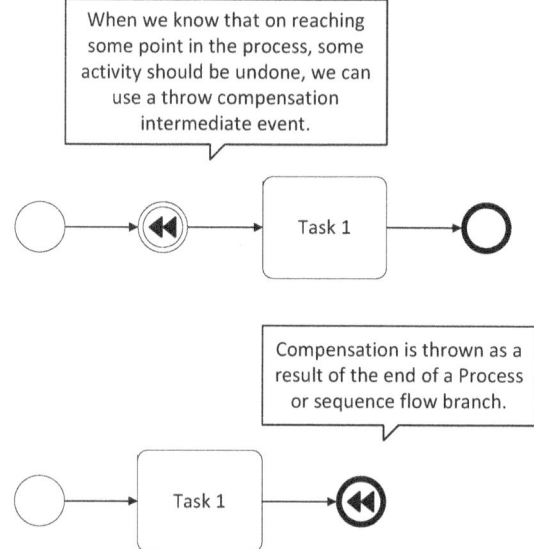

We have now triggered compensation; now we need to catch it so it can be handled appropriately. There are two ways of catching and thus handling compensation:
- A **catch compensation intermediate event** attached to the activity boundary that needs to be compensated. In this case the handler is a compensation activity. The compensation task is dedicated only to undoing the activity with which it's associated. It doesn't have any outgoing flow.

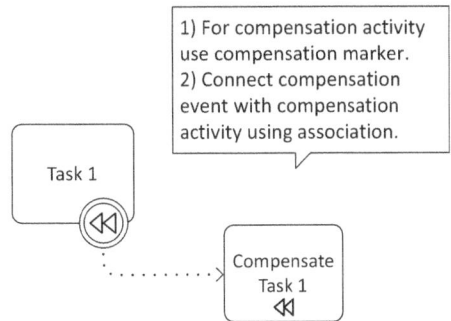

- A compensation start event that triggers a compensation event subprocess (you mustn't trigger a normal subprocess in such a way). Within a subprocess you may define throw compensation events that refer to compensation handlers defined within a parent subprocess; you may also define additional activities that are need to properly handle compensation, e.g. saving data.

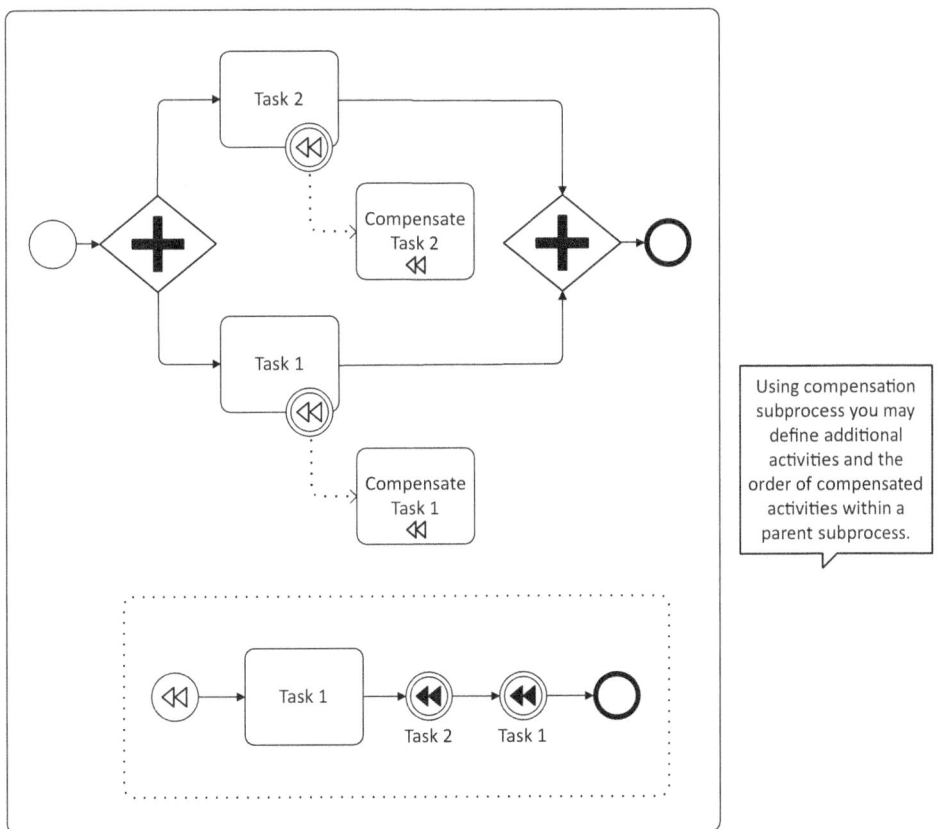

3.1. Borrow book process

Catch compensation events are fired only for an already completed activity. That's why, unlike other events, we have not considered them in the context of the interruption or non-interruption of an activity: we simply cannot interrupt an activity that is no longer active. All other boundary events and other event subprocesses may only be triggered when the activity is active.

So where we can add a throw compensation event that will trigger compensation for the *Reserve book* task? Look at the model in Figure 86.

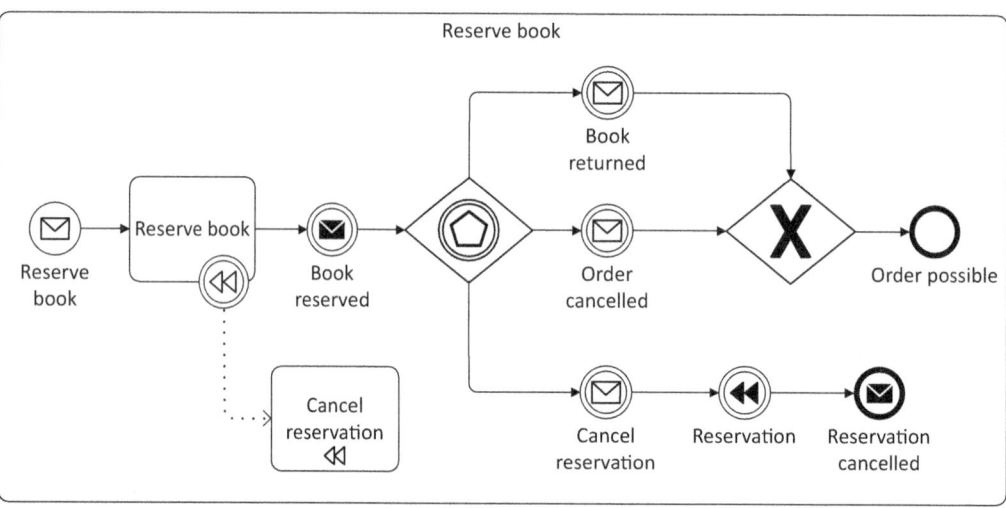

Figure 86: Reserve book process with compensation mechanism

Once again, after a book is reserved, three events may occur:
    a. another customer returns the reserved book
    b. another customer cancels their book order
    c. the customer who reserved the book cancels the reservation

In the first two cases (a, b), if one of the two events occurs, the book is automatically ordered so we go directly to the *Manage book order* subprocess. Case (c) describes the scenario that a customer may decide to cancel a reservation only if the reservation is valid so only if the book is not ordered yet. If the book is ordered then its reservation simply will not exist anymore. The event may occur after a book is reserved and before it is ordered.

We use an event-based race condition modeled using an event-based gateway: whichever event occurs first, wins.

After the event-based gateway, we first use a catch message intermediate event *Cancel reservation*. The throw compensation event cannot be used directly with an event-based gateway. Another point is that the first customer needs to communicate with the library (we don't care if it happens in a library or via the library system) in order to cancel a reservation. We need here a communication point between two participants – a customer and a library – as cancellation may by performed only on the initiative of the customer.

When a customer cancels a reservation, we fire compensation so the thrown compensation event is used. Step by step, this works as follows:

1. Throw compensation *Reservation* event is fired.

2. Compensation is caught by the compensation catch event attached to the *Reserve book* task (Because we have only one throw and catch compensation event within a subprocess, naming them is optional).

3. The compensation catch event fires the flow to the compensation handler *Cancel reservation* task that is responsible for undoing the changes made by the *Reserve book* task.

4. When changes are undone (*Cancel reservation* task ends its execution), the flow proceeds from the place the compensation was thrown: in this case from the throw compensation *Reservation* event to the next throw message intermediate event: *Reservation cancelled*.

Ending the whole process from the child level

After a book reservation is cancelled, an email confirming the cancellation is sent to the customer, and the whole *Borrow book* process should end as it simply makes no sense to keep it active.

If we decide to expose the fact that the subprocess flow ends the whole top-level process instance, we can pull out the different states the subprocess ends in using an exclusive gateway. We've already presented such an approach in Section **3.1. Including all possible process ends**. Look

3.1. Borrow book process

once again at the *Reserve book* process and the fragment of the top-level process that handles this part of the flow. In this case, as we're sure that no other flow branch within the top-level process is active, we use a **none end event** to end the *Borrow book* process with the information that the reservation has been cancelled (Figure 87).

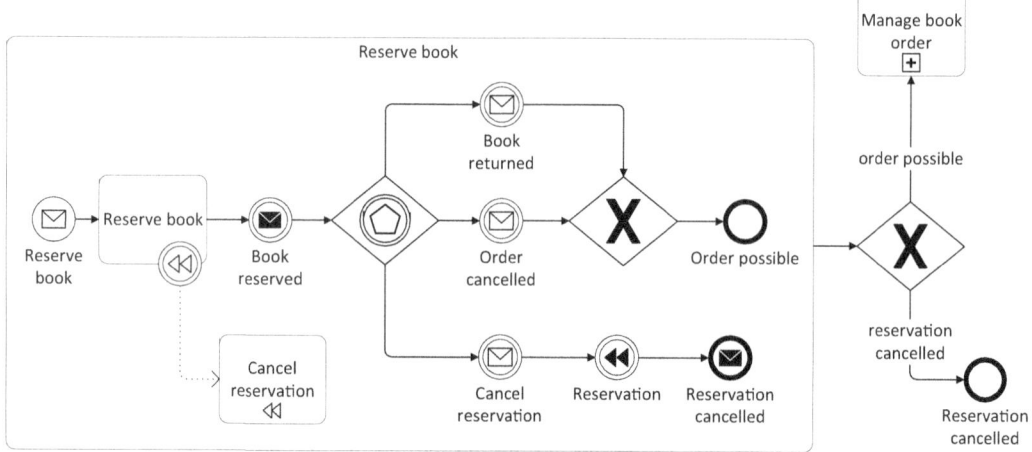

Figure 87: Subprocess end states handled by the parent process

Another way is to use a **terminate end event** directly in a child-level process which end state ends the whole top-level process instance. It doesn't matter at what level of the process the terminate end event is triggered, it ends all process activities immediately. In such case we don't need to introduce *Reservation cancelled* end event in a top-level process (Figure 88).

> **TIP:** Use the terminate end event when:
> - the end of a subprocess flow branch ends the whole top-level process
> - one of many active branches within a top-level process ends the whole process instance

3.1. Borrow book process

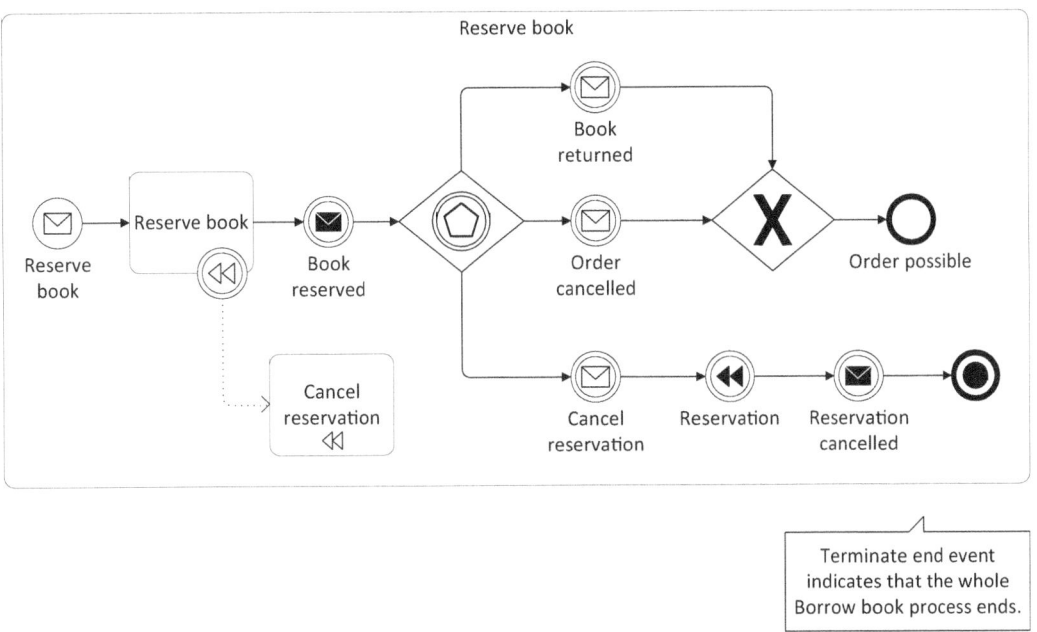

Terminate end event indicates that the whole Borrow book process ends.

Figure 88: Reserve book process with terminate end event

TIP: If performance of a subprocess may end the whole process, use a terminate end event, or transfer this information to the parent process using an exclusive gateway with outgoing flows indicating the subprocess end states.

Joining throw intermediate event and none end event

When the throw event is the last event before the process ends and there is an adequate end event type specified in BPMN, you can 'join' these two events into one (Figure 89). We've applied this for the *Reservation cancelled* event (Figure 87).

3.1. Borrow book process

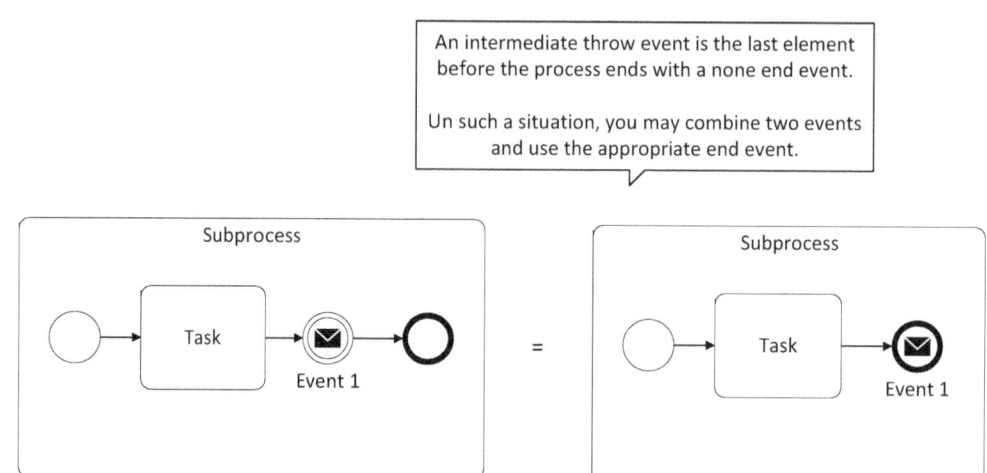

Figure 89: End of the process – two equivalent versions

All differences between end event types and how to use them within child-level processes can be found in section that follows.

THEORY: End events – their effect and usage within processes

BPMN defines nine types of end events. An end event ends the instance of the process or subprocess within which it is triggered. It is the last element in a sequence flow. All end events are throw events.

End events are optional and independently used within processes and subprocesses. We will go through all the types of end events and discuss them, taking into account how they may be handled and how they influence the flow at different process levels.

None end event

The basic end event is the none end event; it is used when we don't need to define the specific end result of the process. With this event you may define an end state of the process.

3.1. Borrow book process

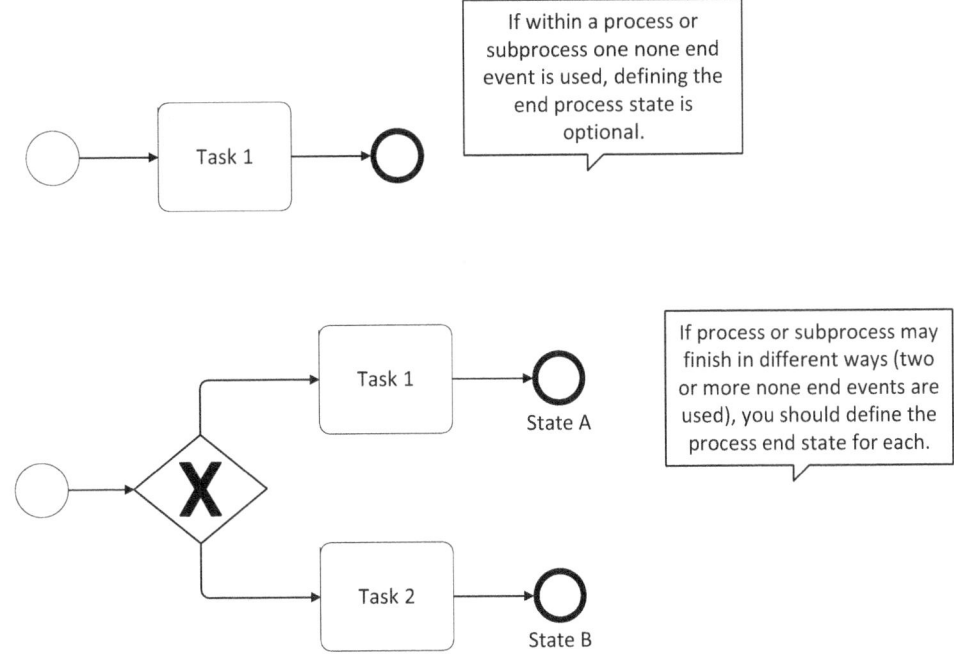

If a none end event with defined end state is used within a subprocess, information about how the subprocess ended is available to its parent process. A subprocess is a part of the normal sequence flow, so you can refer to end states of the subprocess in other parts of the parent process using gateways or intermediate catch events.

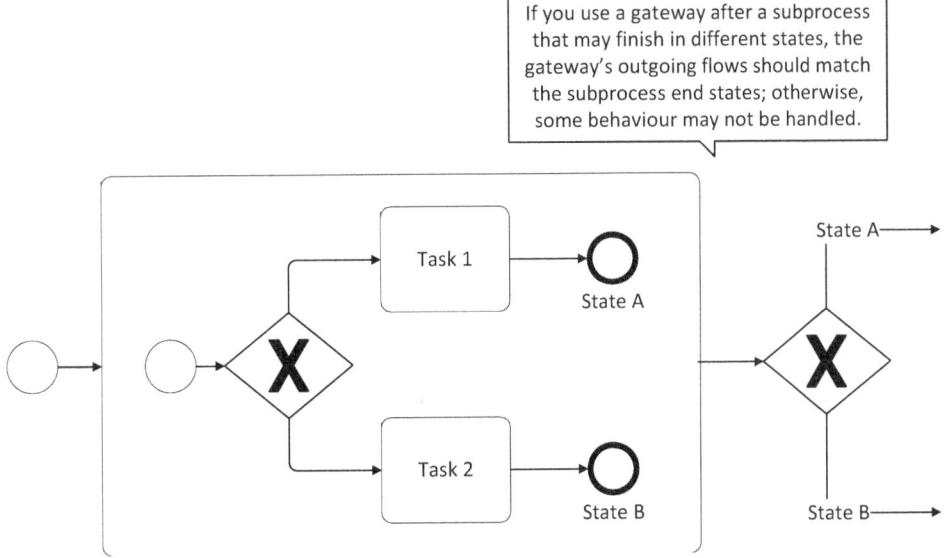

3.1. Borrow book process

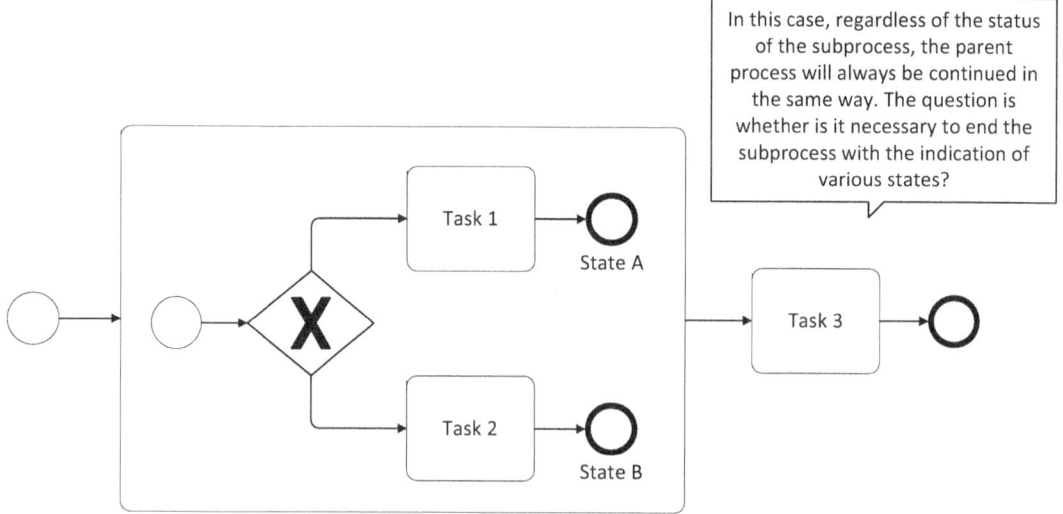

End events with optional catching

The message end event and multiple end event define some additional behavior. Message and multiple end events can be used both within a top-level process and within subprocesses. We group them together as for these end events there is no requirement and no direct mechanism to catch them within a process. You can finish a process or subprocess branch flow with a multiple or message end event, and that's it.

Message end event

The message end event indicates that a process finishes with sending a message to another participant (different process). As we discussed in collaboration (See Section **2.5. BPMN Collaboration**), you cannot use a catch message event (start or intermediate) to catch a message sent within the same process.

Multiple end event

The multiple end event can define many consequences of the process end. It is usually used when many messages are sent as a result of the end of the process, but is not exclusively for this purpose. Using a multiple end event, you can define any number and type of end results, for example: an email is sent, an alarm sounds, a condition is set to true, etc.

You cannot directly catch a message thrown by a message or multiple end event within a process; however, you can use the fact that the end event occurred. There are a number of ways to do this: by using a rule intermediate event, multiple catch intermediate event, or gateways. Such approaches are applicable also for throw intermediate events. Look at the examples below.

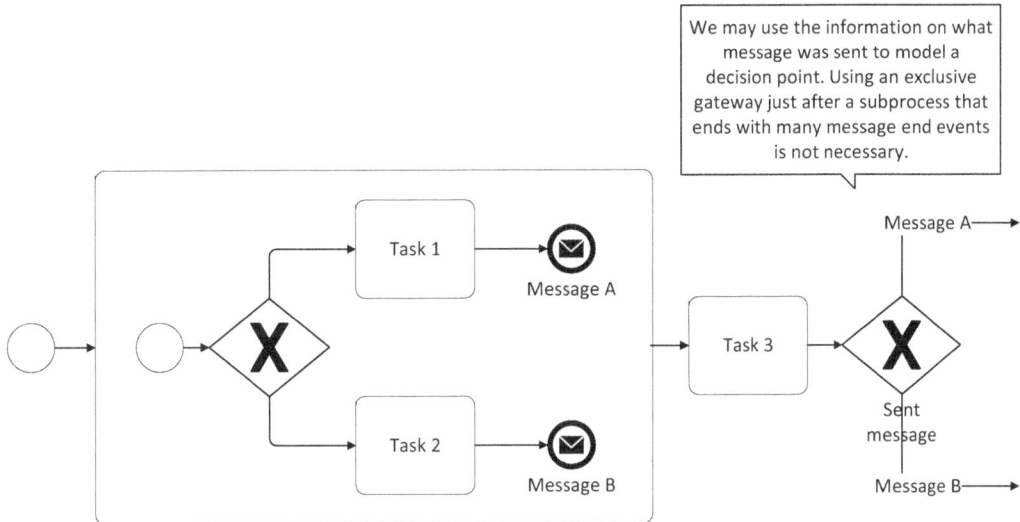

3.1. Borrow book process

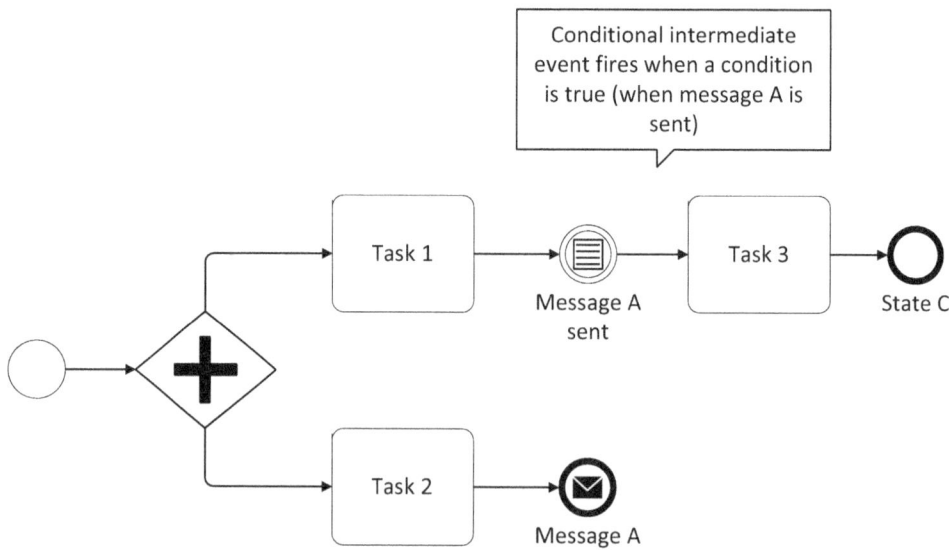

End events requiring catching

The next group are end events that should be handled within the process. This means that there should be a dedicated catch intermediate event that catches a result thrown by the end event.

Error end event

The error end event indicates that a process ends with an error. For error end events used within a subprocess, an error catch event should be defined to handle the generated error. If an error end event is used within a top-level process and there is no handling mechanism, for non-executable processes we may interpret it as an event that terminates the whole process. Good practice is to handle the error that occurs. Using an error end event is the only way to throw an error.

An error end event can be caught only by a **catch error event**. We may model it in two ways.
- Using an error intermediate event attached to the parent activity boundary within which the error end event occurred. Use this solution if you want the higher level process to handle the error. Remember that an error intermediate event may not be directly used in a sequence flow.

- Using an error start event to trigger an event subprocess that handles the error. Use this solution if you want the parent subprocess or other subprocess to handle the error.

Catch error event attached to the activity boundary or triggering event subprocess terminates the parent activity. It is an interrupting event. BPMN doesn't define a non-interrupting error event.

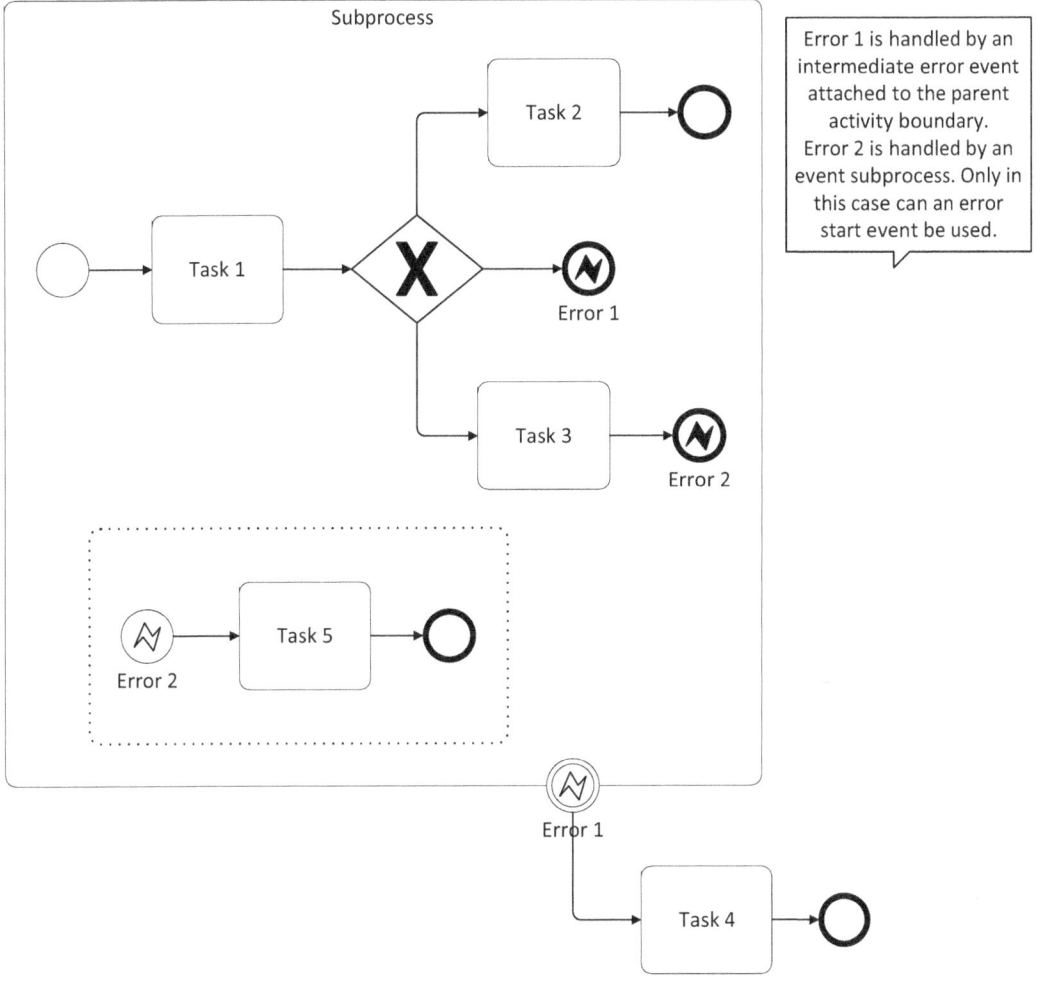

Error 1 is handled by an intermediate error event attached to the parent activity boundary. Error 2 is handled by an event subprocess. Only in this case can an error start event be used.

Escalation end event

The escalation end event means that as a result of the process, escalation is triggered. Escalation must be handled within the process. Analogously to error handling, we can catch escalation using an catch escalation intermediate event attached to the boundary of the parent activity or using an escalation start event that triggers an event subprocess. When catching escalation, the activity doesn't need to be cancelled. We may use interrupting or non-interrupting catch escalation events.

Remember that you cannot use a catch escalation intermediate event directly in a sequence flow; however, using a throw escalation intermediate event is allowed.

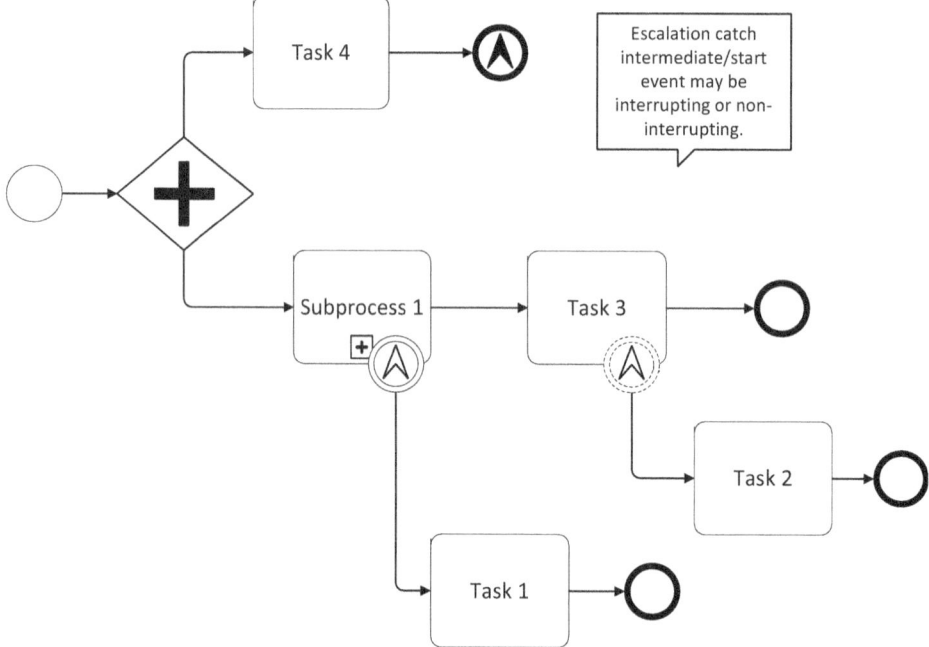

3.1. Borrow book process

Compensation end event

The compensation end event also needs to be caught and handled. We've already discussed the compensation mechanism in Section **3.2. THEORY: Compensation**

Cancel end event

The cancel end event is used in a transition – that is, a subprocess controlled by a transition protocol. Using transition, we may define a specific behavior of the subprocess. Transition is usually used while modeling executable processes rather than non-executable ones, so we won't discuss it here.

End events that can affect the entire model

Signal end event

The signal end event indicates that the process flow ends with a signal that is spread across the whole model. The signal end event is an event that can be caught at any level of the process and also by other processes. We can understand it as an alarm that can be heard everywhere, and it can in fact be used to model an alarm event. To catch a signal thrown by a signal end event (and also the throw signal intermediate event), we use the catch signal event. In this case you may catch the signal in a number of ways:
- Using a signal start event to start a process
- Using a catch signal intermediate event in a sequence flow
- Using a catch signal intermediate event attached to the boundary of an activity – either interrupting or non-interrupting
- Using an interrupting or non-interrupting signal start event that triggers an event sub-process

3.1. Borrow book process

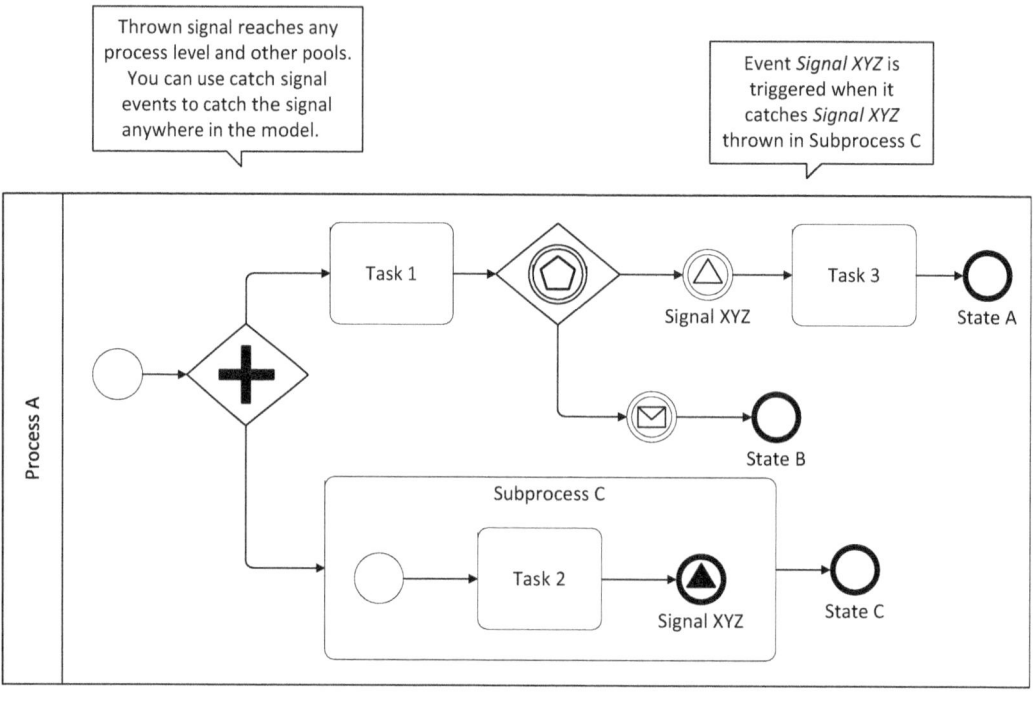

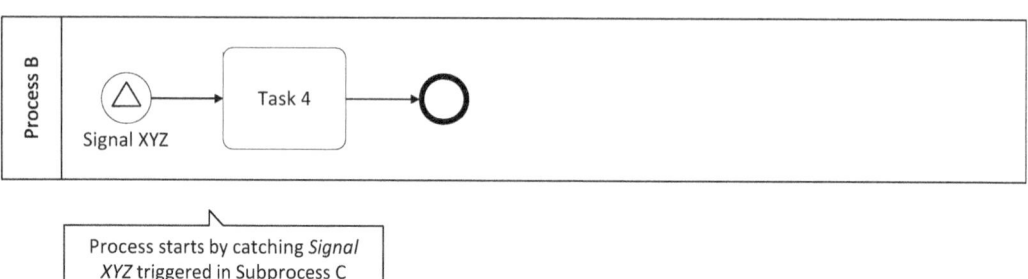

Terminate end event

The terminate end event always influences the whole process within which it's used as it ends the main process instance. It doesn't matter at what level of the process the terminate end event is triggered, it ends all process activities immediately. There is no compensation or error handling. The terminate end event has no influence on other processes.

3.3. Manage book order

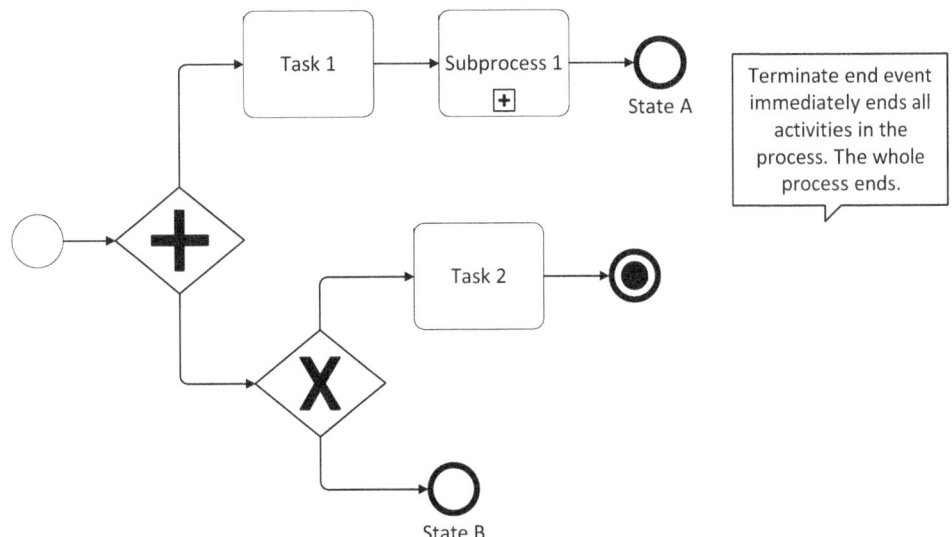

There is no possibility to catch a terminate end event. It stops a process instance.

3.3. Manage book order

The *Manage book order* subprocess should show the part of the flow starting from book ordering and ending with the event when a customer collects the book from the library (in the positive basic scenario). Let's start by analyzing the part of the *Manage book order* subprocess that relates to ordering a book. Part of the process description that contains the order book description is as follows. (The description is a mix of order and reserve book processes.)

A customer can order a book using an online account or directly in the library. Customers may only order available books. If the desired book is already borrowed or ordered, the customer can reserve it; the customer receives an email notification that he/she has ordered/reserved the book.

.... A customer may also cancel an order or reservation from his/her account or at the library; an email with information about the cancellation is sent to the customer.

The next part of the process description says what can happen after the book is ordered till it's picked up from the library.

An ordered book is prepared for borrowing by a library worker, and when it's ready, the customer receives an email notification that the book can be picked up. From this time, the customer has three

3.3. Manage book order

business days to pick up the book from the library. *If the customer cancels his/her order or does not pick up the book, the book is returned to the collection. If the ordered book has not been borrowed within three business days, the order is cancelled.*

When picked up, a library worker provides the book for the customer who comes into the library, the book's status changes to 'borrowed,' the system sets up a borrowing period and the customer gets an email notification about the period of borrowing. Information about the due time is visible in the system for all customers.

Within the top-level process we have already modeled the conditions under which a book can be ordered. The subprocess starts if a customer decides to order a book. Notice that in our model we don't distinguish whether it happens in a library or via the library customer application.

The book is ordered, and then an email confirming the action is sent. The ordered book is prepared for collection from the library. This fragment of the process may look as follows (Figure 90).

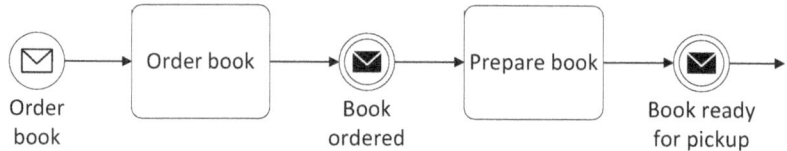

Figure 90: Order and prepare book activities

Use of event-based gateway – advanced

After the book is ready for pickup, one of three events may occur:
a. Customer picks up the book within 3 days.
b. Customer doesn't pick up the book within 3 days.
c. Customer cancels order. (Notice that in the description we have additional information: *If the customer cancels his/her order or does not pick up the book, the book is returned to the collection.* This means that the order can be cancelled by the customer up until the point where the book is picked up (or until expiration of the 3 day period).

If a customer picks up the book (scenario (a)), a library worker provides the book for the customer who comes into the library, and the system sets up a borrowing book deadline and sends required information to the customer.

3.3. Manage book order

In situations (b) and (c), the order is cancelled. We use compensation triggers to trigger compensation for both the *Order book* and *Prepare book* tasks. We add a compensation handler to the task *Prepare book* because if the customer cancels the order, a prepared book is returned to the collection. We interpret it as undoing the changes made by the task *Prepare book*. Analogously we add a compensation handler to the *Order book* task (Figure 91).

Translating this description directly to the model, we get:

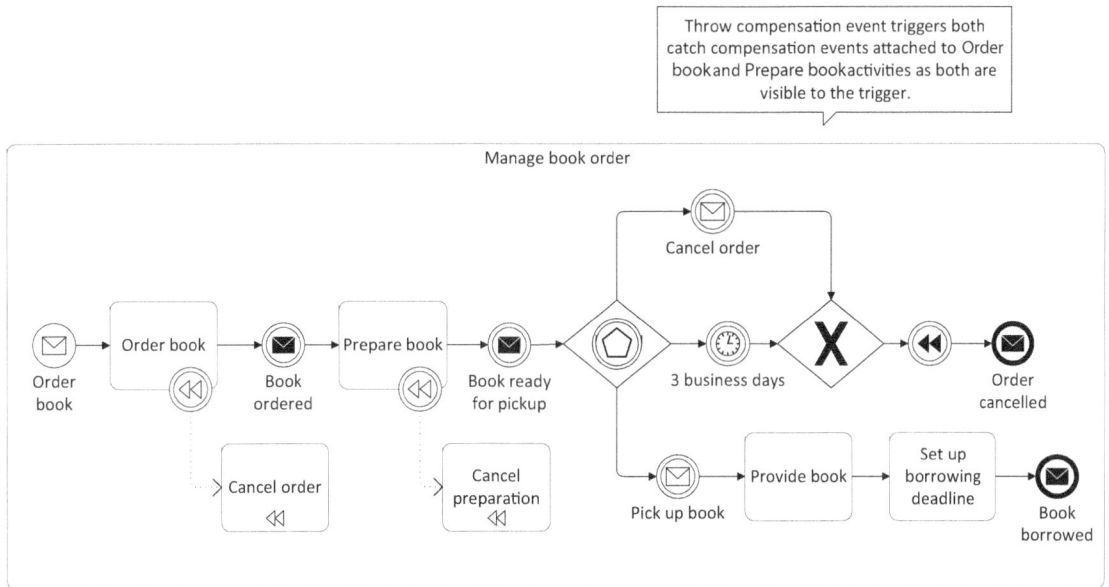

Figure 91: Manage book order subprocess – first version with 2 possible end states of the process

The above diagram (Figure 91) is compatible with the top-level *Borrow book* process from Figure 82, where there are two possible process endpoints of the *Manage book order* subprocess: book borrowed or order cancelled. We may also model a second version of the *Manage book order* subprocess that can end in three ways – book borrowed, book not collected, or order cancelled – and is compatible with the top-level process presented in Figure 81.

3.3. Manage book order

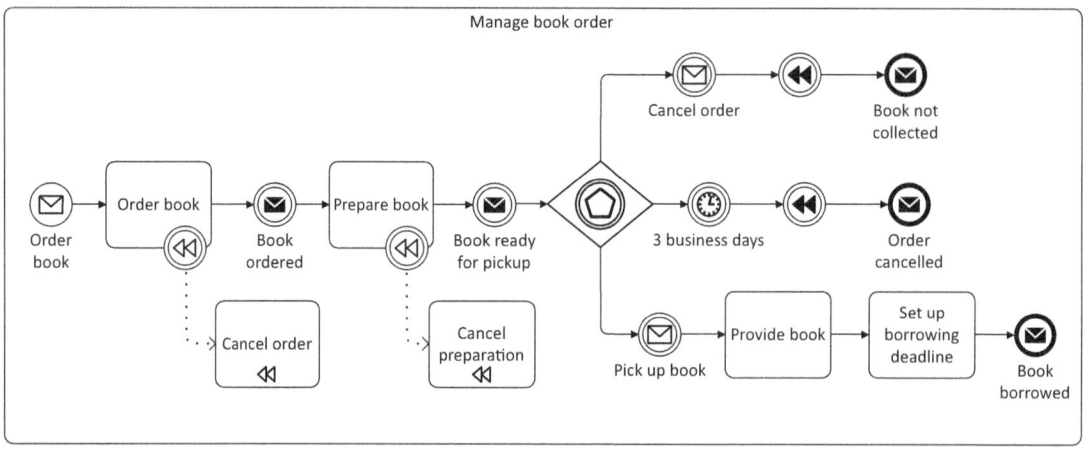

Figure 92: Manage book order subprocess – second version with three possible process end states

In the rest of the example we use the solution in Figure 91.

Compensation of many tasks within the same process

A compensation throw event triggers compensation for all activities that are within its scope. By the scope of this compensation we understand undoing the Order book and Prepare book tasks. Only activities that are "visible" to the compensation trigger can be compensated.

What behavior does the current diagram show (Figure 91)? Let's read it in the context of cancelling an order and achieving compensation.

The customer has ordered a book, and the book is prepared and is ready to be picked up; at the time when the customer could pick up the book, he/she decided to cancel the order. The completed tasks *Order book* and *Prepare book* are compensated in reverse order. Next an email confirming the cancellation is sent, and the whole *Borrow book* process is terminated.

The current model (Figure 91) handles the scenario in which the order is cancelled for a book that is ready for collection. But what about the situation where the customer cancels the order before the book is ready to be picked up? We may imagine that the customer orders a book during the holidays or the weekend when the library is closed, so it may be quite a long time till the book is ready for collection. Even when the library is working normally, it of course also takes time to prepare a book. Such a scenario is not handled. Our model should show that the customer can cancel the order at any time: from the moment the book is ordered to the end of the period in which he/she can pick up the book.

3.3. Manage book order

To handle this we use an interrupting message event attached to the *Manage book order* subprocess boundary (Figure 93). A *Cancel order* message is sent by the customer. This event can be caught at any time while a *Manage book order* is active. It also means that we don't need to additionally model a catch *Cancel order* message event on an outgoing flow from the event-based gateway.

> **TIP:** A compensation trigger defined within an event subprocess is visible for compensated activities modeled within a subprocess that contains the event subprocess.

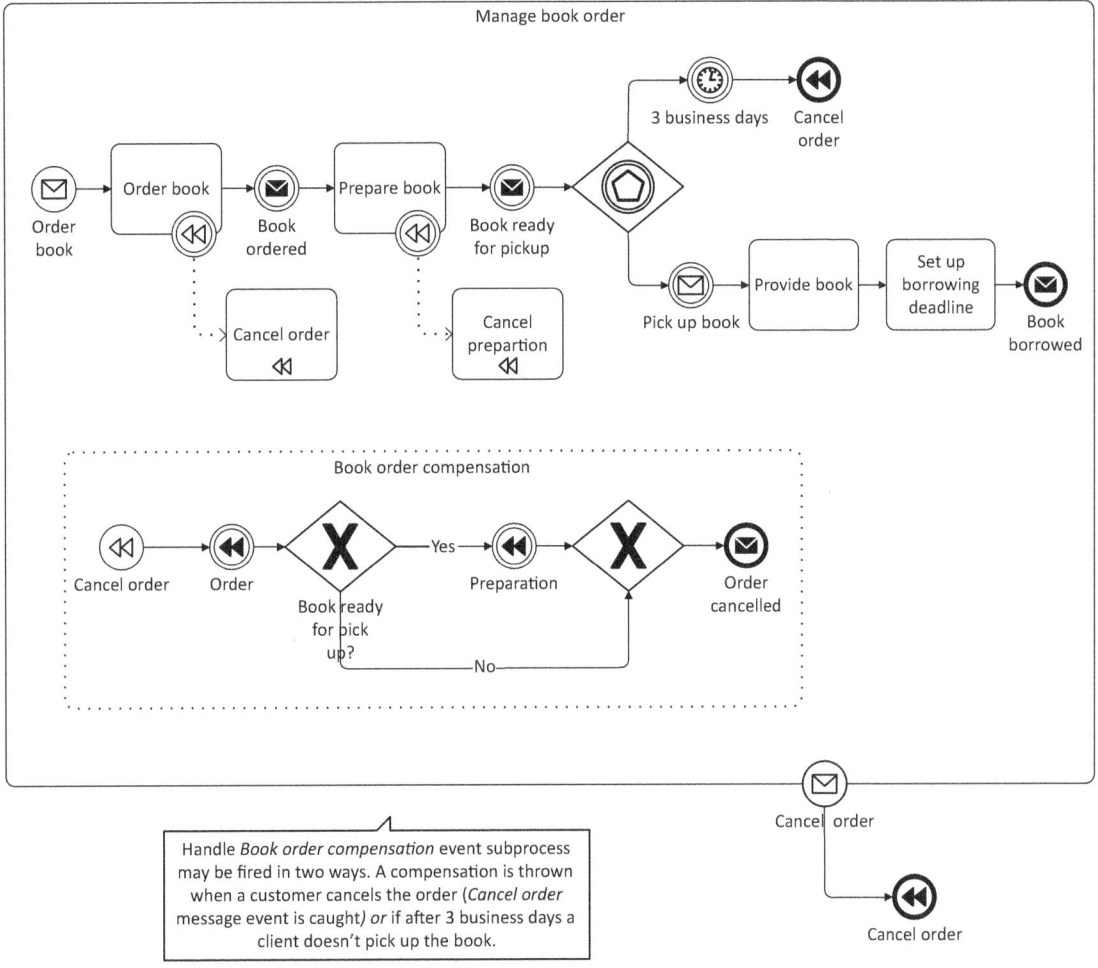

Figure 93: Manage order book process with compensation event subprocess fired from exceptional flow

The *Cancel order* message event fires an exceptional flow that as a result triggers the compensation event subprocess. The *book order compensation* event subprocess may be triggered in two ways: when a customer cancels the order and when a customer doesn't pick up the book within 3 days. Using a compensation subprocess, we can also enforce the sequence that the compensation for the task *Order book* is carried out first, followed by the task *Prepare book* (this is reasonable because first the order is cancelled, and then the library worker gets this information so they can return the book to the collection).

Within the *Book order compensation* subprocess, we additionally check if the book has been prepared to be picked up – in other words, if the task *Prepare book* is complete. Compensation should be triggered only for completed tasks, so if a customer cancels the book order before the book is ready to pick up, there is no need to compensate the *Prepare book* task. It's already cancelled by the interrupting message boundary event.

Following this, a further question arises – what if the *Order book* task has not been completed? In this case, the customer simply cannot cancel an order that does not yet exist, so there is no problem. We don't have this information explicitly provided on the diagram; to show it you may add a text annotation or model the external process for the customer.

We can also model the *Cancel order* message as a start event that fires an event subprocess within the *Manage book order* subprocess (Figure 94). In this case the model is compatible with the top-level process within which we haven't modeled any exceptional flow from the *Manage book order* subprocess.

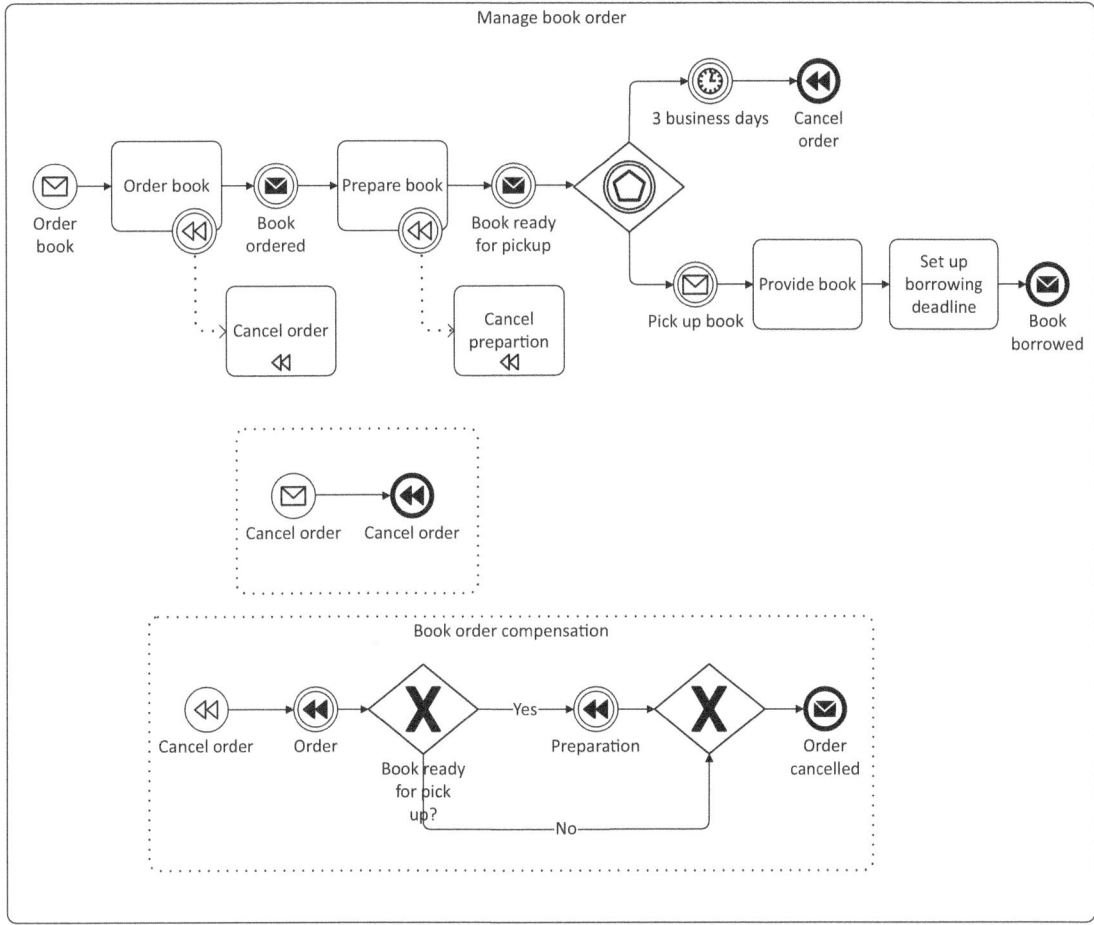

Figure 94: Manage book order process with compensation event subprocess fired from another event subprocess

3.4. Manage borrowed book

The next step in our process relates to the period when a book is borrowed. Let's go through the description of this part of the process:

Library books can be borrowed for a period of 31 days. The library system sends reminders to customers, 7 days and 1 day before the end of the borrowing period, informing them of the end date. The library charges its customers for overdue books. Every two weeks from the time the book becomes overdue, the system sends a message to the customer about the retention and the fee owing.

3.4. Manage borrowed book

A customer may renew a borrowed book a maximum of three times. Renewal can be done only if the book is not reserved by another customer and the customer doesn't have outstanding fees for any borrowed books. Renewals must be made not later than on the day the book's borrowing period ends. The system informs the customer whether the book has been renewed or not.

The subprocess starts after the customer collects the book from the library and ends only when the book is returned. Looking at the process from the library's point of view, we have a sequence of actions that the library system performs based on the book borrowing period:

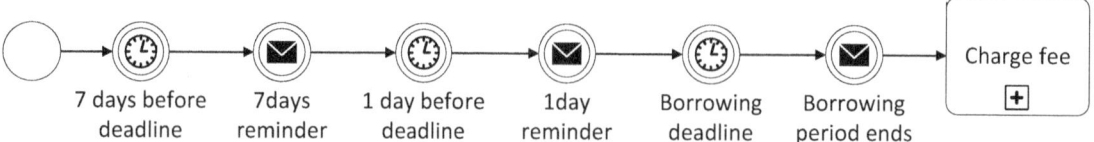

Figure 95: Manage borrowed book subprocess – first version

The system sends messages to the customer based on how the borrowing period progresses. We use a timer intermediate event to indicate when each successive action should be triggered. The process waits at every timer intermediate event till a defined date, then goes on and a message is sent. The first action from the library since the book is borrowed is sending a message 7 days before the borrowing period ends; the next message is sent 1 day before the borrowing period ends; the last message is sent when the borrowing period ends. When the borrowing period is exceeded, the library charges a fee every two weeks from the due date.

Loop subprocess without end event

Let's analyze how to model the *Charge fee* subprocess.

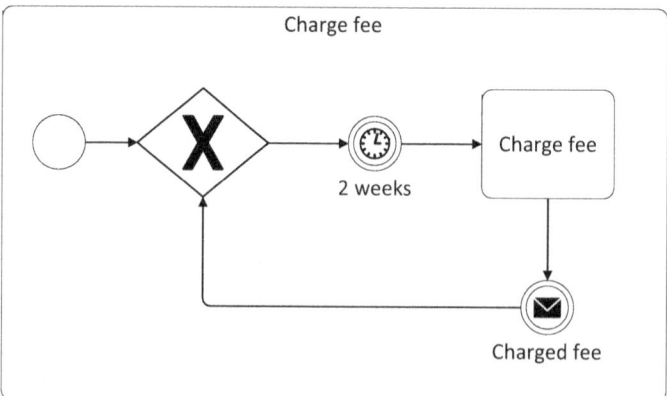

Figure 96: Charge fee subprocess

3.4. Manage borrowed book

The *Charge fee* subprocess is modeled as a never-ending loop. In our example process description, we don't have any information on how many times or for how long the library charges fees. The process starts repeatedly with a timer event that is fired every 2 weeks starting from the borrowing period deadline. Every two weeks, the library charges the fee for a non-returned book and sends information to the customer. Next, the flow goes back to the timer event, waits for two more weeks and is repeated.

This is an example of a process without an end event. We have one process instance that performs the same activities cyclically and never ends. As you can see, this is an exception to the rule that if we use a start event we should also have an end event within the same process: this is not required if the flow returns and creates a loop.

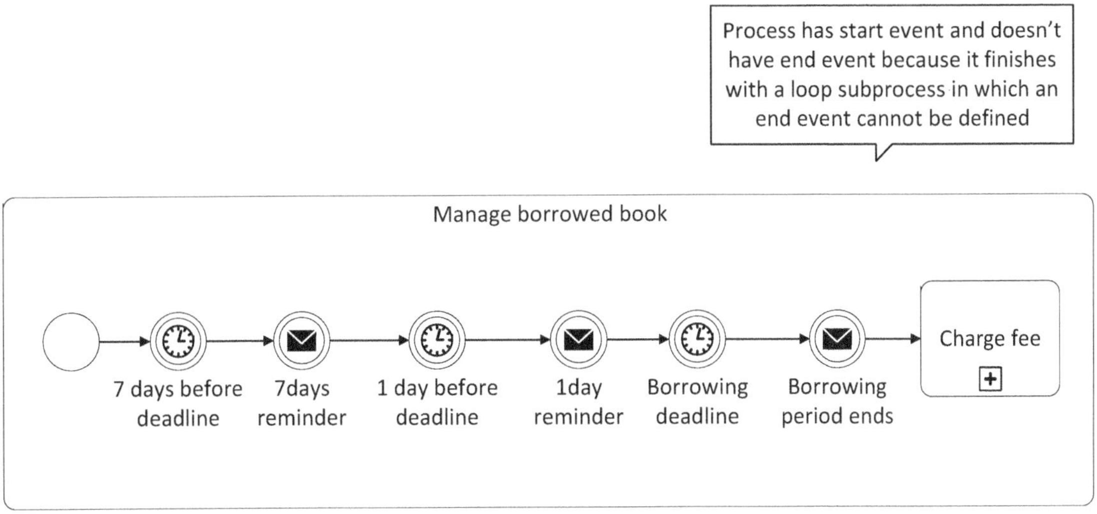

Figure 97: Example of process that is a loop or is finished with a loop so no end event is defined

Process designed as a loop vs. loop activity marker

If the subprocess is a loop, why we don't use a loop activity marker? Loop activities are understood as activities in which an action is repeated continuously, one at a time. However, it is not possible to define a downtime between successive repetitions. That's why in our case, where there is a specific break between the subsequent executions, we cannot use a loop marker.

> **TIP:** In a loop activity (with loop marker), every repetition is made one at a time, without time breaks between the subsequent executions.

143

3.4. Manage borrowed book

Breaking the loop process

So how can we end the *Manage borrowed book* subprocess? There are two external actions that influence the process and lead to its end. The action that definitely ends the process is the return of the book by the customer. This action is external as it depends only on the customer – he/she decides if and when to return the book. Because this is an external action that terminates the *Manage borrowed book* subprocess, we can model it in two ways:
- as an interrupting intermediate event attached to the subprocess boundary
- as an event subprocess that starts with an interrupting message event

We decide to use an event attached to the activity boundary, as the event is a way out of the subprocess and leads to the next top-level subprocess, *Return book* (Figure 98). When the event is fired, the Manage borrowed book process is terminated and the flow should continue to the *Return book* subprocess (we will go back to this issue).

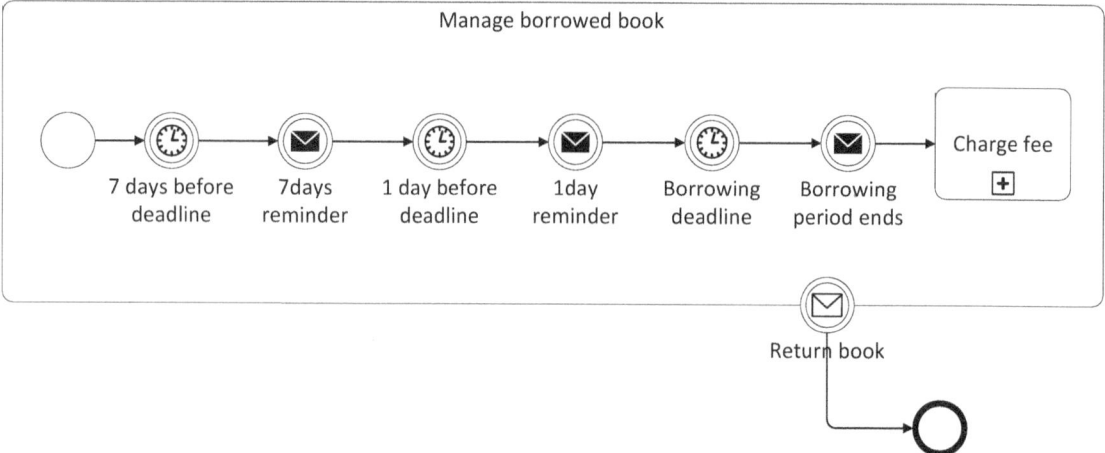

Figure 98: Manage borrowed book process with return book event

Another event that may break the *Manage borrowed book* process is book renewal. Book renewal can be done only till the borrowing period is not exceeded. Every renewal extends the borrowing period of the book. To handle this case, we need to 'unpack' part of the flow that represents the borrowing period and model the possibility to break it by an interrupting intermediate event attached to the subprocess boundary. Let's call this part of the flow *Manage period* (Figure 99). If the book is renewed, it's necessary to define the new borrowing period, so a new *Manage period* process instance should be created.

3.4. Manage borrowed book

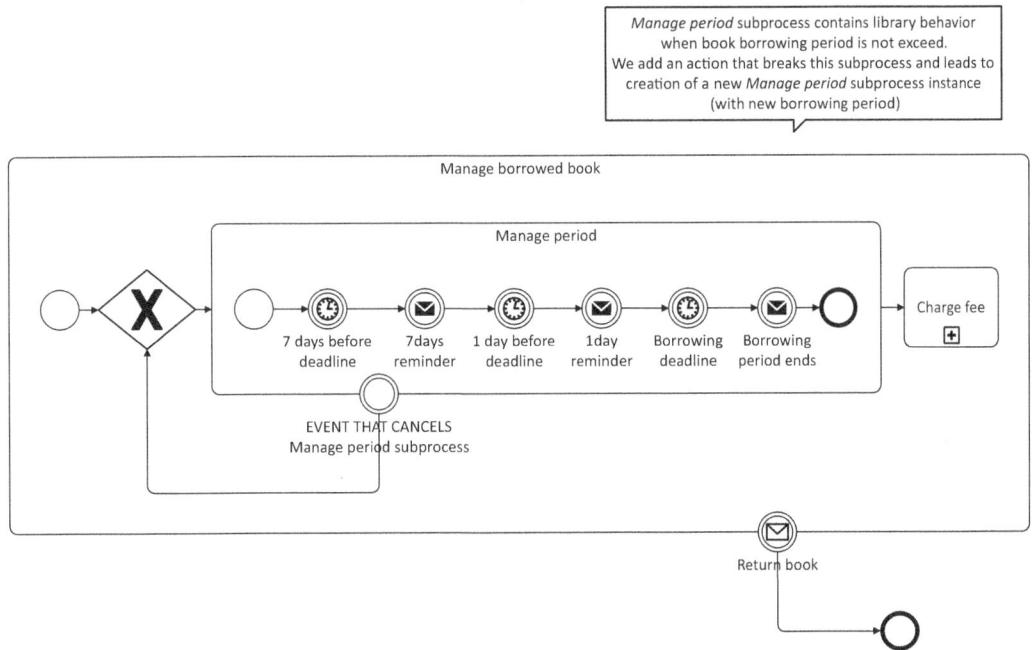

Figure 99: Manage period subprocess with interrupting event attached to its boundary

We deliberately haven't defined the type of boundary event for the "EVENT THAT CANCELS Manage period subprocess" as there is one more issue to analyze. Not every book renewal is finished positively because three conditions must be met. According to the description:

A customer may renew a borrowed book a maximum of three times. Renewal can be done only if the book is not reserved by another customer and the customer doesn't have outstanding fees for any borrowed books. Renewals must be made not later than on the day the book's borrowing period ends. The system informs the customer whether the book has been renewed or not.

This means that firstly, we need to model the part of the process that handles book renewal steps. Let's call this subprocess *Renew book*. Secondly, an event that triggers the *Book renewal* subprocess should be non-interrupting. Why? Because during execution of the *Renew book* subprocess, we gain information on whether the book could be renewed or not. If the conditions are met and the library may renew the book, then the *Manage period* process should break and start again. If the conditions are not met, the renewal cannot be made.

Because this part of the process consists of several steps, we propose to use an event subprocess called *Renew book* modeled within the *Manage period* process, as only when this process is active can a user try to renew the borrowed book (Figure 100).

3.4. Manage borrowed book

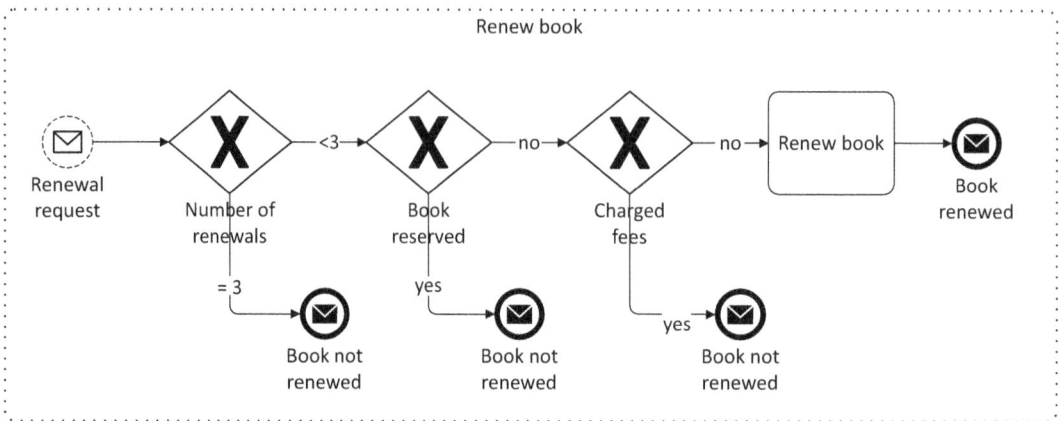

Figure 100: Renew book event subprocess

Conditions on exclusive gateway leading to the same results

We have checked all three conditions using exclusive gateways (Figure 100); if some condition is not met, the book cannot be renewed and the subprocess is ended. But all three alternative paths give the same result: the book cannot be renewed – so we may join them and use only one end event.

> **TIP:** If alternative flows lead to the same end result, you may merge them using an exclusive gateway and use a single end event.

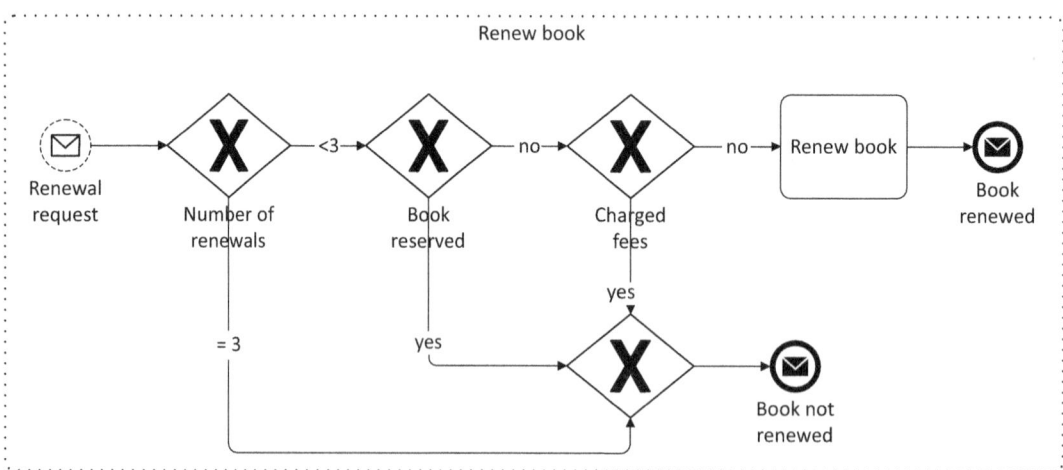

Figure 101: Renew book event subprocess – one end event

The order of conditions at the gateways matches how it's shown in the description. However, we may assume for the purpose of the example that from the flow perspective it doesn't matter at all which condition is checked first. Look at the simplified process:

TIP: If the condition order is not relevant and all lead to the same result, use one gateway that checks all the conditions.

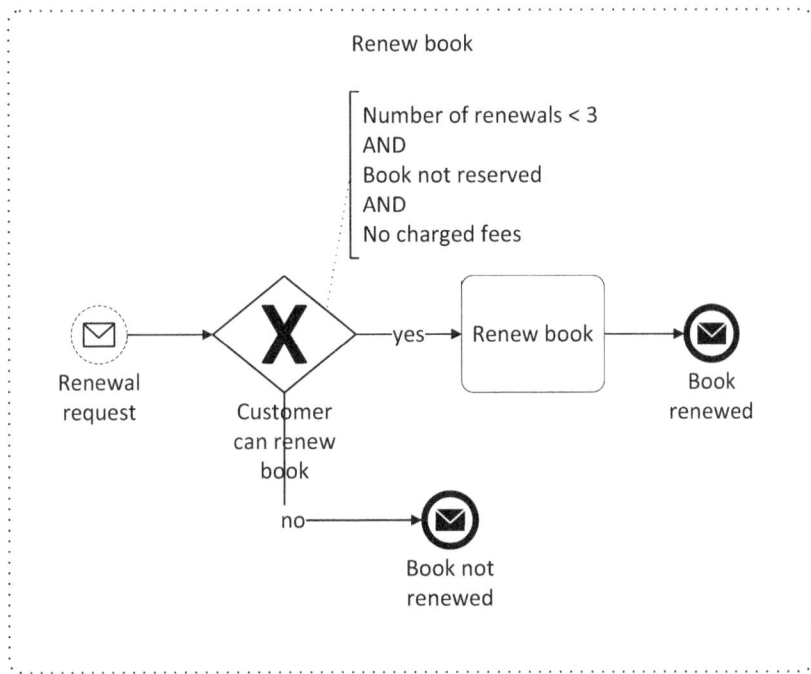

Figure 102: Renew book event subprocess with one Exclusive gateway that represents all conditions

Using a *Renew book* subprocess we show:
- that a book renewal can be made only when the borrowing period is not exceeded
- what conditions must be met so the customer may renew their book

Now we may use a *Renew book* subprocess end state to make it dependent on if the *Manage period* subprocess has terminated or not. Look at the proposed solution in Figure 103. An interrupting conditional intermediate event is triggered if the book is renewed. So the process *Manage period* is cancelled if the book is renewed, and the book renewal itself is triggered by the customer.

3.4. Manage borrowed book

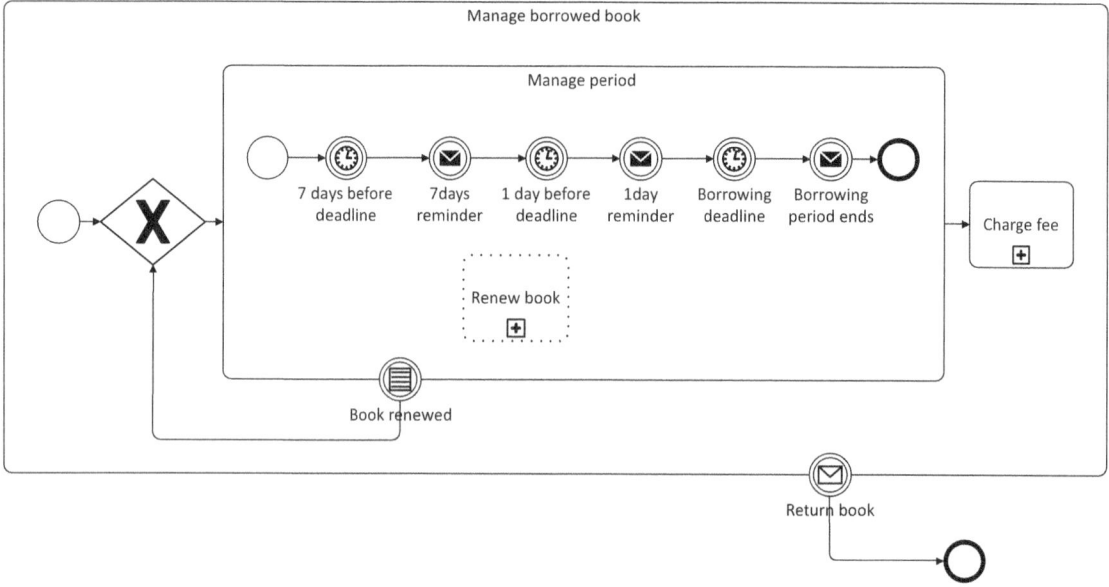

Figure 103: Manage borrowed book process

Consistency with parent process model

The returning of the book, which is modeled within the exception flow, ends the whole *Manage borrowed book* subprocess and provides the link to the next top-level step. Such a model is not only inconsistent with the top-level process but also indicates and can be interpreted as if *Return book* is some exception from the *Manage borrow book* subprocess (Figure 104). Maybe this is some exceptional returning and the basic flow is already handled within the *Manage borrowed book* subprocess?

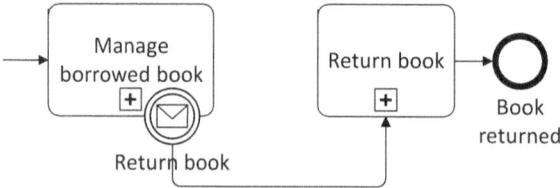

Figure 104: Top-level relations through exceptional flow

In the top-level *Borrow book* process we design the normal flow between the *Manage borrowed book* subprocess and the *Return book* subprocess (Figure 105).

3.5. Return book

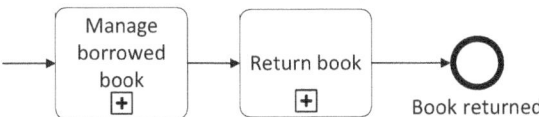

Figure 105: Part of the top-level process showing relation between Manage borrowed book and Return book subprocesses.

To show the relationship between the above two processes in a consistent way, you can simply additionally 'unpack' everything that's inside the *Manage borrowed book* subprocess and derive its end as a standard sequence flow. This is an acceptable solution, but you still have to rename the existing processes. Another way is to use an event subprocess instead of a boundary event.

This is also a good reason to think about including the *Return book* subprocess within the *Manage borrowed book* subprocess.

3.5. Return book

The last step is related with book returning. From the description:

At the time of return, a library employee checks the state of the book and is authorized to charge an appropriate fine if it is damaged. Information about the fine being charged is sent to the customer's email.

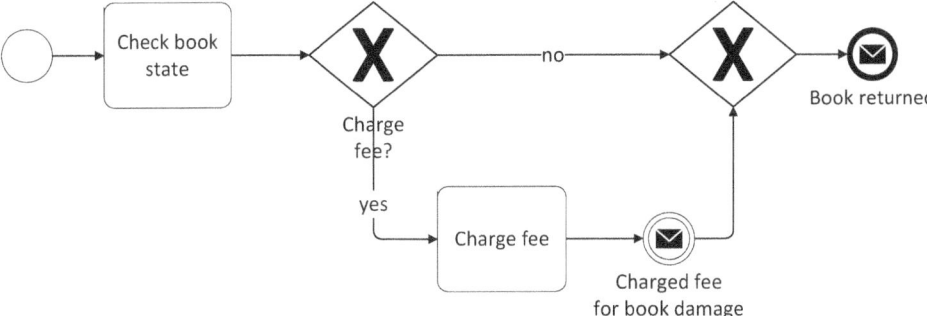

Figure 106: Return book subprocess – first version

There is one more issue: should we provide tasks indicating that the book has been returned – e.g. *Accept book back*? There is no such activity in the process description. However, if we want to indicate that the book state is changed to, e.g., 'available', it's good to explicitly model the activity that changes the status of the book (Figure 107). Still it's not required.

149

3.5. Return book

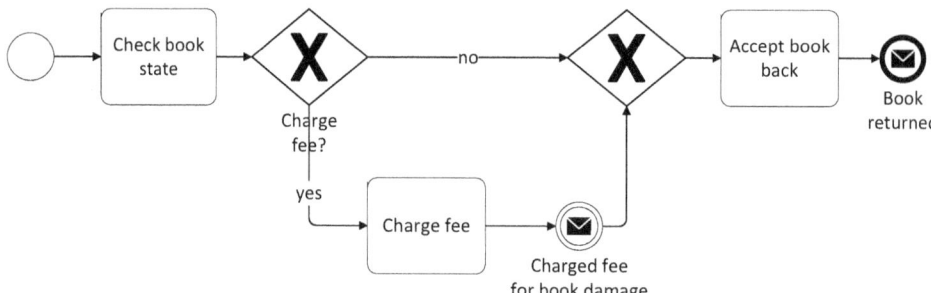

Figure 107: Return book subprocess – second version

TIP: If some activity leads to producing or changing some data, model it explicitly in the diagram

3.6. Collaboration – advanced

Let's sum up all the created models within the *Borrow book* process and try to model Collaboration.

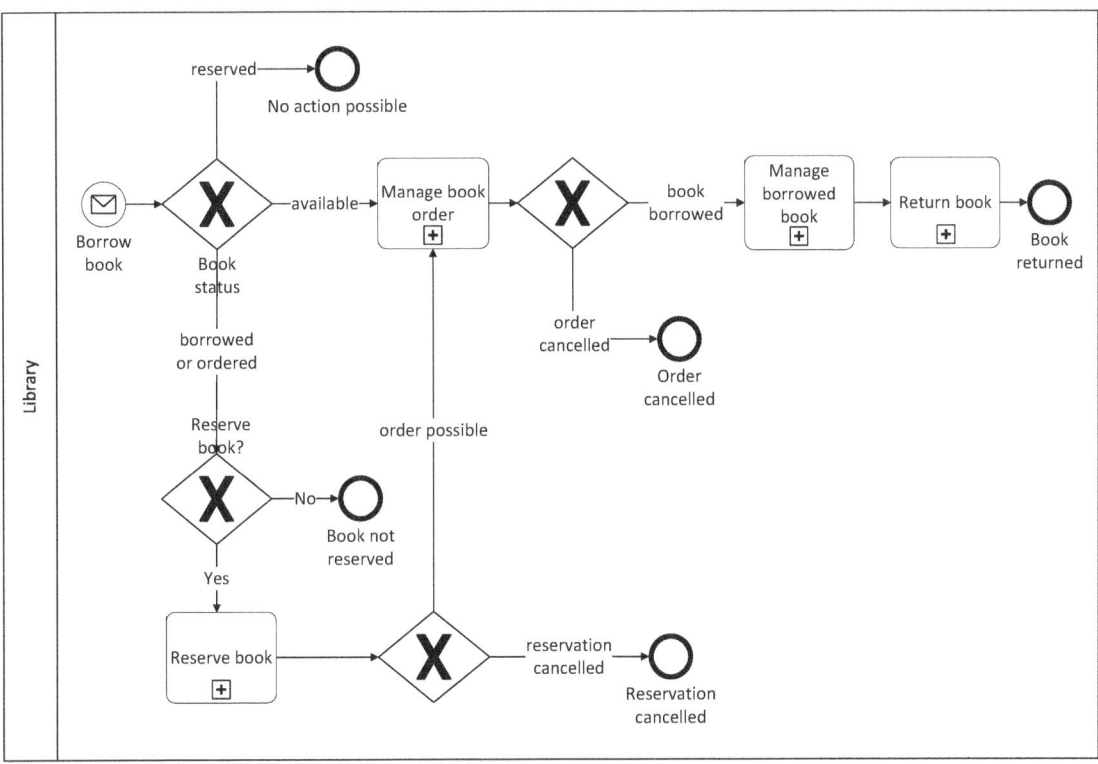

Figure 108: Top-level Borrow book process within pool – Library

Black box external process

All models have been created from a library perspective, so this is the internal participant. A customer represents an external participant that collaborates with the library. We don't know the *Borrow book* process details from the customer's point of view – the process is described only from the library's point of view. We model the customer as a black box pool.

The top-level *Borrow book* process is composed of subprocesses (Figure 108). At every stage of the process, within every subprocess there is some collaboration between the library and a customer. We can model this information within the top-level internal process so every subprocess is associated with the Customer pool (external process participant) through a message flow.

3.6. Collaboration – advanced

If you consider such a diagram to be too general, you can first identify the points of collaboration within individual subprocesses and then transfer this information to the top-level model, naming the individual message flows; alternatively, do not model collaboration in the top-level process.

Different instances of external processes that influence the internal process

Let's model each Library subprocess's collaboration with a Customer as a collaborate black box external process participant. We start with the *Reserve book* process.

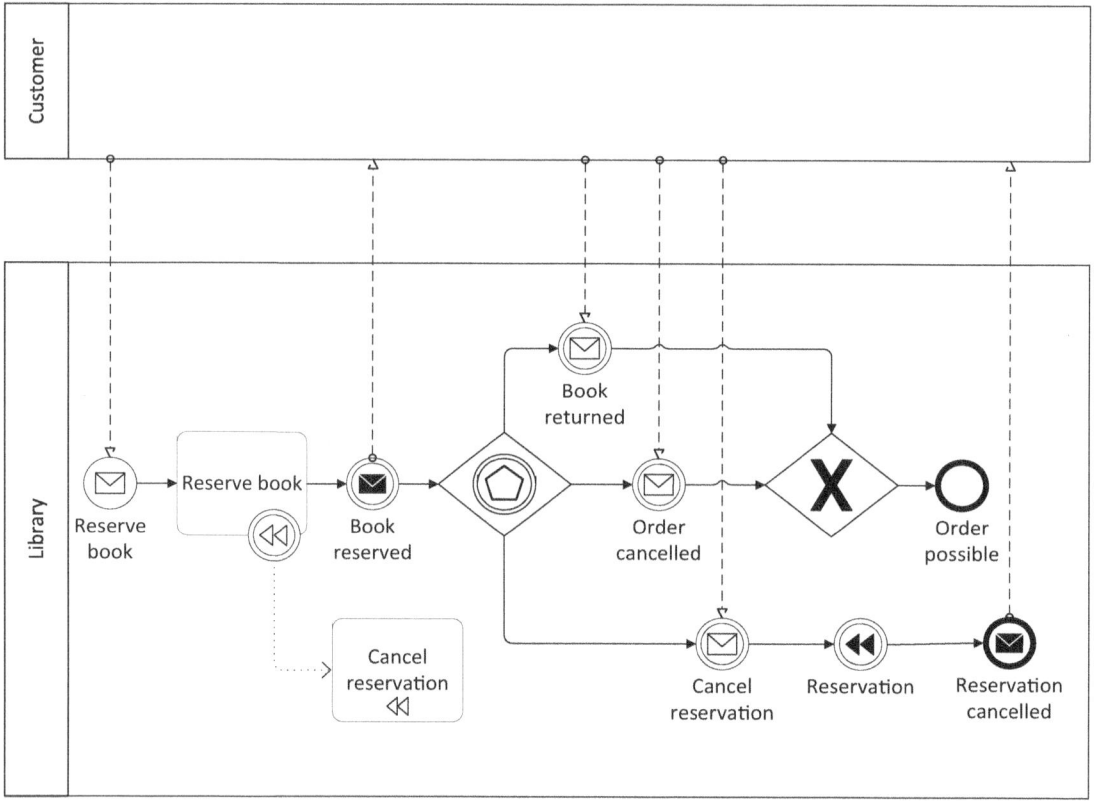

Figure 109: Collaboration – Reserve book process

Is this model (Figure 109) correct? The diagram says that all three message catch events: *Cancel reservation*, *Book returned* and *Order Cancelled* are sent by a customer. And this is true; however, different customers may return the book or cancel an order, and a different customer cancels an already made book reservation. The current model shows that the same customer performs all three actions, which is incorrect.

152

3.6. Collaboration – advanced

> **TIP:** Distinguish external process instances if different instances have influence on one internal process instance.

What are the possible solutions that may arise and what are their meanings?
   a. Add a multi-instance marker to the pool representing external process. This could then be interpreted as different customer actions that are available for various customers and for a given book. This is a correct solution form technical point of view, but still we won't show that different customers may trigger different actions explicitly, so for the reader who doesn't know the process, it can be misleading (Figure 110).

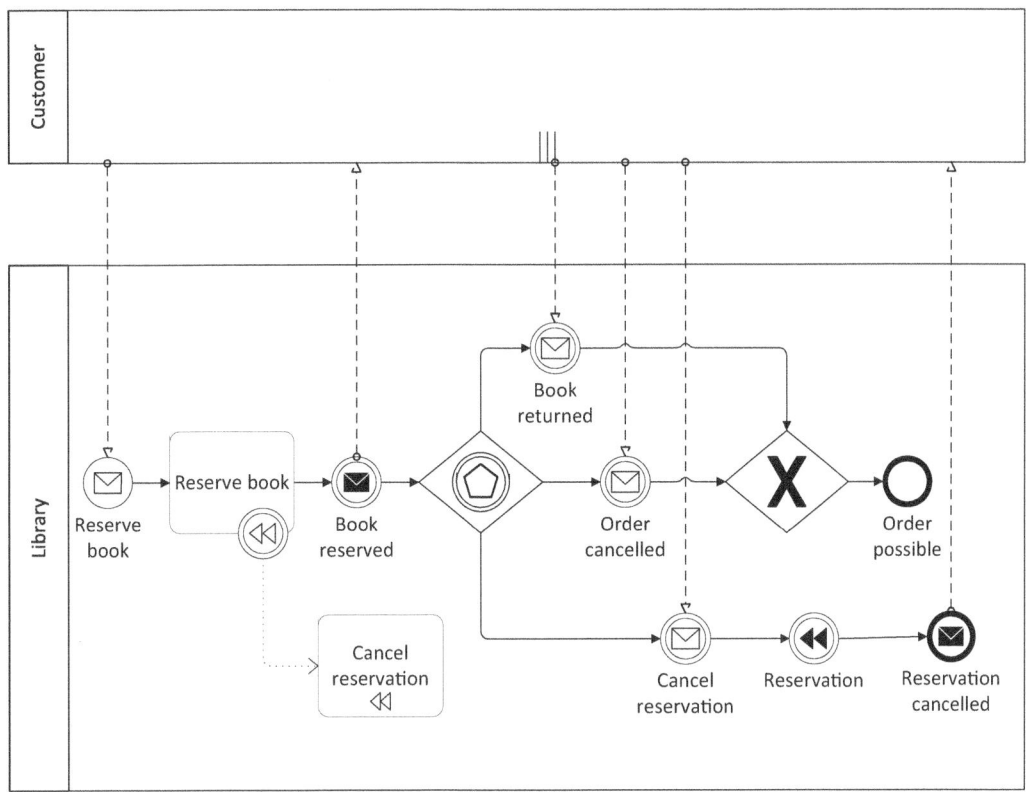

Figure 110: External process as multi-instance process

   b. Create separate pools that represents a customer who reserves a book and a customer who has already borrowed the same book or ordered it. Let's call these pools Customer A and Customer B and explain these differences in text annotation (Figure 111). The benefit of such an approach is that we explicitly show that all three events are the results of Library–Customer collaboration and that separate customer processes handle particular events.

3.6. Collaboration – advanced

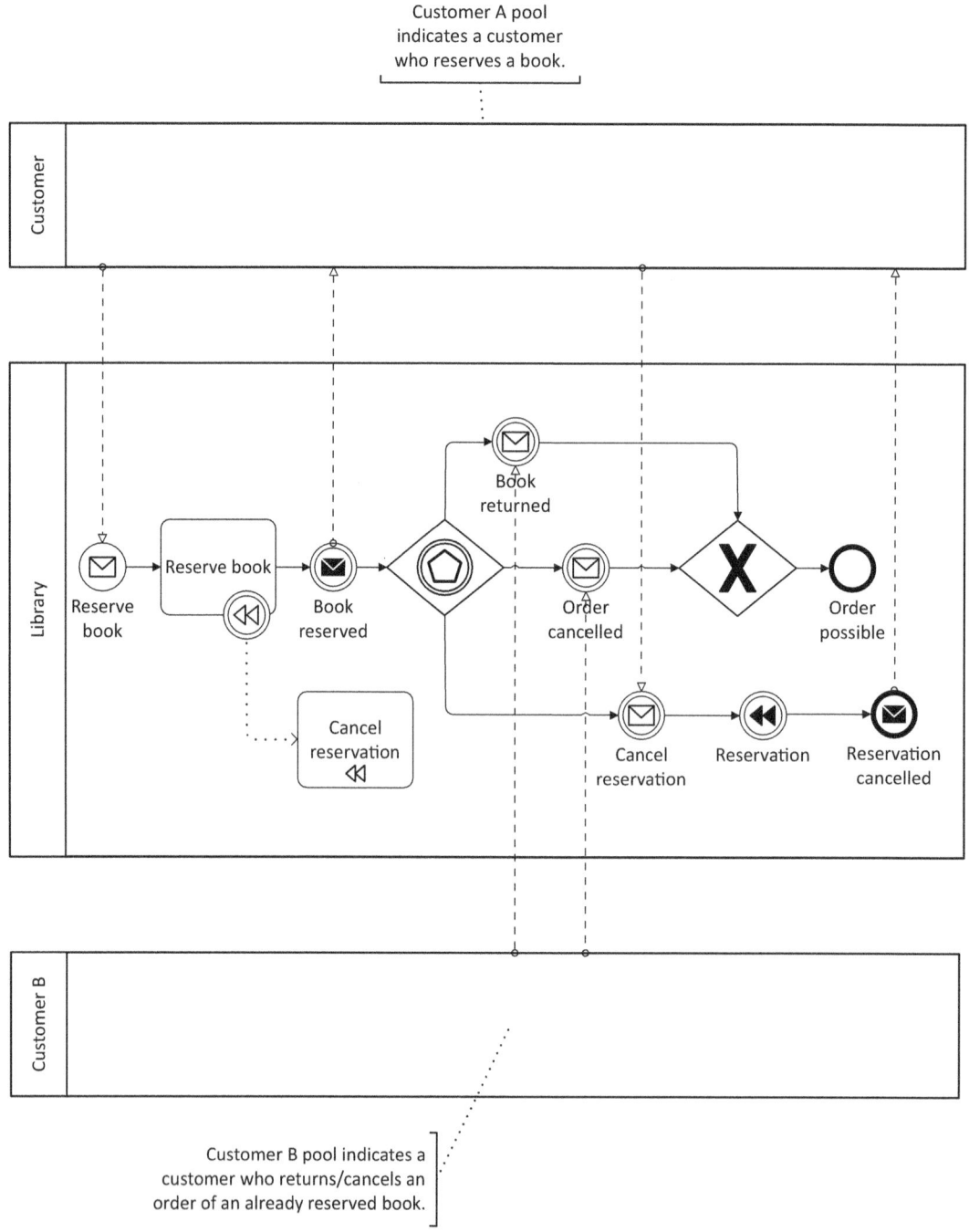

Figure 111: Separate external processes represent the different instances of a Customer

3.6. Collaboration – advanced

c. In this case we model only the collaboration that relates to the *Reserve book* process from both the Library and Customer views (Figure 112). The benefit of this approach is that we provide within the model only information strictly related to the *Reserve book* subprocess from the viewpoint of both the Library and of the Customer who is directly involved in the *Reserve book* subprocess of a specific book.

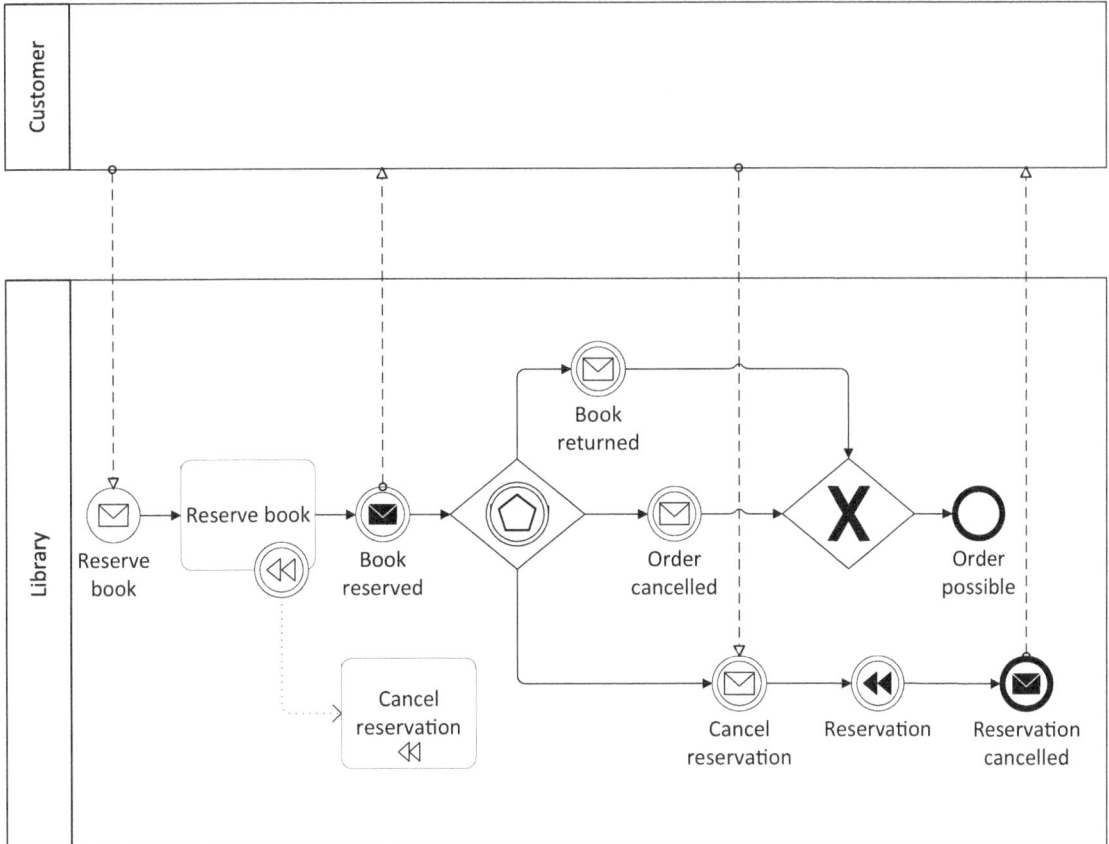

Figure 112: Within collaboration we model only message flows related to the same Customer process instance

Subprocess within a pool – what to do with boundary events

Let's discuss collaboration for the *Manage book order* process. When you present a particular subprocess within a pool, it represents an end-to-end process. The subprocess's graphical boundary doesn't exists in this context. The issue that arises is how to model a boundary event that is

3.6. Collaboration – advanced

attached to the subprocess that we want to present separately within a pool. This issue exactly shows the difference between a boundary event and an event subprocess. You cannot include a boundary event while separately modeling a subprocess within a pool – not only because the boundary doesn't exists but also because a boundary event is handled by the parent process (Figure 113). If you want to handle and also model within a pool behavior triggered by an event, use an event subprocess. Let's do this for the *Manage book order* subprocess (Figure 114).

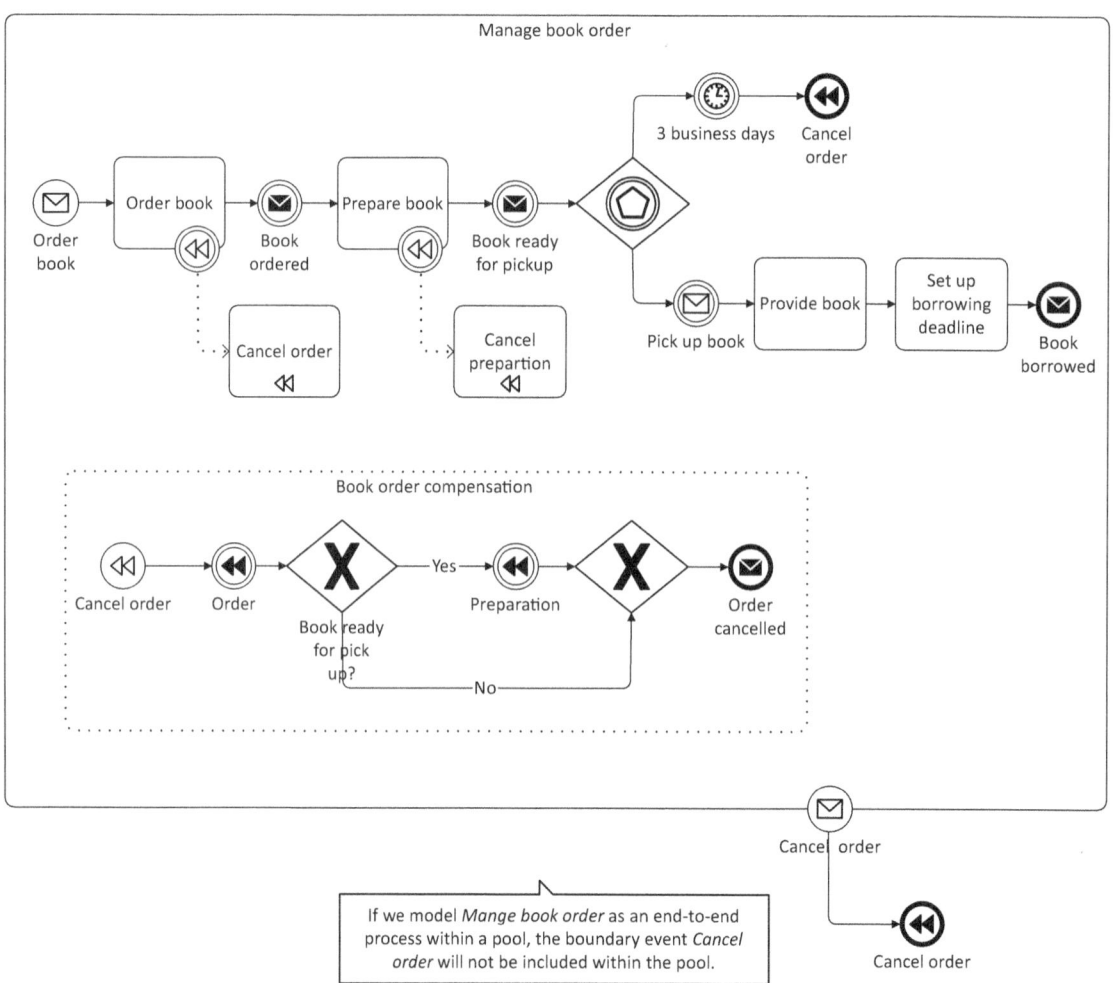

Figure 113: Manage book order subprocess with boundary event

3.6. Collaboration – advanced

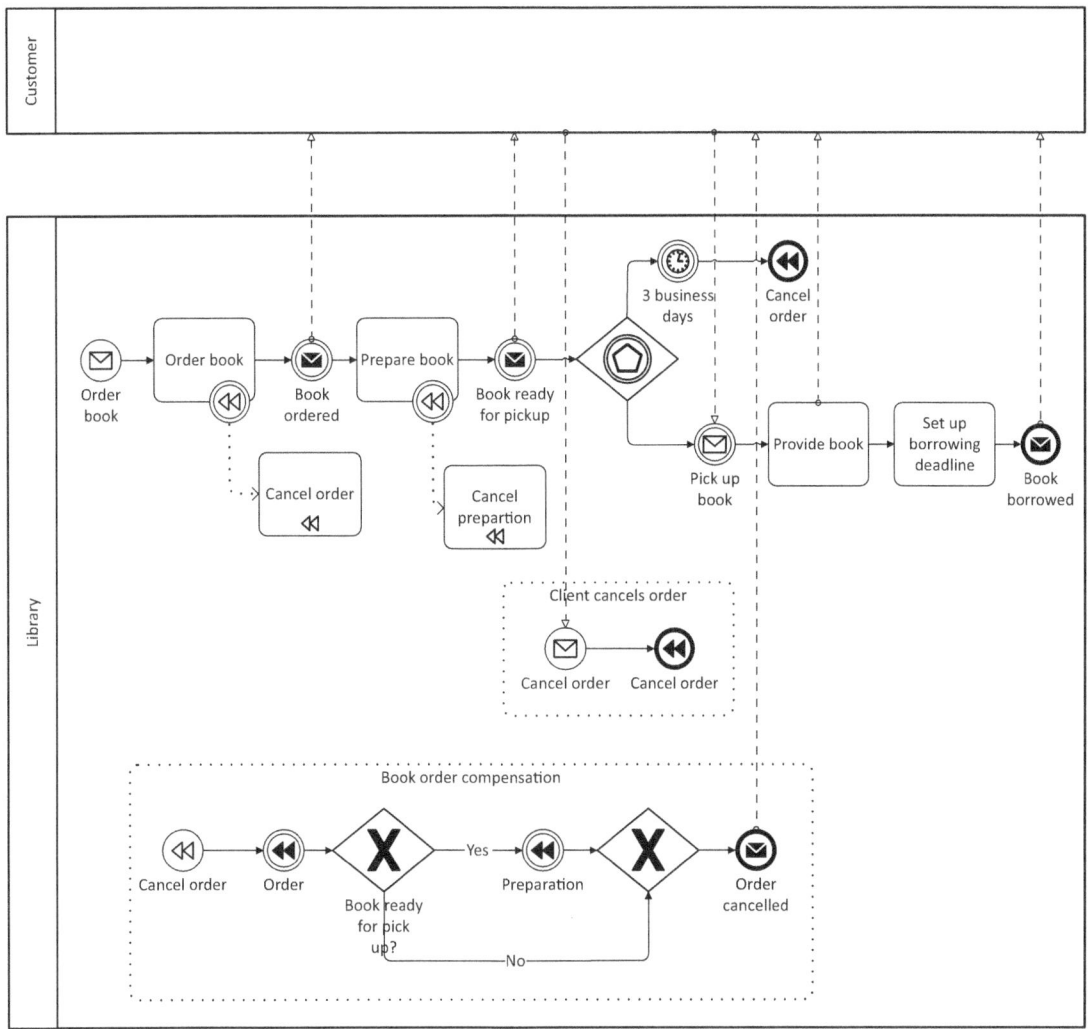

Figure 114: Manage book order process – collaboration

Message flow associated with collapsed subprocesses

In the *Manage borrowed book* process there are two subprocesses: *Charge fee* and *Return book*. We can try to model them expanded; however, the *Manage borrowed book* process then becomes 'overloaded'. Because we know exactly how the interactions inside the process look, we may model all occurring interactions using message flows and additionally labelled them so the user from the parent process level gets information on what kind of collaboration occurs in the child-level subprocess (Figure 115). If you don't know all the collaboration points within a child-level subprocess or there are many of them, you can just draw 'empty' message flows to and/or from a subprocess to inform the reader that there is some collaboration at this level (Figure 116).

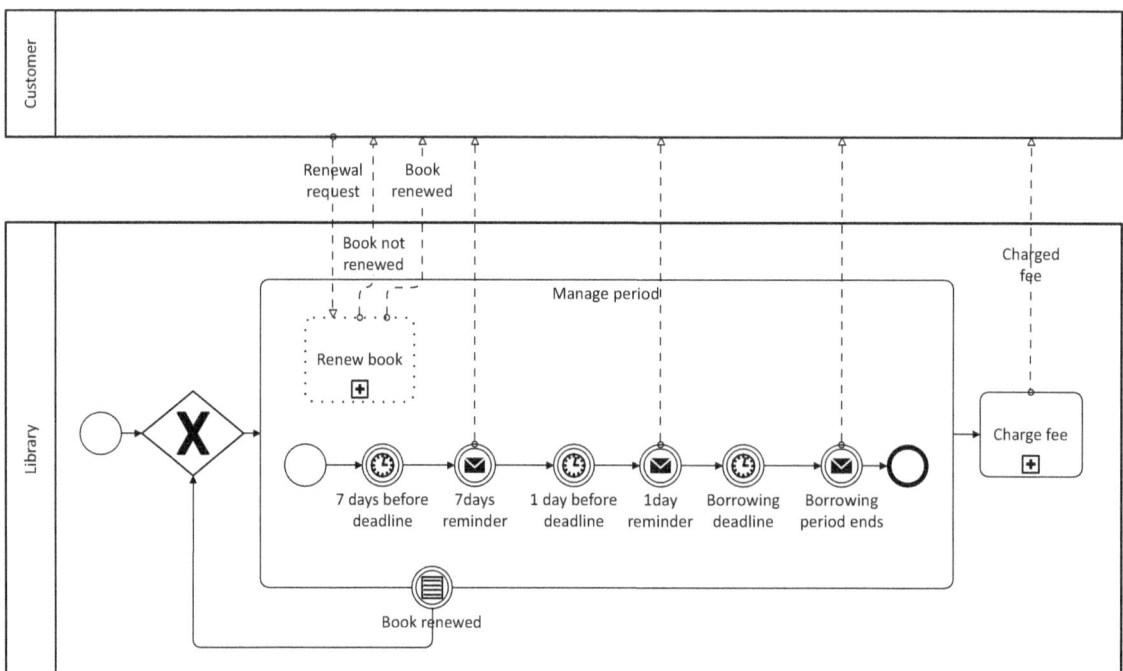

Figure 115: All message flows occurring within a subprocess are presented and labelled on the parent process level

3.6. Collaboration – advanced

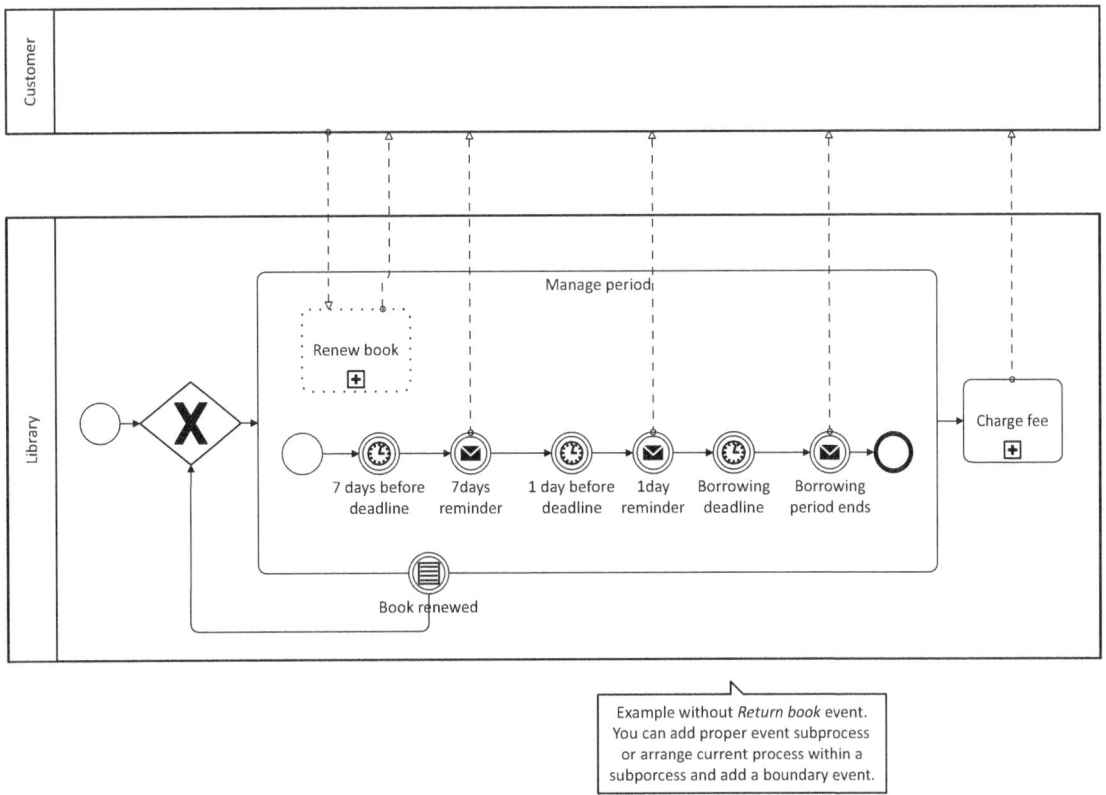

Figure 116: Manage borrowed book process – message flows associated with subprocesses

System-driven and human-driven processes

The *Borrow book* process is described from the library's perspective. Within a library we can distinguishactivities performed by the system and by the library workers. Such a division is related to the organization of the internal process.

Most of the activities modeled in the *Borrow book* process and its subprocesses could be 'assigned' either to the system or to a library worker. Let's take for example the *Order book* task: it could be interpreted as a task made by the system (change book status to order) or by a human (library worker orders the book for a customer who comes into the library). Such an issue usually concerns processes that are mix of steps driven by humans, systems or by humans with the support of systems.

Let's try to organize the process between a library worker and a library system. Note that in a general process description we don't have explicit information on whether the worker, the

3.6. Collaboration – advanced

system or both perform some step. If your model needs to expose human–system interactions, use collaboration and note carefully during analysis which steps are performed only by a human, which are performed by the system, and if the human or system is the trigger for some step.

The model presents two scenarios that are also not directly distinguished in the process description.
1. Customer orders a book using the library system – in this case some of the activities are directly made by the system.
2. Customer orders a book in a library – in this case a library worker triggers some system activities.

The processes models presented in Sections 3.1–3.5 are of course correct – they show the process flow according to the process description. However, they lack information on what exactly is done by a human and by the library system.

The following models (Figure 117 and Figure 118) are an extended interpretation of the process, to show how a human–system-driven process can be modeled. The library system sends messages both to the customer and to the library worker, which means that a customer gets an email with proper information and a library worker sees proper notification/status in his/her library system account (or also gets a system email). A library worker also provides needed information to the system, which is also shown using a message flow and additional catch message events if required. Any user–system interaction is modeled using message flows.

Let's discuss some interesting topics that may appear in connection with the presented models. The first thing you should note is that the activity *Provide book* performed by the library worker is modeled as a subprocess. The reason is that in Collaboration, this activity requires communication with two other participants: Customer and Library system.

Imagine the library worker provides the book to the customer; this is a simple activity: usually he/she just gives the book to the customer (first task – collaboration with Customer) and before doing this provides the information that the book has been picked up to the system – e.g., by scanning a code on the book cover (second task – collaboration with the Library system). Another task that could be included in this subprocess is to verify if the customer is the person who ordered the book – e.g., by checking an identity document or a library card. This could be an additional point of collaboration between the Library worker and the Customer. In other words, we could split the *Provide book* activity into smaller tasks.

3.6. Collaboration – advanced

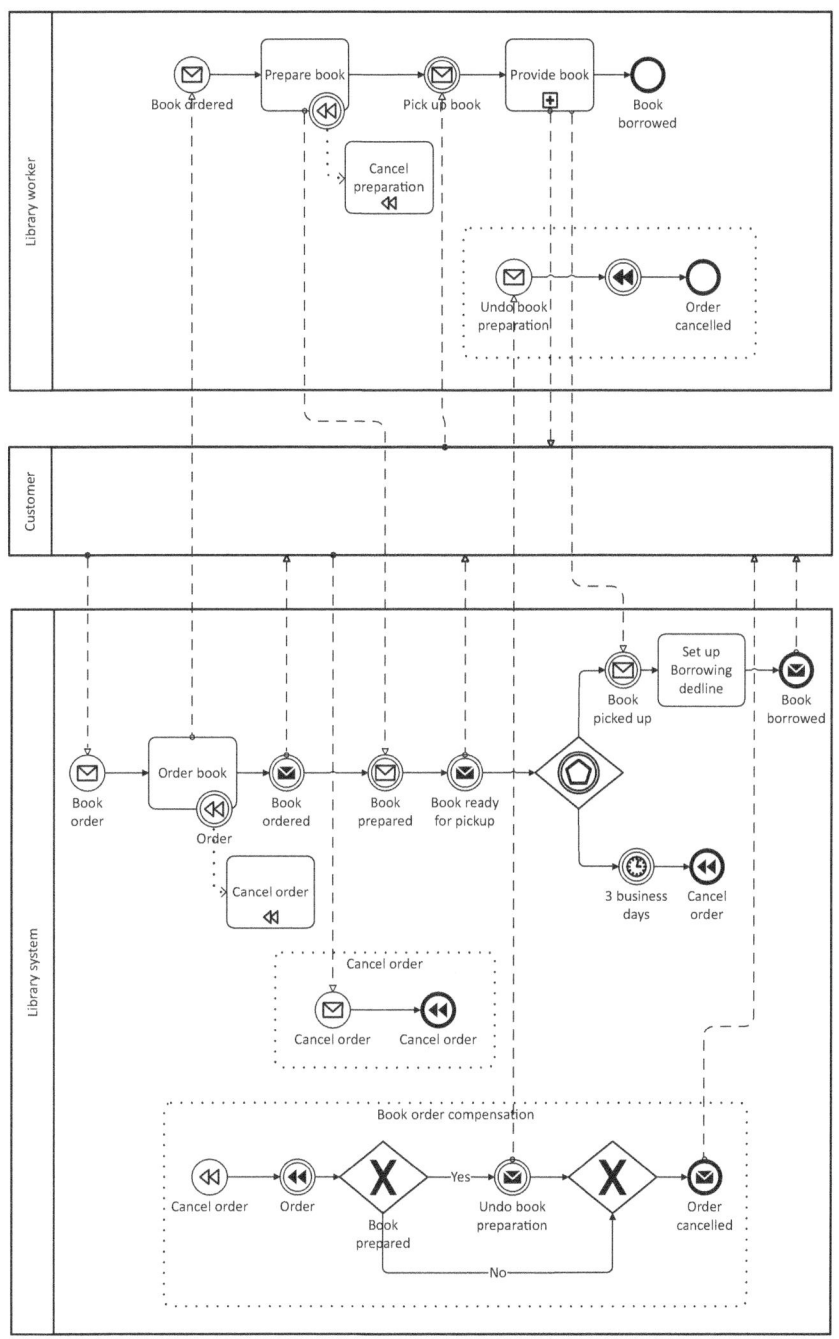

Figure 117: Manage book order process collaboration between library worker and a system – scenario: customer orders a book using the library system

3.6. Collaboration – advanced

Does this mean that while modeling the *Manage book order* process in Section 3.3 and using tasks instead of the subprocess *Provide book* we made a mistake? Well, not necessarily: remember that *you* decide the scope of the process, and you decide how you understand and how you want to present activities within a process. Within Example 3 we've been analyzing and modeling processes on a detailed level that were described directly in the process description, without considering what are/could be other possible smaller tasks. We are not going to do this; however, we want to show within a Collaboration what the interactions between participants look like.

> **TIP:** While modeling Collaboration, if an activity requires communication with two or more participants, it's a good idea to consider splitting the activity into smaller parts or adding a catch and/or throw message before/after the activity.

In comparison, the newly provided *Order book* task in Figure 118, which is performed by the Library worker, has two message flows from and to the same participant – Library system. For such tasks, it is less common to split them into smaller tasks or to use throw/catch messages; however, depending on the purpose and flow of an activity you may consider such a modeling approach.

When modeling Collaboration, you are forced to analyze the activity in terms of how and with how many participants each activity collaborates. This is also a really good test for your model because you consider the process from different perspectives – taking into account different participants of the process – and not only the sequence and dependencies within the process itself.

The second topic concerns introducing new BPMN elements within processes representing different participants – such as message events and tasks – in comparison to the *Manage book order* process modeled in **Section 3.3**, where such elements were either simply not necessary or, in most cases, incorrect because communication within the same process was involved. In both scenarios we provided the BPMN elements that are needed to properly present user–system interactions taking into account how the process or particular step within a process is initiated (by the customer, a library worker or the system) or who is the main performer of the activity.

Third topic – compensation. Notice that processes are modeled in a way that separates the triggering of compensation for the Library worker and for the Library system. The reason for this is that compensation cannot be triggered for a different process. For example, in both scenarios, to trigger compensation of *Prepare book*, the library system informs the Library worker that the book should be returned to the collection (the way it does this is not relevant to our discussion).

Fourth topic – process end statuses. It's your decision whether to use analogous or different end process statuses for collaborating processes. The decision depends on how you organize the whole model and what happens after each process is finished. In our model, in both scenarios we use the same end event names: *Book borrowed* for the basic positive scenario and *Order cancelled* for the second, alternative process end. However, as the Library system is responsible for managing the *Borrow order book* process, you could name the end events differently within the Library customer process: for example, *book provided* (instead of *book borrowed*) or *book available* (instead of *order cancelled*).

The last topic is related to when it is better to use additional message events and when tasks (BPMN specifies special types of tasks that are responsible for sending or receiving messages: Send and Receive tasks; we will not discuss them here). A message event represents an event – a single action – whereas a task represents some activity. If a collaboration is related to some additional activity, it's better to use a task. See at our model examples (Figures 117 and 118).

3.6. Collaboration – advanced

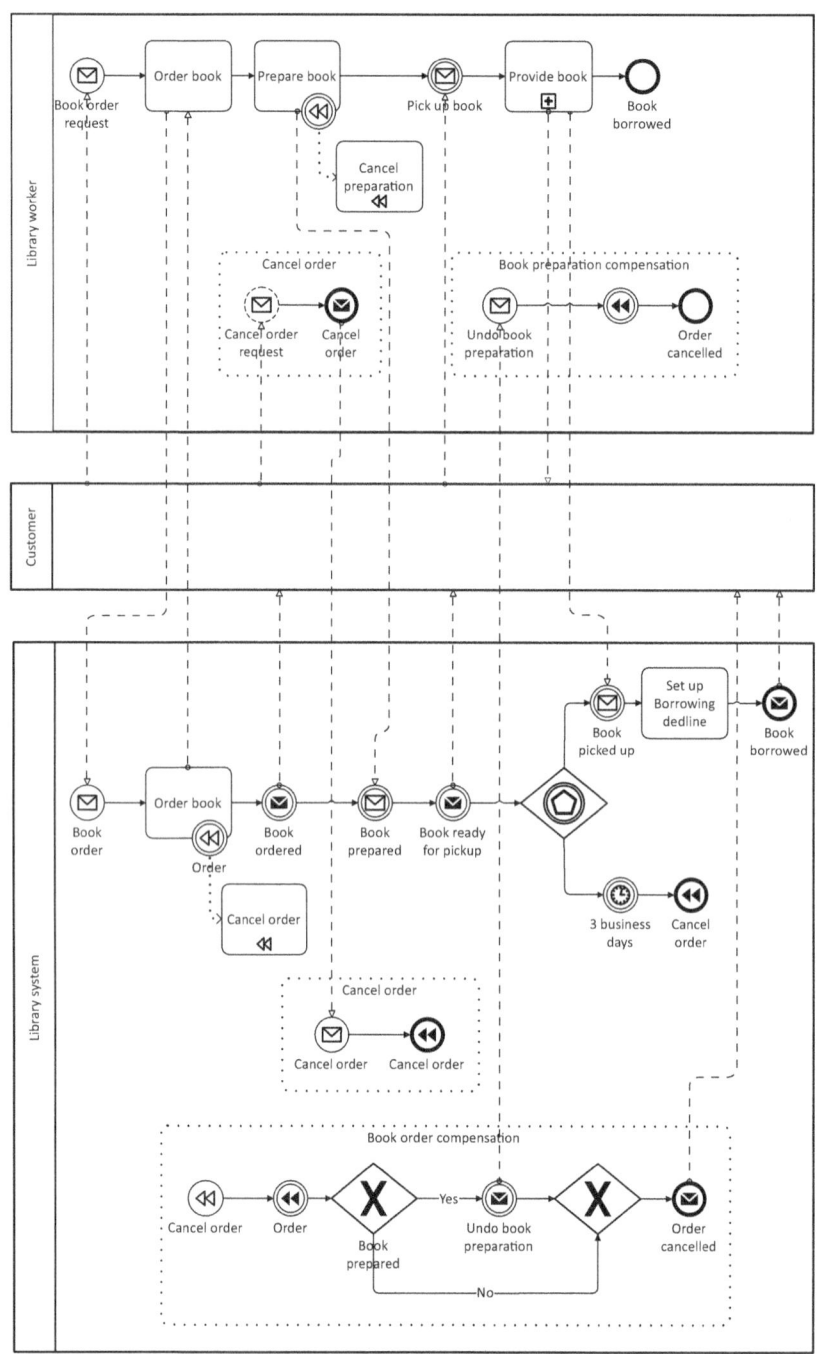

Figure 118: Manage book order process collaboration between library worker and a system – scenario: customer orders a book in a library

What conclusions we can draw?
- If we model a human–system-driven process within one pool, the process may lack information on how exactly some activity is performed. Is it triggered by a human or only system-driven? If you want to model detailed dependences between human and system responsibilities, use collaboration.
- Compensation has to be separately triggered within every process.
- You can associate a collapsed (event) subprocess within a given process with other process participants using message flows. If message flows are not titled, use a maximum of two associations to/from a subprocess.
- If a process may be managed by a human or (mainly) by a system, create separate models for human- and system-driven scenarios.
- Depending on whether a process is managed by a human or a system, the communications between process participants may be different.
- A message event may represent different types of communication between participants, such as an email, a conversation, an alert or message displayed in a system, etc.

Would you like to learn more?

The most effective way to learn is by practicing on solving real-world problems.

If you want to
- learn BPMN from scratch
- exercise and deepen your knowledge about how to model business processes
- discuss your questions and diagrams

... Then visit **www.modelingview.com**

References

1. Business Process Model and Notation (BPMN), Version 2.0, January 2011 https://www.omg.org/spec/BPMN/2.0/
2. The Scrum Guide™, November 2017 https://www.scrumguides.org/scrum-guide.html

Printed in France by Amazon
Brétigny-sur-Orge, FR

16965564R00094